BRADFORD + ILKLEY COMMUNITY
COLLEGE LIBRARY
WITHDRAWN

URBAN EDUCATION IN THE NINETEENTH CENTURY

Child workers in London (from line drawings in *Strand Magazine* in the 1880s). The drawings were originally entitled Picking Sweets, A Child Nurse, At Tea, Packing Chocolate, Throwing Knives, Flower Seller, At The Lyric, At Play.

URBAN EDUCATION IN THE NINETEENTH CENTURY

Proceedings of the 1976 Annual Conference of the History of Education Society of Great Britain

Edited by D. A. Reeder

 TAYLOR & FRANCIS LTD LONDON 1977

First published 1977 by Taylor & Francis Ltd
10–14 Macklin Street, London WC2B 5NF

© 1977 Taylor & Francis Ltd

All rights reserved. No part of this publication may be reproduced, stored in a retrieval system or transmitted, in any form or by any means electronic, mechanical, photocopying, recording or otherwise without the prior permission of the Copyright owner.

ISBN 0 85066 126 9

Printed and bound in Great Britain by
Taylor & Francis (Printers) Ltd
Rankine Road, Basingstoke, Hampshire RG24 0PR

Contents

Contributors	vii
Preface	ix
Introduction D. A. Reeder, University of Leicester	1
Education and Urban Politics c. 1832–1885 D. Fraser, University of Bradford	11
Illiteracy and Schooling in the Provincial Towns, 1640–1870: A Comparative Approach W. B. Stephens, University of Leeds	27
Education and the Social Geography of Nineteenth-Century Towns and Cities W. E. Marsden, University of Liverpool	49
Predicaments of City Children: late-Victorian and Edwardian Perspectives on Education and Urban Society D. A. Reeder, University of Leicester	75
Social Conflict and Urban Education in the Nineteenth Century: A Sociological Approach to Comparative Analysis D. Smith, University of Leicester	95
The History of Urban Education in the United States: Historians of Education and their Discontents Sol Cohen, University of California, Los Angeles	115
Select Reading List	133
Index	137

Contributors to this Volume

Dr D. A. Reeder is Lecturer in the History of Education at the University of Leicester. He was Head of Education at Garnett College of Education for ten years and was editor of *The Vocational Aspect of Education* during that time. An urban historian by training he has contributed articles to journals and books on suburban development. He is also review editor of *The Urban History Yearbook*. He is a member of the History of Education Society.

Dr D. Fraser is Senior Lecturer in History at the University of Bradford. He is an urban historian who has written extensively on social policy, education and politics in the nineteenth century. He has recently completed a major book on *Urban Politics in Victorian England* and edited a book on *The Poor Law in the 19th Century*. He is conferences editor for *The Urban History Yearbook*.

Mr W. E. Marsden is Senior Lecturer in Education at the University of Liverpool. He is a geographer by training, reflecting the influence of urban historical geography at Liverpool. He has undertaken research on Merseyside towns and has contributed several articles on the geographical content of studies in the history of education. He is also interested in the history of geography teaching and is chairman of the curriculum studies group of the History of Education Society.

Dr W. B. Stephens is Senior Lecturer in Education at the University of Leeds. He is a local historian and for several years was editor of the *Victoria County History* volumes. He has written a book on early-modern towns and a guide to sources in local history. He has also written extensively on the local history of education, the most recent contributions being a study of education in early-victorian Coventry and a Leeds University Monograph—*Regional Differences in Educational Provision during the Industrial Revolution*. He is a member of the History of Education Society.

Mr D. Smith is Lecturer in Sociology at the University of Leicester. A historian by training, and a sociologist by profession, he has a particular interest in comparative studies. His writings on education include contributions to a set of Readings on the *Theory of Educational Systems*; and also to the Readings of the Open University, most recently in the text on *Schooling and Capitalism*. He is currently working on a comparative study of urban education in the nineteenth century.

Professor Sol Cohen is Professor of Education at the University of California in Los Angeles. He has contributed extensively to the historiography as well as the history of American education, with articles on industrial and urban education, and a book on American progressive educationalists. He is well known in Britain as well as the USA and is a member of the History of Education Society.

Preface

The History of Education Society of Great Britain have published the proceedings of annual conferences held between 1969 and 1973. This volume marks a resumption of the series, with a new publisher and an editor invited to look after one particular issue. The contents are based on the proceedings of the annual conference at Avery Hill College of Education in December 1976 on the theme of urban education. They include four of the conference papers, annotated for publication, with the addition of two further papers, and a brief introduction, to supplement the proceedings. It is hoped that all these contributions will contain pointers of common interest to colleagues in the USA as well as in Britain. The theme of the conference was a new departure for the Society, as the president pointed out. However, the choice of theme exemplifies the declared policy of the Society 'to encourage and further the study of the history of education in all its wide ramifications'.

Introduction

D. A. REEDER
University of Leicester

The question of what historians are doing to promote the study of urban education has a particular force and urgency in view of contemporary preoccupations. The problems of urban schooling are manifestly a cause of much anxiety. There has been a proliferation of writings about them in Britain as in other older urbanized countries. However, the contemporary debate is generally lacking in historical perspective; it reflects in the main a recent concern with problems that have arisen especially acutely in the inner districts of modern cities. Thus urban education has become a focus for discussion about such controversial issues as compensatory education, resource allocation and priority areas, community education and 'open schooling,' and education for multi-racial groups. Many of the writings on such matters are in effect urban reform tracts, some of them calling into question the assumptions which have informed urban policies as well as educational and curriculum policies in the post war years. Yet there have been relatively few attempts to promote more formal studies of the urban processes affecting education, or to develop perspectives on the ideological viewpoints expressed by current prescriptions for urban schools.

There are methodological difficulties in contemplating more formal analysis because of doubts about what a study of urban education might reasonably cover. The problems of urban schooling can be regarded either as critical instances of fundamental dislocations in the relations between education and a (predominantly urban) society with the city as a mirror that reflects social tensions; or they can be regarded as a specific set of problems, related to and in part dependent on, changes affecting the modern city, whether these are the ecological changes associated with the formation of the inner city, or the related changes in urban economic development that have contributed to the persistence of urban poverty. In the first case, urban education is merely incidental to a larger framework of analysis; in the second case, it is a special field, and an integral component of urban study. Much depends on the view that is taken of the city as a unit of social organization and whether or not the city can be said to embody forces that are generic to it. In practice, however, many different social scientists have come to regard urbanization as a useful if multi-faceted construct, although the most important influences on contemporary urban study have tended to be ecological, stemming from the work of the Chicago school of urban sociologists. Much contemporary urban analysis derives from a view of the early twentieth century city which, in the words of Robert E. Park, 'magnifies, spreads out and advertises human nature in all its various manifestations,' ['The City as a Social Laboratory,' in T. V. Smith and L. D. White (eds.), *Chicago: An Experiment in Social Science Research* (1929), 1, 19]. The ecological, and more recently, the anthropological bases of urban studies, are reflected in the work that has been done of a systematic nature on urban education in studies consisting mainly of inter-cultural comparisons of educational developments in cities, or less frequently, comparisons with pre-industrial societies in the Third World—historical comparisons within the same culture have not really been tried.

The virtual exclusion of the historian from the contemporary analysis of urban education is the more difficult to understand because historians have secured a foothold in several other aspects of urban study, sharing common ground with urban sociologists and urban geographers especially. Moreover, the rise of urban history as a conscious field of study has been connected with discontents about contemporary urban policies, and in the United States, with the so-called 'urban crisis' of the 1960s. In Britain, leading practitioners of urban history, have been challenged to develop a more systematic approach to the urban past by changing attitudes to the city which are themselves expressions of the insidious working out of the forces of urbanization. As the first professor of Urban History in Britain has pointed out, the very differences in form and stress between older terms such as urbane and urbanity and modern terms such as urban and urbanism, suggest 'one of the compelling ironies of urban existence that tug at so many students of urban life—that great gap between the promise of modernity, the vision of abundance and equality, and its fulfilment by the cities which are its agents,' [H. J. Dyos, *Urbanity and Suburbanity* (1973), 5]. The development of education is surely a major aspect of that 'compelling irony,' represented in one form by the contrast to be drawn between, on the one hand, the educational legacy of districts that have become stranded (or 'beached' in Stuart Hall's expressive phrase) behind moving urban frontiers, and on the other hand, the enormous potential for educational and cultural development offered by the historical city. This paradox may have been influential in shaping the attitudes of American historians of education whose recent critical revisions of the development of their school system seem, to an English observer, shot through with references to older ideals of democratic urbanity which are now felt to have been lost.

Urban history is still a relatively youthful field, even if it has rapidly established a corpus of literature and research, and it is only just beginning to have an effect on studies of the educational past. New work on the history of American urban education dates mostly only from the late 1960s. In 1975 an American urban historian could write that 'impressive as the substantive and methodological achievements' of the new generation of urban historians are, the 'unfinished agenda remains long, especially in the realm of interior urban history,' and amongst the neglected items he listed work on the growth and role of public, private, parochial and proprietory schools, as well as the broader spectrum of urban cultural institutions, [Zane Miller, 'Urban History, Urban Crises and Public Policy,' *Urbanism Past and Present*, 1, 1975–6, 4]. That is changing now. From a British perspective, American historians appear more deliberate in the pursuit of urban education and more determined to connect up past and present. The trend amongst leading scholars in this field, as in some other aspects of urban history is, plainly, to construct from the American context a kind of parable for modern times. Hence Professor D. B. Tyack's recent account of the organizational changes in American education is addressed 'not only to specialists but also to citizens curious and concerned about how we arrived at the present crisis in education,' [*The One Best System. A History of American Urban Education* (1974), 4]. In the United States the role of 'myth' in shaping public policy has been an important theme in urban history, and several of the current revisionist interpretations of the origins of the American school system, and the assumptions of its creators are concerned with puncturing the old 'myths.' Such overtly reformist approaches are subjects of a lively debate on the dangers of distorting the past or drawing misleading lessons from it. Professor Cohen's paper in this volume not only summarises the writings but contributes to the methodological debate.

The recent characteristically American entries on the history of urban education reflect the way in which they have been impressed by the role of the city in the institutional and cultural life of the nation. They reflect also the tendency within the professional ranks of educational historians to adopt models that are drawn from social and cultural history. For that reason, perhaps, the city tends to be regarded as encapsulating all the modernizing forces at work in American society, providing a store of themes—the acculturation of migrants, social conflict and mobility, bureaucratic developments, liberal reformism—all of them important to the 'processing' of the American nation. Case studies in urban education are founded on these themes. Here is a *genre* of social history, which would be recognized by British urban historians as making a significant attempt to relate the general forces at work in American society to the specific urban environments in which they arose and found expression. They might think, however, that more ambitious attempts to elaborate a general history of urban education, as with some other studies of the role of the city in the American past, puts over much strain on the concept of urbanization, bearing in mind also that examples are available for only a limited number of cities in a country which has a diversity of urban types.

Although British educational historians recognize the importance of urban influences on educational development, little interest has been shown until very recently in examining the interrelations between urban change and educational development by means of case studies. With a few exceptions, education has not as yet become one of the major concerns of British urban historians. It was not on the agenda for instance of the first conference in 1965. What can be said is that history of education is represented in the bibliographical surveys, particularly of the *Urban History Yearbook*, a volume which functions as a kind of strategy for making connections between the more central elements of the field and a wide range of writings and research that are contributory or incidental to them. History of education is listed under various 'urban' headings—administration, institutions, politics, culture—although it can be argued that such divisions do not altogether do justice to the very many ways in which education in the more extended sense entered into the life of urban communities in the past. Paradoxically, the most explicit recognition of urban educational functions has been made by historians of the early modern city, for whom such matters as school foundations, book production and literacy rates, are regarded as constituting one of the criteria of urbanization. That is why recent surveys of early modern towns, for example, Peter Clark and Paul Slack, *English Towns in Transition 1500–1700* (1976), pay particular attention to charting the fluctuations in the educational and cultural role of towns in the regions and the wider community.

Whilst there are many incidental references to education in more specialized urban historical studies for the nineteenth century, the main source of documentary accounts of schooling in towns and cities in the modern period are local and institutional histories, the greater part of them not extending beyond their particular subjects, and not especially concerned about filling in the historical map of urban education. Many publications on the history of town schools or schooling are celebrations, written to commemorate the achievements of a civic body or to register a landmark in the history of a town or town school, circulated privately or published with the help of subsidies. A sample from these writings is given in a selected reading list at the end of the volume, along with more purposeful or thematic studies by educational and social historians. References in this introduction will be listed there.

Municipal accounts are in many cases the only published sources for the history of educational development and administration in the major cities of the country. They began to be written as a product of the surge of civic consciousness characteristic of late-Victorian and Edwardian Britain. They were attempts to show how municipal education had made good the deficiencies, which an earlier generation of urban reformers had elucidated from statistical surveys of the moral ecology of early- and mid-Victorian industrial towns. The statistical data on school provision and attendance in the major cities was important, as is well known, in preparing the way for the 1870 Act, especially the Parliamentary Return of 1870 'confined to the municipal boroughs of Birmingham, Leeds, Liverpool and Manchester, of all schools for the poorer classes of children,' [H.C. 91 (1870) Liv, 265]. After the 1870s grave homilies on the neglect of elementary education were overtaken by anxieties about secondary schools, investigated by the Bryce Commission and followed up by the town surveys of Michael Sadler in reports that revealed quite an understanding for the times of the ecological determinants of urban school systems. Sadler's reports on secondary education began in Sheffield in 1903 and took in Liverpool, Huddersfield, Birkenhead, Newcastle and Exeter. A related but private study, one of a number of grammar school histories but outstanding as perhaps the first urban based educational history, was the account by A. A. Mumford of *The Manchester Grammar School, 1515–1915, a regional survey of the advancement of learning in Manchester since the Reformation* (1919). The period 1902–18 was particularly important for retrospective accounts of urban educational politics and administration; the classic works, as they now are, by S. E. Maltby, *Manchester and the movement for national elementary education 1800–1870* (1918), by Sydney Webb, *London Education* (1904) and the two accounts of the London school board which set the pace for similar efforts elsewhere by T. A. Spalding and T. S. A. Curney, *The Work of the London School Board* (1900) and by Hugh B. Philpott, *London at school: the story of the school board 1870–1904* (1904). Subsequently education became part of municipal socialism and the provisions made by the Bradford School Board formed the basis for the Bradford Charter of the I.L.P. Now that education has come to be accepted as a municipal responsibility, municipally sponsored accounts tend to be more reflective and factual. They have yielded some informative studies, one of the best represented by Stuart Maclure's recent account of London education based on the researches of David Allsebrook, which manages to break free from some of the more rigid constraints of institutional history to glimpse the schoolchildren as such.

Administrative and institutional history can be one way of developing a history of urban education if researchers are prepared to reach out and make connections with other aspects of town life. However this happens only occasionally. Some reaching out is evident in school history that has been written by educational specialists as with David Lawson's study of Hull Grammar School or Marjorie Cruickshank's vignette on the Manchester Mechanics' Institute and Technical College, or in the institutional account of Nottingham's educational history by David Wardle still perhaps the only thorough study that has been done. However, this kind of published local history is sparse—there has been little attempt to follow up the regional history of Leicestershire for example—and it is inclined, understandably, to deal with districts or institutions in terms of national themes rather than the springs of local initiatives.

One might expect to find local connections emphasized more in writings that are part of an extensive body of local history, contributed not only by specialists but also by people interested in tracing the history of schools as a local pursuit. This wider area of urban study cannot be ignored, even if as it sometimes appears, much of the research is motivated by a kind of searching for roots. A point to remember is that the local interest in the educational past has been stimulated by a profusion of historical societies in towns and cities, separate from but usually related to the larger county organizations, whose activities are a natural outcome of the desire to preserve a sense of belonging or attachment to places that were formerly villages or small towns. No one has yet managed to keep track of all the local historical research, not even the specialized educational part, that comes out in booklets, transactions and proceedings, mimeographed news sheets and other ephemeras. This represents an accumulation of detail on town schools and schooling, including information on topics such as private schooling, which is often difficult to obtain in any other way. The most helpful local research provides insights into the forms and experiences of urban schooling in ways that would not normally find their way into more scholarly work. In addition to specialized accounts, the historians of provincial towns almost invariably make some references to town schools and charitable endowments, including those of the grammar schools whose reorganization in the nineteenth century was frequently a cause of much town strife. Profiles of town schools and schooling often depend heavily on extensive quotations from original records from which educational historians may cull useful information although they cannot expect in most cases that local profiles will take account of modern scholarship. Nevertheless, local history on the small scale extends and amplifies the recording activities of the Victoria County History whose stately progress has now taken in urban areas thus providing the most coherent accounts we have of the additions and adaptations to the educational apparatus of suburbanized or industrialized counties. The value of this work has been illustrated by Margaret Bryant, who explained to the Society, on a previous occasion, how the sources used for one of the Middlesex volumes of the V.C.H., can provide new and sometimes unexpected insights on the history of suburban education. The publications of local historical societies also provide outlets for theses on the history of education, and for other academically sponsored researches as in the occasional papers of the Southampton City Council, although university research into local history is also published separately, as with the Exeter papers in regional and educational history.

There is a sense, in which local history should provide the empirical basis for an urban history of education, at any rate for the smaller or medium sized provincial towns. For this to happen, local educational research needs to exploit more fully the prospect which university local historians have held out for a more comparative and altogether more analytical approach, one that develops themes and does not merely record developments. Alan Everitt's edited essays, *Perspectives in English Urban History* (1973) have many suggestions on how that might be done. Unfortunately, it is doubtful whether the academic skills of local history have been much used to explore urban relationships in the considerable number of theses on educational developments in towns and cities. The main effort of post graduate research in local study, especially for M.Ed. degrees (by part time research) seems to have been concentrated on developmental and administrative accounts based on a linear progression, rather than the more integrative approach of local history. In these circumstances the urban context can only function as a kind of background rather than a means of establishing links between educational institutions and the world they served. Although it is difficult to generalize simply on the impression left from theses read personally, the most fruitful of them, combining scholarly procedures with wider perspectives, have tended to be thematic studies of education in relation to such aspects of urban life as the economy, politics and pressure groups, the poor, and the development of neighbourhoods. There are relatively few of these compared with the number of general developmental accounts and specialized outlines of elementary and technical education, mainly in the nineteenth century.

This is not to suggest that British educational history has been unaffected by similar trends as in the United States: there has been, for example, a growing discontent with older developmental accounts and some criticism of their lack of social content, except that reservations have also been expressed about the tendency of social historians to adopt too readily the concept of social control as a methodological tool. In fact, the most critical assaults on older interpretations—of early-Victorian education especially—have been launched by social historians interested in the ideologies of mass education. The more thorough going of these have put forward interpretations of educational provision for the working classes as the concomitant of the class cultural control of an urban bourgoisie [Johnson, Shapin in the select reading list]. So far this approach has not produced any sociologically based studies of urban schooling in case studies, although references are made to towns and in particular to the influence of members of a London–Edinburgh axis, on definitions of elementary education and demands for state intervention in the first half of the nineteenth century. However, these and related themes, have been significantly advanced in studies published recently by Philip McCann, *Popular Education and Socialization in the Nineteenth Century* (1977). This collection explores 'ways in which various types of elementary education, at different periods in the nineteenth century, attempted to prepare the working-class child for life and labour in an industrial capitalist society'. Although the essays concentrate on utilizing one sociological concept—that of socialization—they are, in effect, case studies in urban education of a particular kind. If the gaps and disclaimers in present accounts are to be filled, there is evidently a need for more local urban based research on the ideologies and nature of the middle class support for education, as on the middle classes themselves, and the extent to which 'social control' was effective in practice. It is necessary also to balance these approaches by exploring the way that educational institutions especially adult institutions expressed or embodied some of the common elements in a mid-Victorian urban culture (if that phrase can be used meaningfully). Social historians with other interests in leisure and religious provision for example have developed approaches which depend upon particular case studies. The importance of doing so for educational institutions is underlined in various pieces of sociological writing, which show how voluntary associations in early Victorian cities acquired a range of social functions important to emergent urban based social 'networks.' Studies of this kind connect up with sociological descriptions of how an urban way of life evolved: firstly, how voluntary associations developed as 'intrinsic structural concomitants of the process of urbanization' [Louis Wirth, 'Urbanism as a Way of Life,' *American Journal of Sociology*, 44 (1938), 22]; and secondly, how these associations especially those disseminating scientific knowledge and instruction, functioned in relation to a provincial urban-based culture [Inkster, Shapin].

On a wider front there are clues for educational historians interested in the urban context of developments in studies of the structural characteristics of urban development, and the interrelations between different structural facets of urban organization, the repercussions for instance of changes in the economic base and physical articulation of towns on the quality of social and political life. The most recent and coherent example of this approach is M. J. Daunton's study of Cardiff 1870–1914, cited along with other examples in the bibliographical references. Apart from direct references to education, this kind of urban analysis suggests that any sustained attempt at formulating a history of urban education on the basis of single or comparative studies of educational developments, in particular towns and cities, needs to take account of a very wide range of structural relationships.

The study of urban relationships should include not only those inhering in local social and political structures, but also those emanating from the interplay between town and country, town and town, above all perhaps, metropolis and provinces. This second category constitutes a set of themes that have hardly yet been explored, whether in terms of the politics or the administration of urban schooling, except perhaps for the division between central and local relationships which have formed some part of urban educational study. There are opportunities also, for a more sociologically based interpretation of the structural variations in the social development of English towns, and how these affected the patterns of formal educational provision in different places. One particular theme might be the influence of different élite groups—a simplified version of a more elaborate hypothesis explored by Dennis Smith in research on the middle classes and education in Sheffield and Birmingham in the second half of the nineteenth century. His paper in this volume elaborates on the theoretical and historical basis of sociological comparisons in urban education. One relationship he discerns is that between a metropolitan orientated and a locally orientated élite, the former associated with support for liberal education and culture, the latter with the promotion of technical and commercial education. The hypothesis is a reminder of the importance of recognizing the cultural conflicts and compromises of an urban society as well as its class relationships. Again, there are many other themes which arise if the focus is enlarged to include not only differences between groups within urban society, but also the shifting balance and interactions of urban and rural interests, a subject that is directly relevant to educational policy making in Victorian Britain, not least perhaps to the genesis of official policies on middle-class education.

It was not practicable to include all the many possible urban themes in the conference proceedings, although the papers given did represent some of the methodological approaches to urban history in Britain. In the time available it was thought better to choose topics mainly from the nineteenth century that had a direct bearing on the changing concerns of British educational historians. The latter have been summarized (by Professor Harold Silver) as 'the greater concern with statistics, with education on a considerably wider basis than schooling, and with the direct and indirect impact of political and religious movements.' Thus Dr Fraser's paper drew on his own wide ranging studies of urban politics in Victorian England, but succeeded also in tapping subjects on which education historians have contributed as for instance, the insights given by James Murphy into Liverpool politics and religion, through concentrating on the Liverpool corporate schools, or those provided by D. K. Jones into Manchester politics and nonconformity through his work on the origins of the National Public Schools Association, or the researches in several unpublished theses on politics, education and the formation of opinion in Birmingham. What Dr Fraser provided and illustrated, was a way of examining these relationships, connecting up national and local politics, also within a framework of comparative studies. He stimulated questions about the impact of different urban and political structures on education, and the reasons why education became more of a political issue in some towns rather than others, especially during the school board era.

The remaining papers were concerned one way or another with the impact of urbanization on education and child life. This is, of course, a very difficult matter to assess. One problem is to know where to draw the boundaries. As Joan Simon has recently suggested this is a matter which has to be searched out in a period before the modern city emerged, and elucidated on a broad front: the urbanization of early modern society was important not only for the impetus given to the rise of the organized school adapted to lay needs, but in more wide ranging ways, affecting the patterns of growing up and influencing too the very concept of development and therefore the possibility of education as a formative process, ['The History of Education in Past and Present,' *Oxford Review of Education*, 3, 1 (1977), 80]. On the other hand, attempts to measure the impact of urbanization on education in the narrower sense of institutional provision have been few and mainly inconclusive. Professor Laqueur concludes his survey of the development of Sunday schools for example by pointing out that factors other than settlement patterns must have been the primary determinants of success or failure, [*Religion and Respectability Sunday Schools and Working Class Culture 1780–1850* (1976), 53]. This question considered more generally, has received less than due attention from economic and social historians, who have focussed mainly on the relations between education and industrialization, rather than urbanization, or at least have seen these two processes moving together. Whilst the interests of social and demographic historians have stimulated local studies of literacy and educational provision, there is much more to be done both in assessing the qualitative significance of literacy, and in accounting for variations in basic measures of literacy (or illiteracy) as between different types of settlement. Dr Stephens' paper emphasized the variety of towns that made up urban provincial England, went back to the seventeenth century, and derived evidence from many local researches as well as official printed sources in coming to an assessment of the impact of urbanization. Whereas Dr Stephens was concerned with variations in literacy rates and educational provision between towns in their regional settings, Mr Marsden examined the forces affecting the distribution of schools within, as well as between towns and cities, mainly in the second half of the nineteenth century. Both papers offer a distinctively British approach, Dr Stephens as a local historian who has developed a geographical and comparative framework for studying local educational provision and school attendance, Mr Marsden as an historical geographer who has developed the study of socio-spatial aspects of urban processes. Mr Marsden's conference paper showed mainly and with the aid of more maps than could be printed here how changes in the internal organization of urban districts affected schooling. He pointed to the emergence of a perceived hierarchy of schools responding to changes in their catchment areas. In a forthcoming article he goes on to argue for a geographical component which goes beyond ecological studies to include behavioural aspects, taking into account subtle relations between school and neighbourhood.

The study of school–community links must surely form a central component of the history of urban education, providing one of the ways in which the history of urban schooling might contribute directly to a more certain grasp of the possibilities available in the urban present. It is sometimes claimed, for instance, that the so-called crisis in city schools arises from an erosion through urban growth of that consensus of values once achieved between school and local community. Is this really so? The answer requires a much better understanding than we have at present of the role and functions of schooling in different communities, and of the attitudes to schooling by parents in different neighbourhoods. On the first matter, it may seem rather surprising that so little has been done to examine the education of ethnic minority groups in nineteenth-century Britain. Even at the level of institutional provision, there are only brief studies of the special initiatives taken on behalf of the children of the Irish poor, and the separate organization of, for example, the Catholic school boards in some cities. The education of Jewish children has also been neglected, despite much current interest in the history of urban Jewish communities more generally, although one study in an unpublished thesis does throw light on the role of elementary schools in the assimilation of successive waves of Jewish migrants in Liverpool, concluding that 'through many vicissitudes, Jewish schools first made Jews Englishmen, but now exist to make Englishmen, Jews,' [Herschon].

On the second matter, that of parental attitudes to schooling and the related question of child labour in the family economy of the working classes, some work is available touching on aspects of these relationships, as in David Rubinstein's pioneering study of school attendance in London, the researches of Eric Hopkins on working class attitudes to education in Midland industrial areas, the work of Dr Stephens on education in early Victorian Coventry, and of Simon Frith on elementary education in Leeds. Yet, here again, instructive approaches are contained in unpublished theses, two theses on ragged schooling in Victorian cities, for example, which provide insights on the problems and curriculum of schools set up in urban slums; and a study by Cheryl Parsons of the connexions between three elementary schools and the urban community, which enclosed them in a district of Sheffield colonized in their own way mainly by steelmen. The latter thesis goes beyond the relatively perfunctory entries in the school log books to the perceptions of the ex-pupils themselves over a time span of nearly 80 years. These Sheffield schools clearly had an uphill struggle, given their inadequate resources, and the floating population of a still developing district, but the chief obstacle seems to have been the indifference of most parents to schooling itself, despite a retrospective pride or even affection for certain schools and individual teachers. This is a hypothesis which needs testing for other schools and neighbourhoods. Professor Harold Silver has raised the problem of how to assess the typicality of any particular urban school in reflecting on the joint study undertaken with Pamela Silver of a National School in Lambeth. In this case, he explains, 'the school sources revealed a more imaginative and more humane approach to children and to school affairs, and stronger school–community links than we had expected, or could explain,' ['Aspects of Neglect: The Strange Case of Victorian Popular Education,' *Oxford Review of Education*, 3, 1 (1977), 58].

A basis for comparative work on school–community links can be laid from studies of the incidence of school attendance in the nineteenth century. Despite the difficulties and pitfalls of using the census enumerator's returns, 1841–71, the details they provide can be used for a quantitative assessment of the patterns of school attendance and child work in relation to particular socio-economic groups in urban neighbourhoods. This would at least provide a start on a subject which requires the historian of education to probe more deeply than he has thought necessary before, into the interstices of family life and urban community structures in the past. After all, the formation of attitudes to schooling, and to children too, was affected not only by changes in the organization of schooling, and the professionalization of teaching, but also by changes in the pattern of familial organization in districts affected by industrial change. A way into this difficult area of research may be to adopt some of the quantitative approaches used by Michael Anderson in his study of family life in mid-Victorian Preston, Lancashire, or those which Michael Katz has grippingly demonstrated in working out patterns of growing up in mid-Victorian Hamilton, Canada. On the other hand, Raphael Samuel has argued for studies based on the qualitative reconstruction of the cultural patterns of child life, entering into the urban milieux which encompassed the lives of children with the help of reminiscences, biographies, and evidence from local sources, including court cases. Raphael Samuel was invited to the conference where he provided members with glimpses of the life style of the children of East London in the nineteenth century. Unfortunately it was not possible for him to make his work available in a paper for this volume within the time available. Nevertheless, it is worth pointing out that the History Workshop Group has been doing much to foster the history of childhood, and there are other workshop publications of interest, issued as part of an endeavour to bring into view areas of urban culture that had previously been thought too esoteric or too inaccessible for research. In more general terms, the approach to local history recommended and exemplified by Raphael Samuel, including the use of oral history to recover the more fugitive aspects of social life in the past, is offered by him as an escape from conventional institutional sources of history, enabling the local historian to develop a more 'vital approach' by 'making their touchstone, the real life experiences of people themselves' ['Local History and Oral History,' *History Workshop*, 1, 1976].

Whatever reservations may be held about this last point, or the concentration of historians of urban culture on particular aspects of working class life, there is a strong case for a history of urban education based on studies both of the realities and images of child life in cities, and of the street culture which encompassed children. My own paper was concerned with suggesting an approach to policy-making based on examining the cultural perceptions and social anxieties of the middle-class observers of the city and its children. It attempted thereby to erect some bridges between historians of education and historians of social institutions and administration. The paper touched on themes which quite evidently need developing, possibly with local studies, but at least they are themes which bring educational historians into touch with current work in the social history of the city. Then, there are other subjects which can also be discussed from the point of view of the formative or socializing agencies brought to bear on city children, not mentioned in this paper, one of the most important being the development and design of schoolbuildings.

A subject of such complexity as urban education requires a variety of approaches, not only those embodied in contemporary research, but a variety of historical approaches too. These are early days yet for pronouncing on the range of approaches or judging the priorities for research, whether they should be the development of urban school systems, or the content and processes of urban schooling, or the study of social perceptions and school–community links. All of them are important, requiring the historian of urban education to broaden out by studying the environment in which schools functioned and the range of 'education bearing' agencies influenced, or brought into being, by the rise of the modern city. Whilst this volume is only an interim report on some of the possibilities, it attempts for the first time in Britain to initiate a discussion on urban education as a focus of historical study.

Education and Urban Politics c. 1832–1885

D. Fraser
University of Bradford

The perspective of this paper is not the history of English education but the history of politics, primarily in those four great provincial capitals of Victorian England—Leeds, Manchester, Birmingham and Liverpool—which were linked together as distinctively metropolitan in the 1867 Minority Clause. We need to understand the context within which elementary education became an important political issue in mid-nineteenth century towns. To this end a model of urban politics is suggested which envisages an institutional political structure of four levels in urban society. At the lowest level are the parochial and township institutions such as the vestry, the improvement commissions and the Poor Law. The next level is that of municipal government and is concerned with the growing importance of town councils. The third stage is the parliamentary election, long considered the only really political element in urban affairs. Finally, political activists were engaged in political agitation in pursuit of reform or some social or economic goal. This layered political system is not only suggested as a mode of analysis but corresponds to the real political world within which urban activists operated in Victorian England.[1] Education, as a political issue, acted as a bore-hole which penetrated the different layers of the urban political system.

Before tracing the way in which education took on political significance in the large towns, two general points need to be made: the first concerns the way the history of education appears to be moving. Traditionally, elementary education in nineteenth-century England was viewed by historians solely as a matter of dispute between Anglicans and Nonconformists and it was a welcome change when that essentially political battle was pushed into the background and historians of education began to chart progress on the ground. This administrative history, which explores statistics of pupils, teachers and buildings, examines syllabuses and teaching methods and computes costs and benefits, may now have gone too far. Rather like administrative studies in the history of the Poor Law, educational history is wrested out of its social and political context and studied internally, almost in a vacuum. This paper is partly a plea for the restoration of the political dimension, in the study of the history of English urban elementary education.

The second general point concerns perspective and its consequent parallax. Just as an arrangement of objects appears differently when viewed from different points, so education in Victorian England takes on a different guise when viewed from the perspective of urban politics rather than the history of education. It may be that in this paper the significance of educational issues will be differently assessed from that normally offered by educational historians. Just because the perspective here is urban politics and not the history of education, the conclusions drawn from familiar episodes will vary somewhat from the norm. Those familiar episodes are four case

---

[1] For fuller details of this approach see D. Fraser, *Urban Politics in Victorian England* (1976).

studies of educational activity which took on political importance. The first concerns the pioneering attempt in Liverpool to promote non-sectarian schooling in the Corporation schools between 1835 and 1841. The second examines the political significance of Voluntaryism—the fire from Leeds—in the later 1840s. The third traces the path of educational agitation which begins in Leeds, crosses to Manchester and finishes up in Birmingham. Finally, a brief glance at the political role of School Boards completes this review. The four case studies correspond roughly to the four levels of urban politics mentioned earlier—the Liverpool episode concerns municipal government, Voluntaryism was significant mainly in parliamentary elections, the education movement was but one of many political agitations which characterized urban society, and School Boards were the 1870s equivalent of parochial and township institutions.

Liverpool Corporation before 1835 was, like so many of its type, exclusively Anglican and Tory. Though many Liberals and Nonconformists had contributed greatly to the mercantile growth of the town, they had no opportunity to fill the posts of honour in town government which were the property of the traditional Tory élite of Liverpool. Municipal reform created the possibility of the excluded élite becoming the political masters and, as elsewhere, the new Council was overwhelmingly Liberal in character. Corporation posts, seats on the bench and aldermanic robes were the rewards for the political victors and of course corporate power. After one year Joshua Walmsley, a leading radical, reviewed what the new rulers had done for the town. What had been the significance of municipal reform? He argued that three things were paramount; first the new regime had economized on public funds; second they had introduced efficient administration, especially in judicial affairs; third they had expressed the popular will. Economy, efficiency and popular election were the common factors which all municipal reformers extolled in towns throughout England, but in Liverpool there was something more, for the reformed council inherited what virtually no other Corporation had acquired—a social role.

That role concerned the education of the poor. During its last dozen years the Liverpool Corporation had established two elementary schools which served the poor of the town. Since there was an Established Church and since the Corporation was exclusively Anglican it was natural for the Corporation schools to be staunchly Protestant and almost all pupils were Protestant. In 1836 the Liberal majority sought to open this Corporate amenity to all denominations, particularly Roman Catholics. They adopted the so-called Irish system, which enabled only extracts of the Bible to be used in teaching but permitted sectarian religious teaching by visiting preachers at certain periods of the day. Walmsley was proud of the Council's achievement in making education available to such needy children:

> 'Under the auspices of the new Council the Corporation schools have been thrown open so that children of every religious persuasion may participate in the benefits of education without doing violence to the feelings of any. ... The great objection made to the system is the withdrawal of the Bible and the substitution of the Irish extracts. It is true the Bible is no longer used as a mere class book for the purpose of teaching children to read, but it may most unhesitatingly be denied that it is withdrawn from the purposes of religious instruction. ... So far from the Word of God being excluded from the Schools there is not a Protestant nor a Roman Catholic child who has not as free an opportunity of reading the Bible as in any other school in the Kingdom. ... By throwing open the Corporation schools to all, whatever their religious persuasion, they have caused a more general diffusion of the blessings of education and have paved the way to the extinction of these sectarian feelings which have given rise to so much bitter animosity.'[2]

Yet of course it was just those sectarian feelings which were raised to a new level of intensity by the Corporation schools question. Many extreme Anglicans were

2 J. Walmsley, *What Have the Council Done?* (1836).

unhappy about the exclusion of the Authorized Version of the Bible and aroused popular opinion against the Council. The Protestant backlash was led by a fundamendalist Ulsterman the Rev. J. M'Neille. Though the Liberal majority was neither pro-Catholic nor pro-Irish, the structure of Liverpool's population made it appear that it was. M'Neille converted the schools question into 'no popery' and in doing so provided a political asset in municipal elections. The Corporation schools became the crucial issue in Liverpool municipal contests in the later 1830s.[3] It must be pointed out that nationally there was a Tory revival and all towns witnessed a spirited fight back by the groups displaced in 1835–36. There was also a local issue, that of dock warehousing, which caused the Liberals to lose some of their support[4], but it was the schools question which gave the real cutting edge to the Tory campaign and enabled the Tories to move from a desolate to a victorious position within five years. The details of the Tory resurgence are provided in Table 1.

Table 1. Tory seats on Liverpool Town Council 1836–40

	Tory seats won at November election	*Total Tories*
1836	8	11
1837	4	15
1838	6	17
1839	9	18
1840	11	25

By the end of 1840 the Tories had actually achieved a majority of the 48 Councillors and so Liberal rule was maintained only by the Aldermanic vote. In 1841 the Tories regained power and immediately changed the rules on religious education at the schools, restoring the Protestant ascendancy. The story of the Liverpool schools experiment is told in two statistics. In 1840 55 per cent of pupils were Roman Catholic: by 1842 only 8 per cent were so.

The historian embarks on a slippery slope when he attempts to assess the sincerity of motivation but it does appear that there was some truth in the contemporary assertion that while the Liberals genuinely believed in open education, the Tories merely used religious prejudice as a political handle. It did appear that Liberal religious faith aimed at harmony where Tory Protestantism provoked discord. As Samuel Wilderspin, a Liberal supporter put it:

'I believe they are the only schools in this kingdom for poor children in which are to be found a system of religious-moral intellectual and physical education united and in which the children of every *sect* may be found learning in harmony, playing in harmony and above all living in Heavenly love and charity amongst each other. Oh how I do lament that Christian men should throw an apple of discord amongst them and that many of the clergy should show the first example.'[5]

Despite repeated Liberal assertions to the contrary, M'Neille and his friends continued to proclaim that the Bible was excluded from the schools. Walmsley even reported that clergymen preached on this theme having watched his wife teaching from the Authorized Version herself.[6] There was much political mileage to be made out of the Bible and Tories adopted the practice of carrying Bibles at their meetings. The 1837 parliamentary election was called 'the wooden Bible election' because Tory processions were accompanied by wooden Bibles on long poles.[7] As M'Neille became more extreme in his language so he pitched his appeal lower down the social scale.

3 See by way of example *Liverpool Mercury*, 4th November 1836, 2nd November 1838, 30th October 1840.
4 B. D. White, *A History of the Corporation of Liverpool 1835–1914* (1951), 25.
5 S. Wilderspin, *A Reply to the Various Speeches . . . on the Subject of National Education* (1837).
6 H. M. Walmsley, *The Life of Joshua Walmsley* (1879), 91.
7 *Liverpool Mercury*, July 1837, *passim*.

Where in many towns there were Operative Conservative Societies, in Liverpool M'Neille organized the Operative Protestant Association. The distinction was important.

In the history of education the Liverpool Corporation schools are rightly termed 'the crucial experiment,' for in that context their significance lay in the attempt to marry education and religion.[8] However, in the urban political context, the schools take on a different role. The distinctive political mark of Liverpool in the middle decades of the nineteenth century was its Toryism. Where Leeds, Manchester and Birmingham were solidly Liberal, Liverpool was a haven of Toryism. The Tory municipal regime begun in 1841 was to last half a century and Conservatives usually had a comfortable passage in parliamentary contests.[9] Why was Liverpool so unlike its fellow provincial capitals? It was a question which puzzled contemporaries, for Liverpool seemed to have the potential to become a Liberal borough. The answer had much to do with tradition. Though there was a traditional endemic Toryism in Liverpool, what sealed the Liberal fate was the Corporation schools question. This fundamentally determined the political contours of party support in Liverpool by exaggerating and confirming the tendency of the Liberals to be pro-Irish and pro-Catholic. The Conservatives were thus able to appeal to anti-Irish, anti-Catholic prejudice and parade in the town as the party with a strong no-popery working-class following. Images die hard and the spectre of Catholic domination which Anglican opponents raised via the schools question was one that would not lie down. The 'crucial experiment' was thus critical in determining the political history of Liverpool in the nineteenth century.

The impossibility of religious co-operation in Liverpool presaged national difficulties which were confirmed in the outburst over Graham's 1843 Factory Bill. In a remarkable display of political strength Nonconformity denied the principle of Anglican domination and forced the government to withdraw its proposals. When the 1846 Minutes occasioned a further threat to religious equality, Dissenters were once more in the political battleground. But the agitation of 1847 was different from that of 1843 in three ways. It was decidedly more virulent, distinctly less united and markedly less successful. The Parliamentary approval of the Minutes in April 1847 understandably mark the end of the story for the historian of education since the pupil–teacher scheme operated and developed rapidly. But since Dissenters refused to accept the Commons' vote as a *fait accompli* the significance of the Minutes in urban politics was only just beginning. Voluntaryism, the belief that all elementary education must be voluntarily provided without state aid, was the adopted principle of Nonconformity and Voluntaryists demanded political vengeance on their betrayers, who were ironically the Whigs and Liberals.

Maynooth marked the first breach between Voluntaryism and urban Liberals and it was in 1845 that one Voluntaryist warned George Wilson, 'the Voluntary friends have hitherto restrained their watchword as a cause of division but they will now be compelled to rally their strength and vote for their own candidates.'[10] This was the policy which Voluntaryists adopted at the 1847 general election. Coming so soon soon after the vote on the Minutes, it provided an admirable opportunity for Voluntaryists to demonstrate their political strength in pursuit of religious belief. Miall piously reminded his flock, 'our principles have been ruthlessly trodden in the dust and we are summoned to bear witness on their behalf,' while the Anti-State Church Association instructed Dissenters to vote 'in indication of those ecclesiastical

8 J. Murphy, *The Religious Problem in English Education. The Crucial Experiment* (1959).
9 C. D. Watkinson, 'The Liberal Party on Merseyside in the Nineteenth Century,' (University of Liverpool unpublished Ph.D. thesis, 1967).
10 J. W. Massie to G. Wilson, 9 April 1845 (Wilson Papers, Manchester Reference Library).

principles which constitute the sole basis of religious freedom and equality.'[11] It was soon clear that politics in 1847 would operate under quite novel conditions. A national dissenting journal reported that candidates were 'subjected to a new and to them most perplexing test, old political organizations are being broken up, new ones are in the course of formation.' Indeed some Nonconformists were willing to remodel politics upon a Voluntaryist base, as one activist explained, 'the Anti-State Church principle . . . has in it sufficient vitality energy and aptitude to the times to become a germ of a new party.'[12] It did appear that education was doing to the Liberals in 1847 what the Corn Laws had done to the Tories in 1846. Yet in seeking for theological truth Dissenters harmed the only party which could aid their cause and so committed political suicide. As the radical Perronet Thompson sharply explained, the Dissenters 'chuse to blow up what they think is an enemy fort, though their own friends and in fact themselves are in it.'[13]

Nowhere were more forts blown up than in the urban heartland of the West Riding centred on Leeds. Contemporaries referred to Voluntaryism as 'the fire from Leeds' and it was this fire which caused divisions in urban politics in Yorkshire. Edward Baines, jun., editor of the *Leeds Mercury*, believed state education to be morally, theologically and politically evil. He committed himself and his paper to the extreme Voluntaryist position that the State had no right to educate. It was on his advice that his fellow believers, the Congregationalists, refused state grants for their schools for a quarter of a century from 1843. The reason why Leeds opinion was so acutely tuned to the education question in 1847 was that local people had been debating it fiercely during the previous year following the publication of a moderate Anglican pamphlet by the vicar of Leeds, W. F. Hook.[14] Hook had arrived in Leeds an uncompromising high churchman but he had gradually moderated his Anglican exclusiveness and by 1846, in the interests of educating the poor, he was proclaiming that Anglicanism had no right to special privileges. Hook's advocacy of equality of treatment within a state education system gained him much support even from some Liberal Dissenters, notably Unitarians and Wesleyans. Baines's counterblast was in the form of very long editorials and open letters which appeared in the *Mercury* in 1846.[15] Thus well before the Minutes had become a national political issue the 'yards of letters' from Baines had made education the key local issue in the West Riding. Baines had no doubt that it should remain so in 1847. The key to the 1847 general election in the West Riding lay in the Yorkshire delegate meeting assembled by Baines in May at East Parade chapel in Leeds. The delegates solemnly vowed to support no candidate 'who shall not be prepared to resist every attempt to renew the grant of public money . . . and who does not maintain the principle that public moneys cannot rightly be appropriated to sustain Educational and Religious Establishments.'[16] Voluntaryism was to be made the shibboleth of West Riding elections and a review of urban contests exposes the importance of education as a political issue in 1847.

At Wakefield the effect of Voluntaryism lay in the choice of candidate. The potential Liberal candidate was told by Dissenters 'we cannot support any man at the next election who held it to be the duty of the state to educate the people' and since Voluntaryists were in a majority in the local party they were able to insist on a Volun-

11 *Nonconformist*, 30th June 1847; *Nonconformist Elector*, 23rd July 1847.
12 *Eclectic Review*, July 1847, xxii, p. 108; *Nonconformist*, 12th June 1847.
13 T. P. Thompson to G. Wilson, 16th June 1847 (Wilson Papers).
14 W. F. Hook, *Letter to the Bishop of St. David's* . . . (1846); see also W. R. W. Stephens, *The Life and Letters of Walter Farquhar Hook* (1880), II, 205–12.
15 *Leeds Mercury*, 25th July–28th November 1846, letters from E. Baines jun. to Russell, Vaughan, Ewart, the *Wesleyan Review*, the *British Quarterly* and the *Morning Chronicle*.
16 *Leeds Mercury*, 8th May 1847.

tary candidate, G. W. Alexander. He was not able to muster the full Liberal strength and so the Tories were victorious. The contest at Huddersfield was between two Liberals, the sitting member W. R. C. Stansfield who believed in state education and John Cheetham a Lancashire manufacturer who was a staunch Voluntaryist. Though Cheetham could command a narrow majority of Liberal voters, the state education Conservatives voted for Stansfield and got him home. Huddersfield had a miniature Liberal–Conservative coalition which was to figure so prominently in Halifax and Leeds.[17]

Bradford was able to avoid a split but only after a very complex compromise was worked out. By a prior pact the Liberals were to run two candidates, the radical T. Perronet Thompson and the sitting Liberal member William Busfeild. The origin of Bradford's difficulties lay in Dissenters' demands that Voluntaryism be the crucial test of both candidates. Thompson was asked about the 'all important' issue, 'Do you disapprove of the Government undertaking the superintendence of the Education of the People and would you resist any attempt to renew the Grant of public money... in the Minutes?'[18] Thompson's reputed atheism caused some sticky moments with the godly people who led the Dissenters, but he passed muster. Busfeild was quite another matter not least because he had voted for the Maynooth grant. He would not state his views unambiguously and refused to come to Bradford to be questioned. His intransigence threatened party unity and even his former supporters cited his age (he was 74) and poor health as a reason for withdrawal. When he bluntly refused to stand down Bradford faced the prospect of a Tory victory and Thompson, ever the pessimist, concluded that their only hope was to ensure that the Tories were Peelites—'when you cannot save the horse you must save the saddle.'[19]

Faced with this dismal prospect, Bradford Liberal activists pieced together a compromise. Dissenters had begun in Bainesite all-or-nothing fashion but had second thoughts when the political consequences became clear. As Thompson put it, 'the leader of the Dissenting party who have overset the coach at Bradford... appears to be just waking to the fact, when one fourth of the Liberals in a constituency chuse to break faith with the other three fourths it is useless for them to think to bring in their man.'[20] The political expediency which suggested compromise was much sustained by William Byles, editor of the *Bradford Observer*. Where Baines in the *Leeds Mercury* proclaimed the dogma of pure Voluntaryism, Byles in the *Bradford Observer* searched for ways of restoring party unity. Byles was committed to alliance where Baines was committed to secession. Both sides were forced to give ground in the Bradford agreement by which Voluntaryists would moderate their demands and Busfeild would commit himself nearer the Dissenters cause. The Voluntaryists certainly gave Bustfeild the weakest dose of voluntary potion, as one of them explained, 'they gave up the question of the separation of Church and State and the educational question... they asked that he would not incorporate any other sect beneath the sanction of the State. That was all they required.'[21] This was certainly weak medicine compared to full bodied Bainesite Voluntaryism and the pledge merely not to vote for further state endowment contrasts sharply with the pronouncement in the *Eclectic Review* that 'it is not enough that no further grants be made, that no new encroachments be

---

17 ibid., 29th May, 3rd, 17th, 31st July 1847; *Nonconformist*, 13th, 23rd, 30th July, 13th August 1847.
18 J. Hanson to T. P. Thompson, 6th, 15th May 1847 (Thompson Papers, Hull University Library, DTH/3/29).
19 T. P. Thompson to G. Wilson 15th June 1847 (Wilson Papers); cf. *Leeds Mercury*, 12th, 19th, 26th June 1847.
20 T. P. Thompson to G. Wilson, 16th June 1847 (Wilson Papers); cf. T. P. Thompson to G. Rogers, 12th June 1847 (Thompson Papers).
21 *Leeds Mercury*, 10th July 1847; cf. T. P. Thompson to R. Milligan, 14th July 1847 (Thompson Papers).

permitted. The existing connection is essentially vicious.'[22] Yet the reports of Busfeild's embarassing cross-questioning suggest that even this modest conversion owed more to desperation than conviction. Busfeild's recantation was the key to the election for as Sir Charles Wood reported to Russell, the prime minister, 'Busfeild gave way on education and promised to abstain from voting in favour of more grants. This secured him and Colonel Thompson.'[23]

This was hardly a victory for Voluntaryism and Henry Forbes, a leading Bradford Dissenter, made it crystal clear that Voluntaryists were giving way on this one occasion in the interests of party unity. He pronounced,

> 'In conceding upon this occasion a point which we hold to be of such vast importance, we have done so simply for the purpose of healing the difference among the Liberal Party and it must be understood we never intend to make such a concession again. . . . Although we give up this point in the present instance to secure a united action yet on all future occasions we shall make it a test to every candidate seeking our suffrages.'[24]

Though Dissenting journals might include Busfeild in their list of favoured sons and even in one case cite him as an anti-state church, anti-state education candidate (which he certainly was not), those nearer home recognized the hard and, for Voluntaryists, unpalatable political facts. As Henry Forbes understood, the victory of Busfeild and Thompson at Bradford was due not to the insistence upon Voluntaryism but to its temporary suspension.

By thus removing the sting from Voluntaryism Bradford avoided the political fragmentation which occurred at Halifax where the virulence of dissent broke the Whig–radical understanding between the radical Edward Protheroe (MP since 1837) and Sir Charles Wood (MP since 1832 and chancellor of the exchequer from 1846).[25] Between them, Maynooth, the 1846 Minutes and Chartism, destroyed the chances of a return of the sitting members. The radicals and Chartists launched the Chartist leader Ernest Jones who was first in the field in the Halifax campaign. Dissenters objected to Protheroe's vote in favour of the Minutes and many of his former supporters followed the radical carpet manufacturer Frank Crossley in support of the Leeds resolutions. Crossley and the Voluntaryists nominated Edward Miall, editor of the *Nonconformist* and so there was a splendid confrontation between England's leading political Dissenter and the chancellor of the exchequer, thus personalizing the conflict between Dissent and the Whig government. Waiting in the wings to pick up the spoils of Liberal schism, the Tories nominated a strong local candidate Henry Edwards, a textile manufacturer, magistrate and colonel in the yeoman cavalry. The permutations were infinite as Halifax voters were wooed by five candidates for two seats, Jones (Chartist), Miall (Voluntaryist), Wood (Whig), Protheroe (Radical) and Edwards (Tory). Though Jones imparted a radical tinge to the election, it was essentially about education and religion. As the *Nonconformist* explained, Miall's supporters were 'acting solely on behalf of religion and prepared to merge all political differences with a view to their religious principles.'[26] Wood was in a dilemma but accepted that education must be the election's central issue, 'five-sixths of my friends are Dissenters and I cannot go up as the representative of a church party . . . I think we must make it a fight upon education for all classes.'[27]

Wood played a waiting game of consummate skill and wanted to keep all options open even an alliance with Miallite Voluntaryism:

22 *Eclectic Review*, May 1847, xxi, 639.
23 Sir C. Wood to Lord John Russell, 1st August 1847 (Russell Papers, Public Record Office, 30/22/6E).
24 *Leeds Mercury*, 12th July 1847.
25 For Halifax politics see J. A. Jowitt, 'Parliamentary Politics in Halifax 1832–1847,' *Northern History*, XII (1976), 172–201.
26 *Nonconformist*, 14th July 1847.
27 Sir C. Wood to J. Stansfeld, 21st June 1847, (Hickleton Mss., Garrowby, A4/50A).

'What I am anxious about more than anything is that we the Whigs should throw nobody over, desert nobody and stand above reproach. I believe the greater part of the dissenters will find out before long that they are in the wrong box. Then they will come round to us again. We must do nothing to render this reconciliation difficult.'[28]

It was a test of nerves and predictably Protheroe cracked first. In withdrawal he identified the new feature '*all other* considerations are disregarded for the sake of this one idea long cherished it is true, but now for the first time brought into political agitation.'[29] By a process of elimination an alliance with the Conservative on a pro-education playform was all that was left for Wood and so Wood and Edwards were returned (one Whig and one Tory), forced into each other's arms by Voluntaryism.

A similar contest occurred at Leeds, the home of the 'very oracle of Voluntaryism.' It had been traditional in Leeds for each section of the Liberal party (the radical and the Whig) to nominate a candidate who would then run jointly with mutual support.[30] In 1847, however, Baines put a proscriptive ban upon any alliance with a state educationalist and urged Voluntaryists to stand alone, pure and unsullied. Baines brought out Joseph Sturge, the Quaker Birmingham corn merchant, who had an impeccable record on reform and religious questions. In insisting upon the primacy of Sturge's Voluntaryism, Baines had to compromise on Sturge's radicalism since the *Leeds Mercury* had always argued forcibly against an extension of the suffrage. State education Liberals, in a minority in their own party, called on James G. Marshall to stand. He was an ideal candidate. A local man of wealth and standing, he was joint owner of the largest flaxspinning firm in Europe, giving much employment to local people. He was radical and believed in suffrage reform, he had been a keen free trader and as a Unitarian, he had supported Dissenting causes. In any other election he would have been overwhelmingly adopted but because he refused to toe the Voluntaryist line the Bainesite section rejected him. In pursuit of religious truth Voluntaryists could not commit the heresy of voting for Marshall, the state educationist. In so doing, the Voluntaryists ironically saved the political skin of William Beckett the sitting Tory member.

Beckett had voted with Peel in 1846 and without the education issue he would have been subjected to much recrimination. Indeed as a local journalist remarked, 'the great question of Education . . . has united a divided party and divided a united one.'[31] The 1847 contest was not between Liberals and Tories, as every other Leeds election was between 1832 and 1885, but between Voluntaryists and state educationists. It was this battle which determined how people voted and caused so many to vote against their normal political inclination. Of something over 4000 who voted, 1600 Liberals plumped for one candidate where they would normally have split between two; about 500 Liberals cast a second vote for a Tory (for the first and probably last time), and 1500 Tories cast a second vote for a Liberal (also a unique occurrence). In a highly politicized town the normally strong party system broke under the strain of Voluntaryism and the education question.

The members of Beckett's and Marshall's committees announced that as individuals they would be voting for the two education candidates. As at Halifax, the Leeds election was decided by this cross-party vote resulting from the independent stand taken by the Voluntaryists. As Wood explained to the prime minister, 'we have done very well upon the whole here and but for the extreme and really incredible

---

28 ibid., 23rd June 1847.
29 *Nonconformist*, 20th July 1847.
30 For further details see D. Fraser, 'Politics in Leeds 1830–52' (University of Leeds, unpublished Ph.D. thesis, 1969).
31 *Leeds Intelligencer*, 3rd July 1847.

violence of the nonconformists we should have been triumphant. They were wrongheaded beyond measure . . . [yet] they formed a very strong opposition and nothing but the support of the Conservatives carried us through at Leeds and Halifax.'[32] Where there was some doubt at Halifax as to the effects of the cross-party vote the Leeds election was more clear cut since, in the words of a dissenting journal, 'Marshall not only consents to come in with a tory but on his very shoulders.'[33] In Leeds the agreed statistical version was that Marshall commanded only about one quarter of Liberal votes and so would have come a poor third if all candidates had stood alone. As it was the high, cross-party vote sent Marshall to Westminster and kept Sturge out yet again. The extent of cross-party voting in the contested two member seats varied directly with the virulence of Voluntaryism. In Bradford where its potency was weakened a normally high cross-party vote was reduced to 4·9 per cent; in Halifax where the cross party vote had been 5·5 per cent in 1841, it became 43·6 per cent in 1847; and in Leeds most significantly of all, the cross-party vote increased from the minuscule 2·33 per cent in 1841 to the phenomenal 51·6 per cent in 1847. Such voting patterns marked the havoc of Voluntary schism in urban Liberalism and it was a sorry tale of failure from a Bainesite point of view. The Voluntaryists had lost a seat at Wakefield because of the extremism of their candidate, had been beaten at Huddersfield by forcing Tories into Liberal arms and had sacrificed safe seats at Halifax and Leeds. The Bradford victory was achieved by a flexibility of conscience and a political expediency which was not displayed elsewhere in the Riding.

In a sense, worse was to follow, for Voluntaryism sacrificed a seat for the West Riding in 1848.[34] The county constituency was always regarded as of great symbolic significance nationally and it was a measure of the achievement of the Anti-Corn Law League that Cobden was returned for the West Riding in 1847. When a byeelection occurred in 1848 the free traders were confident that they could carry this second seat because of the majority they had secured through registration activity. Urban interests forced the withdrawal of Charles Fitzwilliam, son of Earl Fitzwilliam, who usually expected to have deferential authority in the constituency. The Liberals then split along the lines of 1847 and imposed on the county an extreme London Voluntaryist Sir Culling Eardley. Many Whigs, respecting Fitzwilliam, and many radical Liberals, believing in state education, refused to support Eardley. Some even voted Conservative. Despite a potential Liberal majority, Baines and the Voluntaryists had thrown away the seat by making education the sole electoral test. Voluntaryism in 1847–8 was breaking up urban Liberalism in the West Riding on the education question and none was more critical of Baines than Cobden:

> 'Literally speaking he and he alone is the obstacle. By hereditary prestige rather than any native qualities for leading such a constituency he occupies a position from which he cannot be deposed. He has weakened the Dissenting party by severing it from Liberal politics and dividing it against itself and by his fierce opposition to National Education he has enabled the Tory Churchmen to turn his flank. . . . Baines is destined to be a standing obstacle to the success of the Liberal Party in the West Riding.'[35]

The fire from Leeds continued to burn brightly in the 1850s and 1860s but in many ways the centre of gravity of educational agitation was moving in those years on a triangular path, from Leeds to Manchester and thence to Birmingham. The rivalry between Baines and Cobden was symbolic of the rivalry between Leeds and Manchester on the education question. Leeds was the seat of Voluntaryism while Manchester sponsored many organizations in favour of state education. Manchester was

---

32 Sir C. Wood to Lord John Russell, 1st August 1847 (Russell Papers).
33 *Nonconformist Elector*, 3rd August 1847.
34 For full details see D. Fraser, 'Voluntaryism and West Riding Politics in the Mid-Nineteenth Century,' *Northern History*, XIII (1977).
35 R. Cobden to J. Bright, 22nd December 1848 (B.M. Add. Mss. 43649, f. 107).

as divided as Leeds, though along very different lines. In Leeds the question was whether the State should intervene at all, while in Manchester it concerned the form that intervention should take. It will be clear that long after the Leeds dilemma was disposed of the Manchester problem would still have to be resolved. Leeds imposed a proscriptive ban upon state education *per se*; Manchester sought to define the proper goals of a state education scheme that was both necessary and desirable.

The Lancashire Public Schools Association, officially begun in February 1848 under the chairmanship of Samuel Lucas, brother-in-law of John Bright, campaigned for rate-aided, locally controlled, secular education. These three principles were central. Schools should be publicly financed, run by elective boards and wholly concerned with secular education. When it changed its name to the National Public Schools Association it spelled out its commitment clearly:

> 'The National Public Schools Association is formed to promote the establishment by law, in England and Wales, of a system of free schools:- supported by local rates and managed by local committees, specially elected by the ratepayers for that purpose; and which, imparting secular instruction only, shall leave the teaching of doctrinal religion to parents, guardians and religious teachers.'[36]

The secular education lobby did not monopolize local opinion in Manchester, which also boasted a strong movement for state-aided denominational education. Indeed the latter scored a spectacular victory over the L.P.S.A. on its own ground at a meeting in the Free Trade Hall in March 1849.

While Baines continued in the 1850s to preach the evils of state education and the virtues of Voluntaryism, Manchester tried unsuccessfully to resolve locally the issues the nation was to face in the 1870s. Indeed in 1852 when it appeared that the two Manchester proposals would be definitively judged by Parliament, it was argued that 'Manchester will settle this great question for the present on the principles of one or other of the two schemes which Manchester has promulgated.'[37] The two schemes were similar only in that they were based on state aid. The denominationalists accepted some form of central control, wanted the endowment out of public funds of denominational establishments, firmly believed in religious education and opposed universal free access to state schools. The secularists vigorously opposed centralization, believed in strictly secular education, rejected the idea of state endowed religious institutions and were committed to universal free schooling on the rates. Their views may be gauged by the comment of the National Association on the denominational bill of 1852:

> 'It would tax all for the benefit of a part and that part not the most needy . . . would amount to an endowment of various and contradictory forms of religion whilst it would altogether shut out the approvers of purely secular instruction and would totally neglect the lowest class of all . . . there is no hope of bringing up the inert lower classes apart from a national system but that which is paid for by all should be kept free of legal and moral hindrances for the use of all: and that instruction agreeing with this principle and supported by a tax should be secular only.'[38]

Many Dissenters who viewed with horror the idea of banishing religious instruction from the schools were nevertheless equally aghast at state endowment of religion. What was wrong for Maynooth could not be right for Manchester and Salford. In the event neither proposal was adopted and a resolution of these issues was delayed until the late 1860s, by which time the initiative had passed from Manchester to Birmingham.

36 Minutes of the Lancashire Public Schools Association, Report of the Sub-Committee, 22nd November 1850 (Manchester Reference Library). The best account of the Association is to be found in D. K. Jones, 'The Lancashire Public School Association, later the National Public School Association, in its role as a pressure group, with an account of the Manchester Model Secular School, later the Manchester Free School,' (University of Sheffield, unpublished M.A. Dissertation, 1965).
37 Minutes of the National Public Schools Association, 7th January 1852.
38 ibid., 3rd November 1852.

The National Education League, founded in Birmingham in 1869, was in a sense the heir of the Manchester tradition. Indeed one of its moving spirits, George Dixon, believed that Manchester 'ought to have headed, and was entitled to lead a national movement.'[39] Birmingham's admiration of Manchester was evidenced by Francis Adams' comment on the secularist proposal of 1852—'based on the principle that the cost should be thrown on property, that the management should be confided to local representatives and that the people should be taught to regard education not as a bone of contention between churches and sects, but as the rights of free citizens.'[40]

The Birmingham movement brought together prominent radicals, leading Dissenters, and the advocates of the civic gospel. Underlying the pressure for education in the late 1860s lay the reluctant admission by Voluntaryism that it had failed. Baines admitted to Kay Shuttleworth in 1867 that Voluntaryism 'was allowed too absolute a sway and as a practical man I am compelled to abandon the purely voluntary system.'[41] Baines was as much a barometer as a mentor of Dissenting opinion and as his unbending Voluntaryism in 1847 struck a chord in the Nonconformist conscience, so his reluctant acceptance of state aid 20 years later was in tune with contemporary Dissenting attitudes.

In Birmingham the National Education League was partly an expression of a growing urban concern with educational deficiency and many of the civic reformers who rose to prominence in Birmingham politics in the 1860s and 1870s were motivated by a desire for educational reform. Yet significantly enough, when these educational reformers placed the League in historical perspective the context they chose was a political rather than an educational one. Francis Adams explained:

> 'Let me say that the members of the League were not anxious to make this question one of political warfare. It would have been a pleasure to them if for once in the history of this country a great work, having for its object the benefit of the multitude, had been suffered to proceed on its way undisturbed by the bitterness of party conflicts. But, sir this has not been permitted. Our old enemies the enemies of freetrade, of religious liberty, and popular government—the old obstructive party—ever on the watch for an opportunity to impede—has risen up against us to prevent, if possible, the accomplishment of our object. Though we did not seek it—though we would gladly have avoided it—we accept the situation which has been forced upon us, if not without regret, at any rate without despair. . . . We are charged with seeking to revolutionize the country. We hope so. There is nothing we desire more than to effect a revolution; but it will be a bloodless one—one which will put into the hands of the people no weapons but those of peace and industry, one which will break down no barriers except those which impede the way to a higher civilization.'[42]

It was all part of a traditional battle—not the battle for education but the battle of freedom against privilege.

In that battle all three cities prominent in educational agitation, spoke with a divided and not a united voice. Just as the Anti-Corn Law League never spoke for the whole of Manchester, the National Education League never spoke for the whole of Birmingham. Opinions were divided and there was great rivalry between the League and its denominational counterpart the National Education Union. As before, the agitation was placed in its political milieu and Adams explained that:

> 'The Union would have slumbered for ever in the womb of obscurity, had not the League been founded. It was then that the supporters of the Union hastened to the walls to array themselves once more, as the party of which they are composed has so often done before, against the just demands of the people! Their object is the supremacy of class interests, the perpetuation of priestly interference in national concerns and the conservation of the spirit of servility and dependence.'[43]

39 F. Adams, *History of the Elementary School Contest* (1882, repr. 1972), 195. The best account of the League is to be found in A. F. Taylor, 'Birmingham and the Movement for National Education 1867–77,' (University of Leicester, unpublished Ph.D. thesis, 1960).
40 Adams, op. cit., p. 152.
41 E. Baines to Sir James Kay Shuttleworth, 19th October 1867 (Baines Papers, Leeds City Archives, 23/11).
42 Quoted by A. Briggs, Introduction to Adams, op. cit., x.
43 ibid., xxv.

Again the context was the history of privilege and while the Union eschewed radical agitators, its sponsors included two archbishops, five dukes, one marquess, eighteen earls, twenty one bishops and twenty one barons. Sometimes the rivalry went beyond mere words and fighting broke out between supporters of the League and the Union in Manchester Free Trade Hall. These tests of rival strength were necessary, some felt, to win over the mind of W. E. Forster. As George Dixon explained:

> 'We are doing Forster's work for him testing the power of opposing forces in the country ... exactly in proportion to Forster's estimate of the strength of the League will be the liberal colouring of the Bill—he will be afraid of the churches until we convince him that we are stronger. He is not yet so convinced. He thinks that the Manchester Union will grow faster than the Birmingham League.'[44]

Though the League v. Union battle might appear to echo former disputes between Church and Dissent, this was no simple rerun of an earlier conflict because of the confused response to the question of religious education. Baines personified the difficulty well. He had spent his life campaigning against the evils of a state church and Anglican state education. Yet when he reluctantly acknowledged that there must be some state aid he could not follow his fellow Dissenters into the secular camp. As he explained to Kay Shuttleworth in 1867:

> 'I regret to say that not a few Congregationalists are inclined to favour a purely secular and rate support system of National Education as being in their judgement more impartial, more free from clerical influence and more effective; whilst the working classes and strong Radicals have a prejudice against that which is denominational. Now I fear that the Church Schools are too completely under the control of the Clergy, yet I dare not on that account adopt a system which must exclude religion from the schools and sever them from the religious communities.'[45]

Similarly he explained in 1874,

> 'the logical enforcement of the pure Nonconformist principle would require the absolute exclusion of Religion from the Schools ... yet that exclusion seems to me a violation of our duty to God and man and the elimination from the schools of the most precious element of education.'[46]

Since all education was moral education, and all morals derived from religion, then religion was an essential component of elementary education. Hence it turned out that Baines the Voluntaryist finished up arm-in-arm with his former denominational enemies.

Many of his former allies could not tread his path. Most followed the League first to unsectarian then to secular education as the only solution consistent with freedom. Typical of the Dissenting change of heart was the Lancashire Baptists, an association of urban congregations, whose views are a good sounding board of Nonconformist attitudes. In the 1840s they were staunchly Voluntaryist and their faith never wavered in the 1850s when the census appeared to confirm the voluntary achievement in educational provision. By 1870, however, they had renounced Voluntaryism in favour of a shared responsibility between state and churches:

> 'Let it be the aim of the government to sweep the streets of our large towns and gather in those neglected, dirt begrimed arabs whose dense ignorance is the shame of our civilization, and prevent them from growing up with minds as dark as the untutored savages whose sad condition has been wont to move our pity. Let it see that no child shall be defrauded of its right to a fair start in life through the criminal neglect or pauperized condition of its parents, and thus be allowed to grow up in ignorance, to struggle on in the race for bread with such an immense disadvantage or what is far more natural and likely, not to struggle at all, but to glide into the stream of vicious and lawless life and so swell the rising tide of pauperism and crime ... and then having accomplished its rightful portion of the great work, let the State throw upon the Churches to whom it rightfully belongs the responsibility of supplementing that work by teaching the same children the truths of the Gospel of Christ ... let the Government elevate the intellectual and moral condition of the community and then leave it to the Churches to

---

44 G. Dixon to G. Melly, 30th October 1869 (Melly Papers, Liverpool Record Office, 3702).
45 Baines to Kay Shuttleworth, loc. cit.
46 E. Baines to W. Arthur, 6th March 1874 (Baines Papers 16/19).

step in and expound and enforce the spiritual truths which have been committed to their keeping by the mercy of the Divine Lord.'⁴⁷

State secular education in partnership with voluntary religious education was the Nonconformist panacea purveyed by the League, but the 1870 Education Act was a compromise that was nearer in spirit to the Union than to the League. So the mantle of Baines was taken up by Dale and just as Baines refused to acknowledge a parliamentary decision in 1847 so Dale did the same in 1870. He warned ominously

> 'not even at the bidding of a Liberal Minister will we consent to any proposal which under cover of an educational measure empowers one religious denomination to levy a rate for teaching its creed and maintaining its worship.... We are determined that England shall not again be cursed with the bitterness and strife from which we hoped we had for ever escaped by the abolition of the Church Rate.'⁴⁸

Once the 1870 Education Act was in operation Dissenters had two possible political options. One was the 1847 approach of fighting elections on educational grounds in order to force the Liberal party to change its view. This was certainly explored and in a remarkable echo of Baines' delegate meeting in 1847, Nonconformists met at Manchester in 1872 and resolved to support no Liberal who advocated denominational grants and clause 25:

> 'the time has come for the Nonconformist adherents of the Liberal cause to insist on a thorough and consistent application of the principle of religious equality in the public policy of the leaders of their party.... This conference, believing that the cause of religious freedom is of more importance than any ties of party, appeals to the Nonconformists of Britain to declare that they will not accept as a satisfactory representative any candidate who will not accept the provision of the Conference.'⁴⁹

Either there would be a Nonconformist Liberal Party or it would fall apart and the seeds of divisions were indeed sown in a number of Parliamentary elections.

Yet the main weight of the secular education attack came in the School Boards themselves, for two reasons. First it was recognized that the School Boards were quintessentially political institutions. As Dixon remarked, the League's enemies were rejoicing that League principles had been vanquished whereas 'we have secured in the Education Act of 1870 a lever, by the wise use of which their adoption has become merely a question of time.'⁵⁰ School Boards had the power to implement certain policies and so were political. Secondly, School Boards were politicized by issues of educational policy and beyond education lay a more general commitment to popular participation and control. The League was very much aware of this aspect and added to one of its resolution, 'in urging the universal establishment of school boards, we are supporting the principles of popular government and local control.'⁵¹ That School Boards were overtly political institutions was admitted privately by a Conservative minister, anxious in 1874 that pernicious urban influences should not spread to the countryside:

> 'School Boards... in the smaller country towns and in villages... will produce very serious political results. They will become the favourite platforms of the Dissenting preacher and local agitator, and will provide for our rural populations, by means of their triennial elections and Board meetings, exactly the training in political agitation and the opportunity for political organization which the politicians of the Birmingham League desire and which will be mischievous to the State.'⁵²

---

47 *Circular Letter of the Lancashire and Cheshire Association of Baptists Churches* (1870), 8.
48 *Birmingham Daily Post*, 8 March 1870.
49 *General Conference of Nonconformists Held in Manchester* (Manchester, 1872).
50 Quoted by Briggs in Adams, op. cit., xvii.
51 *Birmingham Daily Post*, 21st October 1870.
52 Sandon Memorandum, November 1874 quoted by P. Smith, *Disraelian Conservatism and Social Reform* (1967), 246.

In very similar language forty years earlier Attwood had said that town councils would be training grounds for political agitation. School Boards, like town councils, came to symbolize the political difference between urban and rural society.

That the full potential of the School Board was not immediately utilized by the Birmingham Education League was the result of the cumulative voting system which allowed all fifteen votes to be cast for the same candidate in School Board elections. This was one side of a coin, the other side of which was the Minority Clause of 1867 which gave large towns an extra seat but restricted voters to two votes. The evolution of the Birmingham caucus was a response to *both* the 1867 Minority clause and the 1870 Education Act. It was not until 1873 that National Education League Liberals exploited the voting system and so School Board politics in the early 1870s in Birmingham largely concerned Liberal attempts to reverse through municipal authority the defeat suffered in the first school board election. Chamberlain and his allies held over the Board, first, the threat to refuse to collect the rate and, when this was deemed illegal, the threat to refuse the payment of rates. By one or other the Board was prevented from fully implementing either clause 25 or its bye-law on compulsory attendance. The Liberals were engaged in a holding operation until the 1873 election allowed them to gain control and enforce the even more secularist programme they had adopted in 1872. The key to a Liberal victory lay in the repetition of the methods used in the parliamentary election of 1868, when three Liberals had been returned: the Birmingham Liberal machine had to find a way round the cumulative vote as it had done round the minority clause. Wards were organized so that all voters cast *five votes* for each of three specified candidates. *Voters had to resist the temptation of plumping for Chamberlain in 1873, just as they had to resist the desire to plump for Bright in 1868.* The Liberals nominated only eight candidates but got them all returned and with Chamberlain as chairman a programme of secular schools was begun.[53]

Elsewhere the League's cause did not generally prosper. Manchester elected a clerical board in both 1870 and 1873 and in the twin towns of Manchester and Salford an Anglican–Catholic alliance maintained control for many years. In Sheffield there was one of the fiercest popular resistance movements utilizing a refusal to pay rates, yet Dissenters were cheated out of an expected victory in 1873 by an electoral mishap which left the 1870 denominational board in office. Prior to the 1873 election there had been an agreement between the Reform Association, the Trades Council and the League to support the 'undenominational eight' and with the support of the Liberal Association the undenominationalists secured a narrow majority in 1876. Liberal control was never secure and Liberal victories in 1876 and 1882 were reversed by Anglican–Conservative victories in 1879 and 1885.[54]

In Leeds the initial decision of the official Liberals and Liberal denominationalists to stand separately allowed an Anglican–Catholic victory in 1870. Politically the Board was composed of eight Liberals and seven Conservatives but the message of the election was taken to be that the ratepayers favoured religious education, to which most Liberals were opposed. Local Liberals recognized that the party had to be 'as capable of organizing its forces as is the Liberal Party in Birmingham' and though ward adoption was not used the combined Liberal–unsectarian list was returned in 1873, to give an 8–7 majority over the Anglican–Catholic members.[55] The parties agreed to avoid a contest in 1876 but by then municipal economists led by the fruit merchant Archie Scarr were in full flow and wished to stage an election 'as a protest

---

53 Taylor, op. cit., 151–205.
54 D. E. Fletcher, 'Aspects of Liberalism in Sheffield 1849–1886' (University of Sheffield, unpublished Ph.D. thesis, 1972), 198–9.
55 *Leeds Mercury*, 22nd–30th November 1870, 22nd November 1873.

against the extravagant expenditure of the board.'[56] The religious difficulty reappeared in 1879 when the board was fragmented over the secularist issue and Anglicans, Catholics and Wesleyans joined forces to protect denominational schools. Baines was forced to acknowledge that 'the elements of disunion and disintegration have reappeared among us,' as the Liberals won only three of the 15 seats in 1879.[57] The Conservative-dominated board severely limited the development of unsectarian board schools in the interests of denominational schools. This policy was reversed in 1882 when Liberals regained control when the voters 'condemned the policy carried out by the sectarian majority.'[58]

In 1882 Baines regretted that unnecessary heat had been injected into a School Board struggle which had been fought on lines 'partly political, partly sectarian and unsectarian.'[59] Then in his 80s, he must have been struck by how similar this all was to the politico-religious battles he fought half a century earlier. The politicizing of School Boards in the 1870s had much in common with the politicizing of vestries in the 1820s. They were both characterized by a mixture of religious financial and political issues and they were both an expression of the Nonconformist search for real religious equality. Institutionally too there were important similarities. Though not precisely a parochial or township institution the School Board was rather like one, for it had been deliberately separated from the Town Council. As Chamberlain had found, municipal power did not carry with it control of the School Board.

In time Chamberlain acknowledged the need to distinguish between the political and educational work of the League, but the gulf between education and politics never really existed, since national education involved the exercise of the community's power in pursuit of a policy objective. Education was viewed as a political question in the Corporation affairs of early Victorian Liverpool, in the parliamentary elections of the West Riding in the later 1840s, in the education movement of Manchester and Birmingham in the 1850s and 1860s and in the urban school boards of the 1870s and 1880s. Education *remains* and has not suddenly become a political issue. It was certainly regarded as such in the great cities of Victorian England.

56 ibid., 11th November 1876.
57 ibid., 22nd November 1879.
58 ibid., 21st November 1882.
59 ibid., 20th November 1882.

Illiteracy and Schooling in the Provincial Towns, 1640–1870: A Comparative Approach

W. B. STEPHENS
University of Leeds

Of mid-eighteenth-century British towns the two capital cities, London and Edinburgh, alone had populations of over 50 000, and only 20 per cent of our ancestors at that time, lived in towns of more than 5000 inhabitants. Between then and the beginning of the nineteenth century, Britain became the first urbanized society of the modern world, with a fifth of its citizens living in towns of 10 000 or more inhabitants. By 1801 there were eight towns with populations over 50 000; by 1851, 29 such centres accounted for a third of the nation's inhabitants. In mid century the aggregate urban population exceeded the rural population for the first time, though it is true by only 1 per cent.[1] These changes represented a profound development, not only in the demographic structure of society, but also in its way of life and in the social conditions of its members.

In present times urbanization and industrialization are seen to go hand in hand with the improvement of educational standards. A certain level of general literacy is considered requisite for a backward nation to achieve significant economic growth.[2] It is not clear, however, whether such an economic 'law' can be applied to the experience of eighteenth- and early-nineteenth-century Britain. Indeed it has been suggested that the British industrial revolution may have caused, or at least taken place with, initially falling standards of basic education and that subsequently rising standards were the fruits of industrialization rather than the seeds of it.[3]

Educational historians interested in the relationship between economic and social change and education in the eighteenth and nineteenth century have tended, like economic historians, to concentrate on the industrial towns of the north and midlands, for this was the period of the Industrial Revolution and where else to study the causes and impact of that phenomenon than in the places it occurred? However, Lancashire was not England, and urban economic and social change in the period of the Industrial Revolution was not confined to the Lancashire cotton towns, nor indeed to the woollen districts of the West Riding, or the various coal and metal based communities. The obverse of the rise of the new industrial towns and regions

---

1 E. E. Lampard, 'The Urbanizing World,' in H. J. Dyos and M. Wolff, *The Victorian City*, I (1973) 4; M. I. Thomis, *The Town Labourer and the Industrial Revolution* (1974), 48.

2 See R. M. Hartwell, *The Industrial Revolution and Economic Growth* (1971), 226 ff. and works cited there; M. Blaug, *An Introduction to Economics of Education* (1970); M. J. Bowman and C. A. Anderson, 'Concerning the Role of Education in Development,' in C. Geertz (ed.), *Old Societies and New States* (1963), 252.

3 R. S. Schofield, 'Dimensions of Illiteracy 1750–1850,' *Explorations in Economic History* (1972–3), 453–4; M. Sanderson, 'Literacy and Social Mobility in the Industrial Revolution in England,' *Past and Present*, 56 (1972), and the ensuing debate on this article between Sanderson and T. W. Laqueur, ibid., 64 (1974) (see n. 29 below); Hartwell, op. cit., 229 ff.; C. M. Cipolla, *Literacy and Development in the West* (1969), 68.

was sometimes the decline of more established ones. On the other hand agricultural expansion, especially in the period 1846 to 1871, led to prosperity for certain market towns. If we look at early- and mid-Victorian provincial towns in England and Wales as a whole, south as well as north, west as well as east, we observe an enormous variety in many aspects of social and economic activity.

English towns had their urbanity in common but they were by no means homogeneous: their variety was extensive. Leaving aside London—as indeed I am afraid I shall do throughout this essay—there were the three great industrial giants—Manchester, Birmingham and Leeds—which had witnessed a comparatively recent and very rapid expansion in population and economic growth, but each of which was very different from the others. There were the smaller but booming textile towns of Lancashire and the West Riding, but also other important centres of production—like Nottingham, Leicester, and Coventry—which were ancient industrial towns before the Industrial Revolution and which now experienced an expansion less based on the factory than Manchester and the Lancashire cotton towns. Yet other places, like Swindon, Middlesbrough and Crewe, were virtually creations of the Industrial Revolution, as was St. Helens, a Lancashire town whose mixed economy, like that of neighbouring Warrington, was not tied to cotton manufacture. Then there were the ancient market towns, some of which still depended on the fortunes of local agriculture, surviving or decaying according to the region and the time; while others, the 'Banburys of England,' which had developed mixed economies of trades, crafts and manufactures in the eighteenth and nineteenth centuries, continued to grow in size. Some of these towns, like Banbury itself, acted as regional centres and were clearly different in character from the predominantly industrial towns.[4] Different again were the older centres of industry which decayed or found new functions as market or administrative centres, like Exeter, formerly the hub of the great west country woollen trade. It would be possible to illustrate a multitude of further diversities in towns of this period—spa towns, cathedral cities, ports—all sub-groups of the genus 'town', but with each varying within the sub-group as, for example, between the port of Liverpool and the port of Brixham. Clearly, types of mid-Victorian British towns were manifold, and to the differences of type we might add the likelihood that regional differences were often extremely significant. It has been suggested, for example, that perhaps 'the Victorian city is less of a type than would be the Victorian city of this or that region.'[5]

In the circumstances, one is bound to heed Professor Checkland's warning that 'those who make thumping generalizations about what happened, even within a particular group of [towns] . . . , for example British industrial cities, are likely to find themselves highly vulnerable.'[6] With that vulnerability in mind I will now proceed to see if even tentative generalizations might be made about the state of the education of British town dwellers in the recent past.

Before looking at the levels of basic educational attainment in the mid-nineteenth century, which form the core of this investigation, it may be pertinent to mention something of what has been discovered of such characteristics in towns before that period. Here, the tentative conclusions of those who have interested themselves in the matter appear to be that basic literacy (measured by the ability to sign one's name) was probably higher in towns than in rural areas in the pre-industrial period, but that the impact of industrialization combined with population expansion adversely affected the literacy levels in 'Industrial Revolution' towns and areas (such as coal-

---

4 A. Everitt, 'The Banburys of England,' *Urban History Year Book* (1974).
5 G. F. A. Best, 'Another Part of the Island: Some Scottish Perspectives,' in Dyos and Wolff, op. cit., I, 390–1.
6 S. G. Checkland, 'Towards a Definition of Urban History,' in H. J. Dyos (ed.), *The Study of Urban History* (1968), 359.

mining districts) at some time in the later-eighteenth and early-nineteenth centuries. Thus, although the Sunday-schools and later the voluntary schools, mitigated the situation, educational levels in industrial towns remained lower than those in many other towns and also than in many rural areas through most of the rest of the nineteenth century. The expansion of population, moreover, created the possibility of a simultaneous decrease in the proportion of illiterates in the community with an increase in their absolute numbers.

I do not seek to overturn these conclusions which may well contain basic truths. Nevertheless, it should be pointed out that the evidence for urban superiority in the seventeenth century is fragmentary, while the evidence for the impact of industrialization on educational levels in the next century is complex and by no means clear cut. The quantitative evidence for the seventeenth century is derived largely from the Protestation returns of 1642[7] analysed by Professor Stone. 'If,' as he says, 'one can base a generalization on the single city of Chester, the literacy rate in the towns would appear to have been a good deal higher than in the countryside, at any rate in the lowland zone.'[8] The returns for Chester, however, omit the large parish of St. Peter's, while an incomplete return for Bridgwater gives a level no better than some rural parishes in Buckinghamshire.[9] Moreover, as Stone himself points out, the situation in the north may have been different; a substantial number of civic leaders in Gateshead and Newcastle, for example, were illiterate. Towns in those days, however, were often very small and it is doubtful whether the distinction between rural and urban conditions was always as great as sometimes assumed. It is true that endowed grammar schools tended to exist in boroughs, but clearly there were large numbers of schools of one kind or another situated in small rural places.[10] I have looked particularly at the Protestation returns for Devon and Cornwall which will yield more information than Stone culled from them.[11] In seventeenth-century Cornwall the concept of a distinct urban type of life is difficult to maintain, for no town in the county, chartered or otherwise, had more than 1000 inhabitants.[12] What is evident is that illiteracy tended to be associated with the prosperity or otherwise of the district, increasing as one moved westwards from the Devon border to Land's End. In seventeenth-century Devon I found information on two towns— Bampton and Totnes. Totnes (41 per cent signatures), prosperous at that time, was well above the average for all Devon parishes analysed (30 per cent) and all 15 parish officers could sign their names. However, its literacy level was equalled and bettered by a few rural parishes, while Bampton (33 per cent) was not outstandingly superior and both its overseers of the poor were illiterate. Even in Exeter, the largest town in Devon and Cornwall, with a population of between 9000 and 10 500,[13] some of the parish officers in the poorer areas of the city could not sign their names. In Devon,

---

7 For the Protestation Returns, see W. B. Stephens, *Sources for English Local History* (1973), 38. For a wider variety of 'signature' evidence in the 17th century, see D. Cressy, 'Educational Literacy in London and East Anglia, 1580–1700,' (Cambridge University, unpublished Ph.D. thesis, 1973).
8 L. Stone, 'Literacy and Education in England, 1640–1900,' *Past and Present*, 42 (1968), 100.
9 Indeed Bridgwater's level may be even lower than the level (38 per cent signatures) that Stone suggests. My calculations, based on the transcript: T. L. Stoate (ed.), A. J. Howard (comp.), *The Somerset Protestation Returns and Lay Subsidy Rolls 1641–2* (1975), give just over 27 per cent signatures, lower than many of the rural areas Stone has analysed.
10 See, *inter alia*, A. Smith 'Private Schools and Schoolmasters in the Diocese of Lichfield and Coventry in the Seventeenth Century,' *History of Education*, 5(2) (1976); M. Spufford, 'The Schooling of the Peasantry in Cambridgeshire, 1575–1700,' in J. Thirsk, *Land, Church and People* (1970).
11 W. B. Stephens, 'Male Illiteracy in Devon on the Eve of the Civil War,' *Devon Historian* (1975) 11; W. B. Stephens, 'Male and Female Illiteracy in 17th-century Cornwall,' *Jnl. Educational Administration and History*, IX, 2 (1977).
12 J. Whetter, *Cornwall in the 17th Century* (1974), 8.
13 W. B. Stephens, 'The Population of Exeter in 1641–2,' *Devon and Cornwall Notes and Queries*, 33, 5 (1975).

again, literacy appeared to be at a higher level in the less remote areas, the areas where there was better farming land and where the prosperous woollen industry was concentrated, while the proportion of those making marks was highest in the less heavily populated areas of poorer farming land, particularly those fringing Dartmoor, where one might expect the task of scratching a living from the land totally absorbed the energies of the population. In my opinion then, it is doubtful whether we have enough positive evidence to suggest a general urban superiority in literacy levels in the mid-seventeenth century.

For the period 1754 to 1840 the obligation for spouses to sign the marriage register on marriage, or to make a mark, provides a great deal more evidence on basic literacy levels—for a large number of places over about a century, until this direct parish register evidence is superseded by the same information, provided for registration districts, in the annual reports of the Registrar General of Births, Deaths and Marriages. Much work has been based on this material (the advantages and disadvantages of which need not be discussed here)[14] but it tends to appear in articles and theses (many fairly recent) or embedded in more general works which makes generalizations on my part, in an article mainly devoted to a later period, difficult. On the basis of what has been seen, however, it appears that a serious attempt to collect and analyse such investigations and to make use directly of parish registers generally would be worthwhile, and is indeed being undertaken by the Cambridge Group for the Study of Population and Social Structure. Because so much work is in progress, what follows must necessarily be tentative.

By the mid-eighteenth century, however, it seems likely that average literacy rates had much improved over 1642. The period from 1650–1800 had certainly been one of urban growth.[15] However, evidence for towns does not indicate that levels of literacy were maintained everywhere in the classical period of the Industrial Revolution, say 1760–1830. True, we can provide statistical evidence to demonstrate urban improvement. At Ludlow, for example, male and female marriage signatures increased from 52 per cent in the period 1754–60 to 62 per cent in the period 1821–30 and continued to rise up to 1840.[16] At Plymstock in Devon there was a more or less continuous rise from 48 per cent signatures in 1754–64, to 67 per cent in 1835–40.[17] In the Lincolnshire towns of Gainsborough, Grantham, Lincoln, Louth, Sleaford, and Deeping decennial averages show a gradual rise with only small variations.[18] At Wetherby (Yorks) percentages of signatures rose more or less steadily from 50 per cent in the period 1754–9 to 56 per cent in 1790–9.[19] At Penzance the proportions of marriage signatures rose from an average of 54 per cent for the years 1754–61, to 57 per cent for the years 1800–1804; and to 63 per cent for the years 1832–7.[20]

14 See R. S. Schofield. 'The Measurement of Literacy in Pre-Industrial England,' in J. Goody (ed.), *Literacy in Traditional Societies* (1968), 318 ff; W. L. Sargent, 'On the Progress of Elementary Education, *Jnl. Statistical Soc.*, XXX (1867), 87–8.

15 See C. W. Chalklin, *The Provincial Towns of Georgian England* (1974), 3–31.

16 D. J. Lloyd, 'Popular Education and Society in Ludlow, 1711–1861,' (University of Hull, unpublished M.Ed. thesis, 1974), 132–5. Percentages: 1754–60: 52; 1761–70: 58; 1771–80: 59; 1781–90: 61; 1791–1800: 58; 1801–10: 63; 1811–20: 57; 1821–30: 62; 1831–40: 72.

17 W. B. Stephens, 'Illiteracy in Devon during the Industrial Revolution, 1754–1844,' *Jnl. Educational Administration and History*, VIII, 1 (1976), 2–3. Percentages: 1754–64: 48; 1765–74: 47; 1778–84: 51; 1785–94: 51; 1795–1804: 52; 1805–14: 55; 1815–24: 57; 1825–34: 69; 1835–44: 67.

18 W. Couth, 'The Development of the Town of Gainsborough, 1750 to 1850,' (University of Wales (Cardiff), unpublished M.A. thesis, 1975), xxi. Composite percentages for these towns: 1754–64: 49; 1765–74: 54; 1775–84: 56; 1785–94: 56; 1795–1804: 56; 1805–14: 61; 1815–24: 62; 1825–34: 67; 1835–44: 67.

19 Percentages (for which I am indebited to my colleague, Dr R. Unwin) are for Spofforth parish: 1754–9: 50; 1760–9: 56; 1770–9: 59; 1780–9: 54; 1790–9: 56.

20 R. Edmonds, 'A Substantial Account of the Borough of Penzance and the Parish of Madron, Cornwall,' *Jnl. Statistical Soc. of London*, II (1838), 226–7.

However, W. L. Sargent in a paper given to the Statistical Society of London over a century ago[21] produced marriage register figures for the geographically scattered towns of Oxford, Northampton, Kings Lynn, Bristol, Nottingham, and Halifax, and a number of country parishes for the years 1754–62, 1799–1804, and 1831–37. He concluded that over the period 1754–1837 as a whole, the literacy (marriage signature) rates for towns barely improved, while those for country folk rose from 40 per cent to 60 per cent signatures. Moreover, he says, 'if we compare 1760 with 1800 we see that the towns had actually deteriorated a little, while the rural districts had made a large advance.' Sargent based his verdict on 26 rural parishes[22] which collectively showed a decline in the percentage of marriage marks from 58 in 1754–62, to 46·5 in 1799–1804, to 41·5 in 1837. However, these were averages disguising the fact that in some of these rural parishes illiteracy, at times, increased. Thus at East Acklam (Yorks) the percentage making marks increased from 37·5 in 1754–62, to 50 in 1799–1804.[23] Similarly, in Devon some rural parishes showed considerable decline in standards of literacy in this period. At Eggesford, for example, the percentage making marks increased from 47·5 in 1765–74 to 50 in 1795–1804, and to over 69 in 1815–24; at Kentisbeare they went up from 48·5 in 1754–64 to 70·5 in 1785–94.[24] So that Sargent's conclusions on rural parishes are not universally applicable.

Lawrence Stone using Sargent's figures for grooms only has produced a table showing that in all the towns cited by Sargent, except Halifax, there was 'a slow, unspectacular but persistent upward trend' in literacy between 1760 and 1800, continuing in the years 1800–35.[25] If, however, we combine percentages for grooms and brides the reasons Sargent's conclusions on towns are to some extent justified (Table 1).[26]

Table 1. Percentages of brides and grooms signing their names

	Oxford	Northampton	King's Lynn	Bristol	Nottingham	Halifax
1754–62	67	79	51	51	54	42
1799–1804	71	62	57	59	49	47
1831–7	75	66	61	66	65	24

The decline in Halifax in 1831–7 from the turn of the century is paralleled to a lesser extent at Northampton and Nottingham at an earlier period. Levels in these towns were lower (in Northampton's case markedly lower) in 1799–1804 than in 1754–62. Moreover, evidence for declining standards in some other towns at various times in the later eighteenth and early nineteenth centuries is not difficult to find. Mrs Sylvia Harrap has found that at Mottram, which embraced Stalybridge, though over the period as a whole standards improved, there was a decline from the mid 1770s.[27] Again, at Ashton-under-Lyne, where in 1763 and 1783 the percentage signing was 36 and 34 per cent, in 1803 40 per cent, and in 1823 48 per cent, ten years later in 1833 it had fallen to 10 per cent, and in 1843 to 9 per cent. Investigation shows that the most significant factor involved here was a drop in the percentage of grooms signing from 68 per cent in 1823 to 11 per cent in 1833. J. R. Coulthard, reported to

21 Sargent, op. cit., esp. 90–1, 127–8.
22 One in Yorks., 1 in Leics., 3 in Staffs., 3 in Warwicks., 8 in Northants., 1 in Hunts., 1 in Cambs., 2 in Worcs., 1 in Oxfs., 1 in Sussex, 1 in Glocs., 2 in Somerset, 1 in Dorset.
23 Sargent, op. cit., 127.
24 W. B. Stephens, 'Illiteracy in Devon . . . 1754–1844,' op. cit., 2–3.
25 Stone, op. cit., 103.
26 The parishes concerned were, Oxford: St. Ebbe's, St. Aldates, St. Martin's; Northampton: All Saints, St. Peter's; King's Lynn: St. Nicholas Chapel, St. Margaret's; Bristol: St. John the Baptist's; Nottingham: St. Mary's (Sargent, op. cit., 128).
27 S. A. Harrop, 'The Place of Education in the Genesis of the Industrial Revolution with special reference to Stalybridge, Dukinfield and Hyde,' (University of Manchester, unpublished M.Ed. thesis, 1976) 75–6, 84.

the Royal Commission on the State of Large Towns that 'if writing . . . is to be considered a criterion of the education of a people, verily the inhabitants of this town are in a pitiable condition; and what makes the matter worse and improvement almost hopeless, is the remarkable fact that we are in a state of rapid retrogression.'[28]

There was a similar deterioration in literacy levels in parishes in industrial Lancashire and north Cheshire in the period c. 1754–1815, including the towns of Blackburn, Burnley, Clitheroe, Whalley, Bury, Chorley, Preston, Kirkham, Deane, Eccleston (embracing St. Helens), Stockport, Manchester and Bolton, and a probable decline in other industrial centres in the area including Rochdale, Wigan, Warrington, Leigh, Oldham, and Winwick.[29] York, according to the researches of M. Yasumoto, had the remarkably high rate of 93 per cent signatures in 1754–59, but this percentage fell to 37 in 1760–69, and to 42 in 1770–79, thereafter rising until in 1800–1809 it was 96.[30]

Superficially, at least some conclusions seem clear. Literacy levels were manifestly related to some extent to the economic function of the town. Towns which experienced an expansion of industry seem also to have suffered a decline in literacy levels at various times in the later-eighteenth and early-nineteenth centuries. However, these included not only the textile factory towns, but also towns like Northampton and Nottingham where industrial expansion was not associated with factory production.

Nottingham, where the population probably rose from some 10 000 about 1740 to nearly 29 000 in 1801 and continued to expand quickly after that, developed in that period from a predominantly market and administrative centre with some domestic industry, particularly framework knitting, into a large industrial town; its industrial expansion combined a growth in the domestic hosiery industry with an expansion of lace-making in small-scale factories and workshops.[31] At Northampton the population rose from 10 000 to 26 000 between 1821 and 1851 when half the labour force was engaged in the shoe trade, organized in small workshops.[32]

These were places where the existing school facilities may have been unable to meet the needs of increased population. What Sargent said of towns generally was at least true of these towns: 'the towns had so far outgrown the means of instruction that the educational efforts made had effected no improvement.'[33] They were also often the towns where there was plenty of scope for child labour. As far as the textile towns were concerned, moreover, the shift from domestic to factory production may have further affected the opportunities for education by depressing the standard of living of the handloom weavers who could no longer afford money to educate their children and needed their help or wages.[34]

It may be, too, that in the early stages of industrialization opportunities for social advancement were not necessarily connected with the acquisition of schooling, so that for a period, investment in education was not as attractive as it may have been earlier or was to become later. Clearly, the value of education would differ anyway according to the economic and connected occupational structure of the particular

28 *First Report, Royal Commission on State of Large Towns and Populous Districts*, (1844) xvii, App., 86.
29 M. Sanderson, 'Literacy and Social Mobility in the Industrial Revolution in England,' *Past and Present*, 56 (1972); T. W. Laqueur: 'Debate,' and M. Sanderson, 'Rejoinder' in ibid. 64 (1974).
30 M. Yasumoto, 'Urbanization and Population in an English Town: Leeds during the Industrial Revolution,' *Keio Economic Studies*, X, 2, (1973), 84.
31 R. A. Church, *Economic and Social Change in a Midland Town: Victorian Nottingham, 1815–1900* (1966), chapters 1–4.
32 W. Page (ed.), *V.C.H., Northants*, iii (1930), 29; J. Foster, 'Nineteenth-Century Towns—A Class Dimension,' in H. J. Dyos (ed.), *The Study of Urban History*, op. cit., 291.
33 Sargent, op. cit., 91.
34 M. Sanderson, 'Social Change and Elementary Education in Industrial Lancashire, 1780–1840,' *Northern History*, III (1968), 136 ff.

town.[35] Industrialization in the early stages of the Industrial Revolution would not particularly encourage and might well discourage indigent education, and would not usually attract large numbers of educated immigrants: as Sanderson has put it, Lancashire underwent industrialization 'with workers whose education was steadily deteriorating.'[36]

The probability that the extent of basic literacy was connected with urban occupational structure is reinforced by the tendency for a high female industrial employment (as in the textile towns) coinciding with a much lower literacy rate for women than for men.[37] At Halifax, for example, nearly double the number of brides as grooms made marks in the periods 1754–62 (77 per cent) and 1799–1804 (70 per cent). At Nottingham the proportions of women making marks actually increased from 61 to 69 per cent between these periods, compared with 32 and 33 per cent for men. At Northampton, too, there was a large increase in the proportion of illiterate brides in the same period.[38]

Conversely, to give examples from non-industrial towns, at Bristol while in 1754–62 some 62 per cent of brides made marks (and 34 per cent of grooms), by 1799–1804 only 50 per cent could not sign (32 per cent of grooms). At King's Lynn there was a similar decline in the proportion of women making marks: 60 per cent in 1754–62; 53 per cent in 1799–1804.[39] The same tendency for non-industrial towns to show increasingly better standards is also demonstrable with smaller market towns, like Ludlow and Wetherby, the places in Lincolnshire mentioned above (essentially market towns), and market towns in Bedfordshire and elsewhere,[40] which all experienced a steady rise in literacy. Here, the stimulation of occupations connected with the expansion of trade (itself stimulated by increased agricultural and industrial output), probably encouraged the acquisition of a degree of education. Market towns contained a larger proportion of tradesmen of one kind and another for whom the three Rs were a business necessity. Moreover, they were often ancient boroughs, traditionally centres where schools existed and educational standards were superior[41] and where population growth was now not so rapid as to cause dislocation of educational facilities. It is noticeable that many of these towns had benefited from improvements in road transport (as, for example, Wetherby) and canal construction (for example, some of the Lincolnshire towns) which stimulated trades in which the keeping of accounts and records and the ability to communicate by letter were useful. Oxford, a market centre, might for other obvious reasons have been expected to have a disproportionate share of educated people.

Not all towns, however, fit easily into this pattern. York, a cathedral city, provincial capital, and social centre for the gentry of the region, suffered a catastrophic decline in literary levels.[42] There was a decline, too, between 1775 and 1784 at St. Paul's,[43] a fairly prosperous parish in Exeter, another cathedral city and a port whose

---

35 cf. Schofield, 'Dimensions of Illiteracy,' op. cit., 452–4; and see references to Sanderson and Laqueur in note 29 above.
36 Sanderson, 'Social Change . . . Industrial Lancashire,' op. cit., 153.
37 cf. Schofield, 'Dimensions,' op. cit., 453; Sargent, op. cit., 111–12 (for the 1860s). This tendency continued in the West Riding into the later 19th century—in 1866, e.g., there were nearly 27 per cent more illiterate brides than grooms in the Huddersfield registration district, 26 per cent in Bradford district, 20 per cent in Dewsbury district: Jennifer H. Robson, 'Educational Attainment of the Working-Class Female in the West Riding of Yorkshire, 1850 to 1870,' M.A. research exercise, University of Leeds, 1976, p. 14 (based on Registrar General's annual reports).
38 Sargent, op. cit., 128.
39 ibid.
40 Schofield, 'Dimensions,' op. cit., 449.
41 P. Laslett, *The World We have Lost* (1965), 194–5.
42 See above.
43 Stephens, 'Illiteracy in Devon . . . 1754–1844,' op. cit., 2: percentage marks: 1754–64: 56; 1765–74: 59; 1775–84: 46; 1785–94: 65; 1795–1804: 65; 1805–14: 65; 1815–24: 73; 1825–34: 84.

trade was still very important and at the time was flourishing.[44] Bristol, however, a far greater seaport, trading city and market centre, fourth largest English provincial town in 1801, a regional capital (if by then losing ground) saw a gradual improvement of its literacy rate over the periods 1754–62; 1799–1804 and 1831–7.[45] Again Ottery St. Mary in Devon is a good example of the difficulties of urban categorization: it was a market town that experienced a decline in literacy rates in the period 1775–84 and probably in the years 1805–14. However, it was also the centre of a lace-making district where domestic child labour was prevalent and, moreover, had the experience, unusual in Devon, of having a large textile mill erected in the 1790s.[46]

Since levels of urban literacy in this period varied so greatly there is no longer any clear-cut over-all distinction between rural and urban levels. What can be said is that where town levels were relatively good they were better than most rural areas. In Bedfordshire, for example, illiteracy declined more in those parishes where there was a greater proportion of non-agricultural occupations;[47] in Lincolnshire rural parishes were inferior to the market towns.[48] The newly industrialized towns of the north, however, were by now inferior to many northern country districts. Levels in the East and North Ridings were better than those in Leeds, and for much of the period, than those in York, and even those of the rural West Riding were superior to those for Leeds. This conclusion is confirmed by the fact that a much higher proportion of immigrants marrying in Leeds could sign their names than was the case with native brides and grooms.[49] Similarly in Lancashire by the 1830s rural areas were much more literate than industrial districts.[50]

For the period from 1840 it is possible to obtain more comprehensive information covering the whole country, for it is from then that we have the Registrar General's annual reports which include marriage register statistics. It was on the basis of these that Professor C. M. Cipolla in his *Literacy and Development in the West* (1968) suggested that in the mid-nineteenth century levels of illiteracy did not vary significantly from one part of England to another, and that 'leaving aside the two extreme cases of London on the one hand and Wales on the other ... England offered an essentially homogeneous picture.'[51] He based his conclusion on a comparison of county averages for marriage signature percentages. It is a patently misleading conclusion. Certainly, as he says, 'the rates of illiteracy of the different counties varied within a relatively narrow range, namely from a minimum of 31 for the south-eastern counties to a maximum of 49 for the north-western counties.' However, county averages disguise wide variations within county boundaries. The county, had in some parts of the country a degree of homogeneity, but it was often defective as a statistical unit for illiteracy. Some counties contained diverse areas—cities, towns, mining districts, farming communities—and discernible economic regions did not necessarily coincide with county boundaries. Illiteracy levels within counties varied considerably. Thus, to give two examples, in the West Riding in 1870 a county average of 28 per cent illiteracy on marriage embraced Hunslet (part of Leeds) with 35·9 per cent and Sedbergh with only 3·7 per cent, and in Devon, while the average illiteracy rate for the six years 1865–70 was 21·2 per cent, the 20 census districts ranged from

---

44 W. G. Hoskins, *Industry, Trade and People in Exeter, 1688–1800* (1935), 78–81.
45 cf. W. E. Minchinton, 'Bristol—Metropolis of the West in the Eighteenth Century,' *Trans. R. Hist. Soc.* 5th ser., IV (1954).
46 Stephens, 'Illiteracy in Devon ... 1754–1844,' op. cit., 3.
47 Schofield, 'Dimensions of Illiteracy,' op. cit., 447–9.
48 Couth, op. cit., xx–xxi.
49 Yasumoto, op. cit., 83–5.
50 Sanderson, 'Literacy and Social Mobility,' op. cit., 84–5.
51 loc. cit., 80.

Exeter (12 per cent) to Torrington (29·3 per cent).[52] In the same way, as we shall see, over the country as a whole there were great differences between individual towns and cities.

Table 2. Towns with more day-school pupils than 1 in 6 of the population, 1851

Population	Town	County	Day-school pupils: one in
5187	Andover	Hampshire	4·97
2748	Arundel	Sussex	5·10
4026	Banbury	Oxfordshire	5·89
5775	Bideford	Devon	4·91
2504	Blandford	Dorset	4·60
2544	Calne	Wiltshire	5·39
7101	Chesterfield	Derbyshire	5·24
8662	Chichester	Sussex	5·66
2932	Chipping Norton	Oxfordshire	5·79
6394	Dorchester	Dorset	5·98
4953	Falmouth	Cornwall	5·93
4595	Faversham	Kent	4·78
6726	Folkestone	Kent	5·83
6740	Guildford	Surrey	5·22
3395	Helston	Cornwall	5·34
6605	Hertford	Hertfordshire	4·98
3882	Huntingdon	Huntingdonshire	4·89
2857	Hythe	Kent	5·53
11 829	Kendal	Westmorland	5·52
3397	Launceston	Cornwall	5·44
17 536	Lincoln	Lincolnshire	5·75
2651	Lymington	Hampshire	4·86
4558	Maldon	Essex	4·51
3908	Marlborough	Wiltshire	3·39
4096	Morpeth	Northumberland	5·41
3959	Penryn	Cornwall	5·71
9255	Poole	Dorset	5·59
2943	Retford, East	Nottinghamshire	3·92
4106	Richmond	Yorkshire	5·37
6080	Ripon	Yorkshire	5·97
2080	Romsey	Hampshire	5·30
5911	Saffron Walden	Essex	5·78
6525	St. Ives	Cornwall	5·03
2503	Shaftesbury	Dorset	3·80
2109	Southwold	Suffolk	5·29
8933	Stamford	Lincolnshire	5·57
1867	Stockton	Durham	5·82
6043	Sudbury	Suffolk	4·99
3901	Tenterden	Kent	5·63
4075	Thetford	Norfolk	5·95
4419	Totnes	Devon	5·39
9458	Weymouth	Dorset	5·49
9596	Windsor	Berkshire	5·96
3588	Wycombe	Buckinghamshire	4·86
8674	Caernarvon	Caerns.	5·43
1927	Llandovery	Carms.	3·83
		Average of these towns	5·25

Derived from *1851 Education Census*, Table T: Municipal Cities and Boroughs: England and Wales, pp. cxciv–ccvii. Pupils here are pupils 'on the books.'

52 W. B. Stephens, *Regional Variations in Education during the Industrial Revolution, 1780–1870*, (University of Leeds Museum of Education, 1973), 5; W. B. Stephens, 'An Anatomy of Illiteracy in Mid-Victorian Devon,' in J. Porter (ed.), *Education and Labour in the South-West* (Exeter Papers in Economic History, 10, 1975), *passim*.

Today, of course, we are aware of geographical variations in the provision of education in this country and even more so on a global scale. Modern educationists, perhaps rightly, tend to accept without great thought the likelihood of a direct relationship between the extent of schooling and literacy levels. It would be tempting to assume without further investigation that in the same way variations of literacy levels in nineteenth-century British towns merely reflected differences in the extent of schooling available or enjoyed in them. This likelihood is worthy of some attention.

A simple comparative analysis of the information provided by the 1851 education census[53] is sufficient to demonstrate that, as with the extent of illiteracy, there was indeed a considerable variation in educational provision (in terms of children at school) between one English or Welsh town and another. These variations often appear, as with illiteracy, to bear some relationship to social and economic factors.

Table 2 lists those 44 English and 2 Welsh towns individually reported on in the education census, where the proportions of children at day school in 1851 were greater than 1 in every 6 of the population. Certain observations may be made about the characteristics of these towns. Geographically nearly all of them were in the south. Nearly half (20) were in the West Country counties of Devon, Cornwall, Dorset, Hampshire, Oxfordshire, Berkshire, and Wiltshire; another 15 were in counties close to London—Essex, Hertfordshire, Huntingdonshire, Buckinghamshire, Surrey, Kent, and Sussex. The only towns in *Table 2* situated in the north or the midlands were Chesterfield, Kendal, Lincoln, Morpeth, Retford East, Richmond (Yorks), Ripon, Stamford, and Stockton—9 towns, a mere 20 per cent of those listed. Moreover, of the 12 English towns with the very best proportions (i.e. those where every 5 persons or less included a child at school: Marlborough, Retford East, Shaftesbury with one pupil in every 4 or less, and Andover, Bideford, Blandford, Faversham, Hertford, Huntingdon, Lymington, Sudbury and High Wycombe with one pupil in every 5 or less) all were in the south of England except Retford East. In addition, Llandovery in mid Wales, had a better proportion than all the English towns except Marlborough.

There also appears to have been some connexion between the size of population and school attendance. Only two of the 46 towns had more than 10 000 inhabitants (Kendal and Lincoln—the largest of the towns); only 6 others had populations over 8000 (Chichester, Poole, Stamford, Weymouth, Windsor, and Caernarvon) and another 8 over 6000—(Chesterfield, Dorchester, Folkestone, Guildford, Hertford, Ripon, Sudbury, and St. Ives). Two-thirds of the towns had fewer than 6000 inhabitants, 12 of them less than 3000—so that by modern standards they were very small places. It would seem that educational provision was better in smaller than in larger towns, where incidentally the rate of population growth was also usually faster.[54]

The size and geographical position of this group of towns clearly had some relationship, too, to their economic complexion. None of the 46 were Lancashire cotton towns; none were West Riding woollen towns—that is to say school attendance in the many 'industrial revolution' textile centres was at a lower level than in the towns represented in *Table 2*. A glance at the table will indicate that the towns listed in it include both a large number of ancient boroughs and market towns,[55] which were usually centres of agricultural regions; and also a fair number of sea and river ports, some of which were also market towns. Chesterfield, it is true, had metal industries and coal mines in its vicinity, but it was also significant for its markets and cattle fairs. Llandovery was a centre for a mining area but it was also an ancient borough which

---

53 *Report Commissioners for Taking a Census of Great Britain on Education*, 1852–3, xc, henceforward cited as *1851 Education Census*.
54 cf. B. I. Coleman, 'The Incidence of Education in Mid-Century,' in E. A. Wrigley (ed.), *Nineteenth-century Society* (1972), 404–5.
55 cf. ibid., 400.

had experienced a recovery from economic decay during the first half of the nineteenth century largely due to the expansion of its markets and fairs.[56] More typically, Andover was an agricultural centre with important markets and fairs, as were, to name a few others, Ripon, Romsey, Stamford, and Totnes. Arundel was not only a

Table 3. 'Principal boroughs and large towns,' 1851: proportions at day school

Town	Population	Day-school pupils: one in
Ashton under Lyne	30 676	11·88
Bath	54 240	7·20
Birmingham	232 841	11·02
Blackburn	45 536	10·93
Bolton	61 171	10·22
Bradford	103 778	10·83
Brighton	69 673	7·38
Bristol	137 328	7·67
Bury	31 262	7·93
Cheltenham	35 051	7·44
Coventry	36 208	12·90
Derby	40 609	7·81
Devonport	38 180	7·44
Dudley	37 962	10·80
Exeter	32 818	6·77
Halifax	33 582	7·68
Huddersfield	30 880	7·66
Hull	84 690	8·37
Ipswich	32 914	7·74
Leeds	172 270	7·88
Leicester	60 584	10·81
Liverpool	375 955	8·56
Macclesfield	39 048	9·72
Manchester	303 382	11·60
Merthyr Tydfil	63 080	17·17
Newcastle-upon-Tyne	87 784	9·65
Norwich	68 195	8·78
Nottingham	54 407	9·68
Oldham	52 820	13·08
Plymouth	52 221	10·82
Portsmouth	72 096	7·57
Preston	69 542	9·05
Salford	63 850	12·17
Sheffield	135 310	8·66
Southampton	35 305	6·40
South Shields	28 974	6·66
Stockport	53 835	12·34
Sunderland	63 897	8·57
Swansea	31 461	8·55
Tynemouth	29 170	9·64
Wigan	31 941	8·47
Wolverhampton	49 985	11·96
Yarmouth (Great)	30 879	8·69
York	36 303	6·27
Average		9·37

Calculated from information in *1851 Education Census*, Table P: Day schools and scholars in the principal boroughs and large towns, pp. clvii ff. Pupils here are pupils 'on the books.'

---

56 G. Evans, 'The Story of the Ancient Churches of Llandovery,' *Trans Hon. Soc. Cymmrodorion, 1911–12* (1913), 204–8. It was also the seat of a public school (founded 1848) and a printing press.

market town, but also a port exporting corn and timber and connected by canal to the Thames. Other market towns that were ports included Bideford, Falmouth, Lymington, Penryn and Southwold, and river ports like Faversham, Maldon, Stockton and Sudbury. Many of these had ancillary industries and crafts often connected with the agriculture of their hinterland, such as the making of gloves and woollens at Chipping Norton, the breweries of Guildford, the woollen manufacture of Kendal, the flour mills of Lincoln, and furniture making at High Wycombe. Dorchester, Guildford, Hertford, Huntingdon, and Lincoln were ancient county towns. In fact the towns in *Table 2* represent to a considerable extent the traditionally important centres of trade and agriculture of pre-industrial England. This suggests that while economic growth is usually associated with the boom towns of the new industrial areas, culturally the towns of the old England, sometimes prospering as a result of expanding trade and agriculture, were superior.

If we now analyse the situation in those places which the educational census lists separately as 'principal boroughs and large towns,' a category which embraced the main new industrial and commercial centres of the north and the midlands, the other side of the coin is revealed. Forty-four such towns are distinguished, (see *Table 3*) each with a population of over 28 000, and half of them with more than 50 000 inhabitants. In none was the proportion of children at day school to total population better than 1 in 6. Moreover, only nine (20 per cent) of these towns were in the south of England, while 16 were industrial towns within the Lancashire–Cheshire–Yorkshire industrial conurbation. In addition, there were the ports serving these areas— Liverpool and Hull; and also York, then developing as a railway and route centre.[57] A further seven were manufacturing towns in the industrial midlands, and other industrial towns were Sunderland, Merthyr Tydfil and Swansea in south Wales, and Norwich. Fourteen of the towns were major seaports—including such significant places as Bristol, Devonport and Plymouth, Hull, Liverpool, Newcastle, Portsmouth, Southampton and Swansea. The only towns in *Table 3* which did not bear heavily the stamp of industry or trade were Bath, Brighton, Cheltenham and Exeter, where the ancient woollen manufacture had virtually ceased by 1831 and where its trade as a port had dwindled.[58] Exeter, Southampton, York and South Shields, a port and market town, were the only towns represented in *Table 3* with better proportions than 1 in 7.

Within the group of large towns represented in *Table 3*, however, the proportions of populations on school books do not correlate very strongly with the size of populations. Of the three great provincial centres with over 200 000 inhabitants each, while both Birmingham and Manchester had proportions worse than 1 in 11, Liverpool where, unusually, the corporation ran two large elementary schools,[59] had as many as one child on the books for every 8·56 of its population. Moreover some smaller towns had worse proportions (Coventry with 1 in 12·9 and a population of about 36 000, Oldham with 1 in 13·08 (53 000), Stockport with 1 in 12·34 (54 000), and Merthyr Tydfil, by far the worst, with 1 in 17·17), while others with over 100 000

---

57 P. H. Tillott (ed.), *V.C.H., Yorks, City of York* (1961), 269 ff. The effect of the railway on York is, however, debatable: A. Armstrong, *Stability and Change in an English County Town* (1974), 37 ff.

58 R. Newton, *Victorian Exeter, 1837–1914* (1968), 74 ff. The interpretations placed by this author on the figures for children at school in Exeter, however, are incorrect. He has taken 1 in 6·77 to mean that 6·77 per cent of Exeter's population were on the books of schools, and consequently declared Exeter to have a smaller proportion at school than York, Birmingham, Leicester, Newcastle, and Sunderland, when in fact the opposite was the case—ibid., 103–4.

59 J. Murphy, *The Religious Problem in English Education: The Crucial Experiment* (1959), *passim*. Cf. *Mins. Committee of Council on Education, 1844* (2), 272 where the provision of church day schools in Lancashire and Yorkshire industrial towns it is said: 'we find Liverpool the only one of those mentioned approaching the right standard'; and also *Royal Commission on Popular Education*, iv (1861), 379: 'there is a fair supply of schools ... within reasonable reach of almost every child in Liverpool.'

inhabitants like Bristol (1 in 7·67, population[60] 137 000) and Leeds (1 in 7·88, population 172 000) had relatively good proportions.

It is possible, of course, that, especially in the booming industrial towns with mushrooming populations, the proportions of children in the population were greater than in older, smaller and less fast growing centres, and also likely that towns varied in this respect one from another. Thus the use of raw proportions of

Table 4. Children at school on census day, 1851 in certain 'principal towns' (expressed as percentage of children aged 5–14)

Town	Percentage	Town	Percentage
Bath	60·4	Liverpool	48·2
Bedford	64·1	Macclesfield	41·8
Birmingham	35·5	Maidstone	56·0
Blackburn	36·8	Manchester and Salford	32·3
Bolton	36·3	Newark	65·3
Boston	62·9	Newcastle-upon-Tyne	41·7
Bradford	36·9	Newport (Mon.)	40·8
Bridgwater	50·1	Northampton	53·0
Bristol	59·1	Norwich	52·0
Bury St. Edmunds	38·2	Nottingham	43·0
Cambridge	54·8	Oldham	21·4
Canterbury	60·1	Plymouth and Devonport	47·7
Carlisle	45·6	Poole	73·0
Chester	52·4	Portsmouth	62·0
Chichester	73·9	Preston	42·8
Colchester	45·6	Reading	62·0
Coventry	29·8	Salisbury	64·5
Derby	46·1	Sheffield	42·3
Dorchester	75·2	Shrewsbury	57·1
Dover	41·2	Southampton	59·8
Durham	55·7	South Shields	57·4
Exeter	64·4	Stafford	49·5
Gateshead	45·4	Stockport	33·8
Gloucester	61·4	Sunderland	52·3
Halifax	77·2	Truro	65·6
Hereford	58·1	Tynemouth	40·0
Hull	48·7	Wakefield	67·3
Ipswich	56·8	Winchester	63·4
Kendal	66·2	Wisbech	59·8
Kings Lynn	44·9	Wolverhampton	30·3
Lancaster	49·4	Worcester	51·1
Leeds	48·0	Yarmouth, Gt.	48·5
Leicester	35·8	York	66·8
Lincoln	69·7		
		Cardiff	40·0
		Caernarvon	73·1
		Pembroke	49·4
		Swansea	44·6

Average for these English towns 51·9
Average for these Welsh towns 51·8

Calculated from information in *1851 Education Census*, Table T, Day Schools and Sunday Schools . . . in each of the Municipal Cities and Boroughs, pp. cxciv-ccvii, and *Census, 1851*, 1852–3 lxxxviii (pt. I), Table V, pp. cxcviii–cc, Ages of Males and Females in the Principal Towns. 'Principal Towns' (Table V) for which the education census does not provide statistics of children actually at school (as opposed to 'on the books') are Brighton (pop. 69 673); Chatham and Rochester (43 362); Dudley (37 962); Huddersfield (84 690); Whitehaven (18 916); Merthyr Tydfil (63 080).

[60] In 1859 Bristol was said to be well off for schools: 'long famed for its charities and the zeal of its inhabitants for education, besides which it is surrounded by the wealth and charity of Clifton and its neighbourhood': *Royal Commission Report on Popular Education*, iii (1861), 21.

children at school to total population may be too crude an indicator. It is difficult, however, to provide the statistics for industrial towns that are really required—that is, indexes of proportions of children of school age at school—since children are numbered in the population censuses at this time only in quinquennial groups. It is not possible therefore, to work out the proportions at school of children in the age group, say, 3 or 4 to 11 or 12, which was perhaps the normal school age range at the time. All we can do is to take the numbers of children in each town or other census district aged 0–4, 5–9, and 10–14 and express the numbers of school children as proportions of these totals. There is, however, a further complication here, for the 1851 education census provides two sets of figures of school attendance for each place: number of children 'on the books'; and numbers of children actually in attendance on census day. All the proportions I have so far used are based on children 'on the books'. These, of course, are bound to be defective to some degree, since they indicate children who perhaps rarely attended, or had ceased to attend altogether, or whose names were duplicated by being enrolled on the books of more than one school. On the other hand the number of children actually present on census day omit sick children normally perhaps regular attenders.

Bearing these caveats in mind I have in *Table 4* expressed, for the sixty-seven 'principal towns' in England and four in Wales, the numbers of children at day school on census day as a percentage of children aged 5–14 in each town.[61] This age group omits some younger children at school, and includes some older ones not at school, but hopefully the one will offset the other. It is the best one can do with the data available.

If the towns in *Table 4* are divided into six groups according to the percentage of children 5–14 at day school on census day, the following emerges:

Table 5. Percentage of children aged 5–14 at day school on census day
(to the nearest whole percentage)

Group	Percentage of children	Number of 'principal towns'
1	40 or less	13
2	41–45	10
3	46–50	12
4	51–55	6
5	51–60	10
6	61 and over	21
		71

In group *1* all but one town, Bury St. Edmunds, was an industrial centre. The group includes in the midlands, Birmingham, Wolverhampton, Coventry, and Leicester, and in the Lancashire–Cheshire–Yorkshire textile areas, Blackburn, Bolton, Bradford, Manchester and Salford, Oldham, and Stockport.

In group *2* only the two ports Dover and Kings Lynn were not industrial towns, while the rest included such industrial centres as Macclesfield, Preston, Sheffield, Gateshead, Newcastle-upon-Tyne, Nottingham, Swansea, and Newport (Mon.).

Group *3* contained more of a mixture. Those towns outside the chief industrial areas were Bridgwater, Carlisle, Colchester, Lancaster, Plymouth and Devonport, Great Yarmouth, and Pembroke, but also Derby and Stafford in the industrial midlands, Leeds, and Hull and Liverpool.

---

61 This is the age-group used by R. J. Smith in 'Education, Society and Literacy: Nottinghamshire in the Mid-Nineteenth Century', *University of Birmingham Historical Jnl.*, XII (1969), 45.

In the three groups *4*, *5*, and *6* (comprising 37 of the 71 towns), where school attendance was over 50 per cent, there were only four industrial towns—Sunderland, Halifax, Wakefield, and Northampton. Some large towns (Bristol,[62] Bath, Portsmouth, Exeter, Halifax, York) were also in these groups, but the remainder had fewer than 25 000 inhabitants each and the group included 14 ancient cathedral cities and a high proportion of towns in the south and outside the industrial areas. Of those in group *6* the only northern towns were Halifax, Wakefield, Kendal and York.

Calculations of the percentages of children aged 5–14 at Sunday school are not as useful as day-school figures. The age range of children at Sunday school was much greater than for those at day school. At Coventry in 1838 many Sunday-school teachers claimed that their pupils entered aged 5 or 7 and remained until 16.[63] Indeed in parts of the country, especially in Wales, young adults clearly attended.[64] T. W. Laqueur suggests that 'increasingly the Sunday school became the province of adolescent boys and girls.'[65] Thus the formula used for day school figures above, applied to Caernarvon, results in an equivalent Sunday-school attendance of 141 per cent of children aged 5–14.[66] I have, therefore, not tabulated these figures. It may be of some significance, however, that of the 23 towns where the percentage of children by this formula was greater in Sunday schools than in day schools (*Table 6*),

Table 6. Towns where % children at Sunday-school on Census Sunday 1851 greater than that of those at Day School

Blackburn	Leeds	Oldham
Bolton	Leicester	Portsmouth
Bradford	Macclesfield	Preston
Bridgwater	Manchester and Salford	Stafford
Coventry	Newark	Stockport
Derby	Northampton	Truro
Lancaster	Nottingham	Wolverhampton
Caernarvon	Swansea	

9 fall into group *1* (above) for day schooling, 4 in group *2* and 5 in group *3*—that is 18 of the 23 that had comparatively high Sunday-school attendances had comparatively low day-school attendances. This lends support to the view that Sunday schools were often used as a substitute for day schooling.[67] Nevertheless, it is interesting to note that Newark, Portsmouth, Truro and Caernarvon, all of which had a larger percentage at Sunday school than at day school, were in group *6* (above) for day

---

62 It is interesting that at Bristol in the 1860s there were said to be 'but very few children employed': *5th Report Royal Commission on Children's Employment*, (1866) xxiv, at Fry's Chocolate Factory an evening school was provided for a time: ibid., 67.
63 W. B. Stephens, 'Early Victorian Coventry: Education in an Industrial Community, 1830–51,' in A. Everitt (ed.), *Perspectives in English Urban History* (1973), 170. The employment of very young children was still common in the Coventry ribbon trade in the 1860s: *5th Report Royal Commission on Children's Employment*, (1866) xxiv, 114–17.
64 cf. J. A. Davies, *Education in a Welsh Rural County, 1870–1973* (1973), 10; R. W. Unwin and W. B. Stephens (eds.), *Yorkshire Schools and Schooldays* (1976), 41; Sanderson, Social Change . . . Industrial Lancashire,' *Northern History*, III (1968), 151–2; *Minutes of the Committee of Council on Education 1847–8*, 30.
65 T. W. Laqueur, *Religion and Respectability: Sunday Schools and Working Class Culture, 1780–1850* (1976), 90, 100.
66 cf. Smith, op. cit., 51.
67 Sanderson, 'Social Change . . . Industrial Lancashire,' op. cit., 146 ff.; Stephens, *Regional Variations*, op. cit., 10–12. cf. W. B. Stephens (ed.), *V.C.H., Warwicks*, VII, (*City of Birmingham*) 215–16. But see Laqueur, *Religion and Respectability*, op. cit., 259–60.

schools—over 61 per cent—suggesting a high degree of school attendance of one sort or another in these towns.

The level of attendance at day school in a mid-Victorian town was clearly no exact indicator of the extent of the educational experience of the inhabitants.[68] Moreover Sunday school attendance varied very considerably from place to place, even in the industrial areas. In Lancashire in the 1820s and 1830s, for example, the levels of Sunday-school predominance over day schools were highest in towns (especially textile towns) rather than rural areas, but even higher in rather obscure places, formerly rural, which had become industrialized.[69] Other educational variables included night schools and provision for adult education.[70]

Again the statistics of children at school on census day in 1851 omit the indeterminate number of children not then at school, but who nevertheless had previously enjoyed a year or more of education, or in perhaps fewer cases would later have some schooling. We have no evidence as to whether the proportion of such children varied from one town to another, but it is not unlikely that it differed according to the type of occupational structure.[71] It is certainly likely that it varied also according to the prevailing economic conditions of prosperity or slump.

The hypothesis that the extent of day schooling is only a partial factor in determining comparative urban levels of education is reinforced if we compare the index of day schooling with literacy levels based on the Registrar General's annual reports on marriage signatures. These indeed might be regarded as more significant than the statistics of schooling, for, as Sargent wrote over a century ago, under the heading 'Results are What we Want', 'It seems to me that . . . the great question is, not how many children are at school, but how many children are educated, and retain their instruction.'[72]

Since the average age of marriage was in the late twenties it is necessary to use marriage signatures/marks for a period some time after 1851 to allow for children then of school age to have reached the age of marriage. I have chosen the year 1866 to allow a gap of 15 years.[73] Unfortunately, whereas the 1851 education census statistics cited above are for boroughs, the Registrar General's marriage statistics are for registration districts. In the case of many towns, therefore, direct comparison is not possible. For 24 places, however, I have found that the 'town population' and the 'registration district population,' as indicated in the 1861 census, are identical or very close, and these I have tabulated in *Table 7*. This table shows clearly that there is not necessarily a relationship between the proportion of brides and grooms unable to sign their names in any particular town in 1866 and the proportion of children at day school there 15 years before. All that can be said is that there was a tendency over-all for towns with high percentages of 'marks' to be places where there had been a low percentage of children at day school 15 years before. Thus, in towns where 25 per cent or more made marks on marriage in 1866, an average of 43.8 per cent of children aged 5–14 had been at day school in 1851; in towns where marks occurred in 19–24 per cent of cases, averages at day school had been 48.9 per cent; and where there were 18 per cent or less marks, 56.1 per cent on average had been at day school. Again, of the twelve towns with the highest percentage of marks in 1866, eight were among the worst for percentage of children at day school in 1851; and of the twelve with the lowest percentage of marks, eight were among the best twelve for children at day school.

68 cf. Smith, op. cit., 54–6.
69 Sanderson, 'Social Change,' op. cit., 147–51.
70 Stephens, '*Regional Variations*,' op. cit., 20 ff.
71 See Sanderson, 'Social Change,' op. cit., 151–2.
72 Sargent, op. cit., 85.
73 For an analysis of literacy levels in London and the larger towns in 1864, see Sargent, op. cit., 108.

Table 7. Marriage marks and percentages of children at school in certain towns

Town	Percentage Marks in Marriages in 1866	Percentage children 5–14 at day school on census day 1851	Percentage Marks in marriages in adjacent or nearby counties in 1866	
Birmingham	31·7 ⎱ 28·0	35·5	Warws. 27·1 ⎱	
Aston	24·4 ⎰		Staffs. 39·9 ⎬ 31·7	
			Worcs. 28·0 ⎰	
Bristol	22·3	59·1	Som. ⎱ 23·6	
			Glos. ⎰	
Bury St. Edmunds	15·6	38·2	Suffolk	29·3
Cambridge	12·9	54·8	Cambs.	27·9
Chester	27·5	52·4	Ches.	29·7
Colchester	20·6	45·6	Essex	26·7
Coventry	27·5	29·8	Warws.	27·1
Derby	17·7	46·1	Derbys.	25·1
Exeter	13·6 ⎱ 14·8	64·4	Devon	19·8
St. Thomas	15·9 ⎰			
Ipswich	15·1	56·8	Suffolk	29·3
King's Lynn	24·1	44·9	Norfolk	29·4
Leeds ⎱	37·1	48·0	West. R.	31·0
Hunslet ⎰				
Leicester	25·2	35·8	Leics.	25·2
Newcastle-upon-Tyne	22·8	41·7	Durham	31·3
Norwich	23·6	52·0	Norfolk	29·4
Nottingham	26·1	43·0	Notts.	27·8
Plymouth and Devonport	20·7	47·7	Devon	19·8
Portsmouth	16·7	62·0	Hants.	16·1
Reading	15·0	62·0	Berks.	22·2
Shrewsbury	17·7	57·1	Salop	31·6
Southampton	11·5	59·8	Hants.	16·1
Sunderland	32·2	52·3	Durham	31·3
Worcester	24·2	51·1	Worcs.	28·0
Yarmouth, Gt.	25·0	48·5	Norfolk	29·4

Derived from 1851 Education Census; Census, 1851; Registrar General's Rep. for 1866, (1867–8) xix.

Some of the same economic and demographic factors we have noted for earlier periods are evident also for literacy levels in the 1860s. Of the towns in *Table 7* with 18 per cent or fewer marks, only Derby was not in the south, and only Derby was a manufacturing town. Those towns with 25 per cent marks and more, however, were all (except Great Yarmouth) in the midlands or the north, and all but Great Yarmouth and Chester were industrial towns. Those towns falling between (19–24 per cent marks) were more mixed geographically, though none was really an industrial centre, except perhaps Newcastle-upon-Tyne where shipbuilding and the manufacture of ships' goods was important.

As for the relationship of population size and proportions of marks, there was again a tendency for larger towns to have worse records. Of the twelve largest towns in *Table 7*, eight were among the worst twelve for illiterate brides and grooms; of the remaining twelve towns four were among the worst dozen for marks.

Thus, to sum up, all the evidence points to larger towns, northern towns, and industrial towns having a smaller percentage of children at day school in 1851 than smaller, southern, market and smaller port towns; and there was a two-to-one chance that the proportions of illiterate brides and grooms 15 years later were greater in large towns, northern towns, and industrial towns. However, while there was thus a general relationship between lack of schooling in a community and later illiteracy it was by no means an automatic relationship. The number of exceptions to the tendencies discerned are too great to prove any 'iron-law' at work. School attendance figures emerge as a significant but by no means the only factor in the determination of the levels of urban educational achievement of young adults of marriageable age. Apart from the imponderable impact of other educational factors, however, it is well to note that the marriage signature statistics themselves embrace persons who had not lived as children in the district in which they were married. Migration is, therefore, an important variable here. It has been suggested, for example, that one reason for the high level of literacy in the metropolitan area and the low level for some rural counties around London is that better educated young people tended to migrate to the urban areas where they later married.[74] It may be, too, that the marriage signature figures for Lancashire towns were distorted by the influx of better educated young persons from Scotland and the extreme northern counties of England where almost all male adults were literate.[75] On the other hand it is likely that such persons were outnumbered by ill-educated migrants, 'too indifferent' as Bishop Sumner put it in 1838, 'to education.' Large numbers of Irish of the roughest sort tended to be concentrated in the industrial towns of Lancashire, Cheshire, the West Riding, Staffordshire and Derbyshire, many of them drifting from place to place in these areas.[76]

Even in Lancashire, however, apart from the Irish, such migration was short distance,[77] and in this context it is interesting that nearly every town in *Table 7* had better marriage-signature statistics than the average for those surrounding or contiguous counties, from which it might be expected to draw a large proportion of immigrants. This reinforces the likelihood that better educated young people were creamed off into the towns, at a time when there was a decline in agricultural employment,[78] perhaps in some places augmenting in the statistics the results of better educational facilities enjoyed by native brides and grooms, or in others offsetting the effects of poor educational standards available to the town's natives. Thus in Devon in the 1860s it was remarked of rural areas that 'the best young men, i.e., those who are the best educated, go away to the police, railways, etc.'[79]

Table 7 suggests, too, that the differences between levels in towns and neighbouring counties were greatest where the town was a smaller traditional market centre set in a predominantly agricultural area.[80] In some of these districts the local market town might be a haven of culture and civilized behaviour. Thus the difference between Bury St. Edmunds and Suffolk as a whole was 14 per cent, and for Ipswich likewise; for Shrewsbury *vis à vis* Shropshire 14 per cent; for Cambridge (and Cambridgeshire) 15 per cent. For Colchester (and Essex), Derby (and Derbyshire), Exeter (and Devon), King's Lynn, Norwich (and Norfolk)[81] and Reading (and Berkshire) differences ranged from 4 to 9 per cent. The figures for the port town of Newcastle-upon-Tyne

74 Stephens, *Regional Variations*, op. cit., 9.
75 Laqueur, *Past and Present* (1974), op. cit., 102.
76 Sanderson, 'Social Change,' op. cit., 141–2, quoting J. B. Sumner, *Charge* (1838), 33; A. Redford (ed. and revised, W. H. Chaloner), *Labour Migration in England, 1800–1850* (2nd edn. 1964), 150 ff., map G1; J. A. Banks 'The Contagion of Numbers,' in Dyos and Wolff, op. cit., i, 118.
77 Redford, op. cit., vii–viii, 62 ff., 182–4. Cf. for the late 18th century: R. S. Schofield 'Age Specific Mobility in an Eighteenth Century Rural English Parish,' *Annales de Demographie historique* (1970), 270–1; J. E. Buckatzsch, 'The Constancy of Local Populations and Migration in England before 1800,' *Population Studies*, 5 (1951–2), 68.
78 cf. E. H. Hunt, 'Labour Productivity in English Agriculture, 1850–1914,' *Economic History Review*, 2nd ser., xx (1967), 284.
79 *2nd Report Royal Commission on Employment of Children, Young Persons and Women in Agriculture*, (1968–9) xiii, p. 111.
80 cf. C. A. Anderson, 'Patterns and Variability in Distribution and Diffusion of Schooling,' in C. A. Anderson and M. J. Bowman (eds.), *Education and Economic Development* (1966), 330–2.
81 For the backwardness of rural Norfolk see D. Jones, 'Thomas Campbell Foster and the Rural Labourer; incendiarism in East Anglia in the 1840s,' *Social History*, I (1976).

were much better than those for nearby County Durham, reflecting the known low level of literacy in the coal mining areas.[82]

On the other hand, for the large towns generally, there was a tendency for marriage signature figures to be nearer those for the neighbouring county averages. Plymouth with Devonport was somewhat worse than Devon as a whole, the urban average brought down considerably by the inclusion here of East Stonehouse, the slum dockland area, one of the least literate registration districts in the whole county.[83] Industrial and populous Birmingham was no better and perhaps worse than Warwickshire and Worcestershire as a whole; Nottingham little better than Nottinghamshire; Leicester and Coventry slightly worse than Leicestershire and Warwickshire respectively; Leeds (with slum Hunslet) than the West Riding (which was by no means all industrial). Moreover in areas where there was a great deal of rural manufacture in industrial villages and in mining communities the distinction between town and county was blurred and the educational situation may well have been worse outside the towns than in them. Thus a witness before the Select Committee on the Education of the Poorer Classes in 1838 attested that there was 'very little education of any sort' in West Bromwich. This was three or four miles from Birmingham, with 20 000 inhabitants, though it is 'hardly a town; but over the whole surface of the parish there are nailers and other small manufacturers,' and 'there is coal under ... West Bromwich; it is close to the great mining district of Staffordshire,' where 'the same lamentable want of almost any education prevails.'

W. F. Hook, vicar of Leeds, in 1846 wrote of the populous industrial villages around that city, 'go to our poorer districts, not to our towns, but to our manufacturing villages and there you will perceive how great our educational destitution really is.'[84] The same was so in Lancashire where children in such areas tended to attend Sunday rather than day schools.[85] Similarly in Radford, an over-spill area adjoining Nottingham the population of which had increased from 4000 to 27 000 in the first half of the nineteenth century, schooling was much less common in 1851, and illiteracy in 1855–64 greater than both in Nottingham itself and in a nearby farming district.[86] Indeed the commissioners investigating child and female labour in agriculture reported in 1867 that the demand for education among the labouring classes in country districts in Nottinghamshire and Leicestershire 'is exceedingly active ... but as we approach the neighbourhood of Nottingham and Leicester seaming and framework knitting absorb almost the whole population while the large overgrown villages in the suburbs of the towns ... are most ill-supplied with schools. The girls especially can begin such work as young as 6 or 7 years old and many never attend school at all. The instances of ignorance in these districts ... far surpass anything I met with even in ganging villages.'[87] The same tendency is seen clearly, too, in Staffordshire, a county containing a great deal of rural industrial slumland where the population was unusually ignorant and degraded to a much lower level than, for example, in the Lancashire cotton areas. Thus Staffordshire as a whole had an illiteracy level much higher even than Birmingham (*Table 7*). 'I suppose,' wrote Revd. J. P. Norris, of the Potteries in the early 1850s, 'there is no district in Europe than can show so large a proportion of children six to seven, and eight years of age

---

82 The same pattern is now, however, observable with Sunderland, another coal port.
83 Stephens, 'An Anatomy of Illiteracy,' op. cit., 12–14.
84 *Report Select Committee on Education for the Children of the Poorer Classes in Large Towns*, (1837–8) vii, 94–5; W. F. Hook, *On the Means of Rendering More Efficient the Education of the People—A Letter to the Lord Bishop of St. Davids* (1846).
85 Sanderson, 'Social Change,' op. cit., 151.
86 Smith, op. cit., 44, 49–53.
87 *1st Report Royal Commission on Employment of Children, Young Persons and Women in Agriculture*, (1867–8) xvii, 85.

engaged in manufacture,' children, moreover, outside the scope even of the educational clauses of the Factory Acts. Here there was a lack of interest in, and a general neglect of, education among a comparatively well paid workforce.[88]

So there emerges the general picture of, on the one hand, older market towns and the like as centres of superior educational standards set in more backward farming areas, and, on the other hand, of industrial towns, especially in the north and midlands where the standards of education were lower sometimes much lower, than in neighbouring agricultural districts. Yet these manufacturing towns might well be surrounded by twilight hinterlands of industrialized countryside where educational facilities and standards were at an even lower level than the urban centres themselves.

The social problems attached to the heavily populated manufacturing towns and industrial villages were wider than educational, and in the minds of contemporaries the spectre of paganism loomed large among them. Since elementary education was so much in the hands of the churches it might be expected that there would be a connexion between the extent of religiosity in a community and the level of education. The contemporaneous religious and educational censuses of 1851 enable us to test possible relationships between church-going and school attendance in mid-century towns. An analysis of urban church-going based on the religious census has already been undertaken by K. S. Inglis.[89] According to the index of attendance at worship adopted by him (total attendances as percentages of population) there was a national average of 61, but while rural areas and small towns averaged 71·4, towns of over 10 000 inhabitants averaged only 49·7.

Of the larger towns only three—Colchester, Exeter, and Bath—all in the south and not industrial, exceeded 71·4 (the average for small towns and rural areas) and only a further 11 exceeded the national average of 61. Of these 11 towns all except Wakefield and York were south of the Trent. Moreover, only Wakefield was in an area described in the census as a 'chief manufacturing district,' though two others Nottingham and Leicester, were centres of industry. The average population of these 11 towns was below 30 000 and Leicester (60 584) was the only one with a population over 40 000.

Another 21 towns had a better index than for all large towns (49·7). These had an average population of nearly 50 000, and included Bristol (137 328). A third of them were in 'chief manufacturing districts' and in addition, Derby and Nottingham were industrial centres. About half of them were in the south and east.

Those large towns with an index below 49·7 included all eight London parliamentary boroughs and 28 other towns, all but seven of which were in 'chief manufacturing districts,' and five of the seven were themselves centres of industry. Even excluding London the average population was much higher than in the other groups, and included in the 28 were Liverpool, Manchester, Leeds, Birmingham, and two other towns with populations of over 100 000 each, Sheffield and Bradford. These towns in which church going was lowest included all the places described in the census as cotton towns and the two great woollen towns of Leeds and Bradford, every large coal town (except Wolverhampton), the two great metal towns of Sheffield and Birmingham, and every large town in Lancashire, except Wigan and Rochdale.

This picture corresponds markedly with the pattern of education, with its worse standards in the north and midlands, in larger towns, and in towns connected with industry. Such a relationship can be demonstrated by applying Inglis's religious index to those towns in *Table 3* for which he gives separate figures. For the seven

---

88 *Mins. of the Committee of Council on Education, 1847–8*, 2, 182; E. S. Bellamy, 'Elementary Education in the Staffordshire Potteries, 1780–1870,' University of Hull, B.Phil. dissertation, 1974. cf. *V.C.H., Staffordshire*, viii (ed. J. G. Jenkins) (1963), 257.

89 K. S. Inglis, 'Patterns of Worship in 1851,' *Journal of Ecclesiastical History*, XI (1960), 78 ff.

much larger towns with better church attendance indexes than the average for rural areas and small towns, the average proportion of children at school to total population was 1:7·52. For the further 12 towns with church attendance indexes above that for all large towns the school attendances averaged 1:8·83. For the 23 large towns below the average for their kind the school figure was 1:9·92.

Again if we compare Inglis's indexes with the percentage of children at school as shown for 46 towns in *Table 4*[90] we find that one-third of the towns were below average for both school and church attendance,[91] and one-third above average for both—that is there was a distinct correlation in two-thirds of the cases.[92]

An analysis of the towns in *Table 7* produces the following:[93]

Table 8. Analysis of towns in *Table 7*

Towns with marriage marks of	Average percentage children 5–14 at day school	Church attendance index (Inglis)
25% or more	43·8	49·7
19–24%	48·9	58·0
18% or less	56·1	66·0

Once more we can discern no 'iron law,' no easy categorization, but only a tendency against which to set the unique history of each particular town. Although the comparative approach is useful in illuminating history, it thus has its limitations, and this essay supports the view that we need not fear that the writing of urban histories will 'result in the same tale told many times.'[94]

---

90 It is possible to do this only for 46 of the towns in Table 4.
91 Average of the 46 towns for children at school: 47·7 per cent; average religious index: 52·6.
92 In the remaining 15 towns, 8 had better than average school attendances but worse than average church attendance, and 7 vice versa.
93 For only 2 towns in Table 7 (Bury St. Edmunds and Shrewsbury) Inglis does not provide information on church attendance.
94 S. G. Checkland, 'English Provincial Cities,' *Economic History Review*, 2nd ser., VI (1954), 202.

Education and the Social Geography of Nineteenth-Century Towns and Cities

W. E. MARSDEN
University of Liverpool

Nineteenth-century Britain experienced the most savage onslaught of urbanization that the world has yet witnessed, the impact of which polarized opinion throughout the period. In the 1840s, Robert Vaughan was presenting a reassuring view of this change, looking upon cities as centres of intellectual opportunity.

> 'Every intelligent person must have observed, that apart from any technical means of instruction, there is much in the nearer, the more constant, and the more varied association into which men are brought by means of great cities, which tends necessarily to impart greater knowledge, acuteness and power to the mind, than would have been realized by the same persons if placed in the comparative isolation of a rural parish.'[1]

However, favourable interpretations could invariably be countered by the mounting evidence that unchecked urban growth was creating social problems of a frightening order. Sixty years after Vaughan, for example, C. F. G. Masterman was bemoaning the effects of the rapid transformation of the people from a rural to an urban state.[2] The enormity of the nineteenth-century city provoked not only conflicting views, but also ambivalent feelings within individuals wavering, as Stedman Jones expresses it, between complacency and pride over 'the sheer size of an immense human artifact' and dread 'at the terrible threat that such an aggregation represented.'[3] Such ambivalence can be found in Charles Booth, one of the best qualified contemporaries to judge, who confessed:

> 'There seems something subtle, an essence, pervading great metropolitan cities and altering everything so that life seems more lively, busier, larger, the individual less, the community more. I like it. It does me good. But I am not surprised when people feel crushed by the wickedness of it, the ruthlessness, heartlessness of its grinding mill.'[4]

---

1 R. Vaughan, *The Age of Great Cities: or, Modern Society Viewed in its Relation to Intelligence, Morals and Religion* (1843), 146. See also E. Baines, *The Social, Educational and Religious State of the Manufacturing Districts* (1843). Both Vaughan and Baines were defending cities against attacks in Parliament. See B. I. Coleman (ed.), *The Idea of the City in Nineteenth Century Britain* (1973), 87. Other writers drew attention to the special advantages of London as a centre of intellectual opportunity. See, for example, J. Fletcher, 'Moral and Educational Statistics of England and Wales,' *Quarterly Journal of the Statistical Society of London*, XII (1849), 176; A. Conan Doyle, 'On the Geographical Distribution of British Intellect,' *The Nineteenth Century*, XXIV (1888). See also D. J. Olsen, *The Growth of Victorian London* (1976), 20–21.
2 C. F. G. Masterman, 'The English City,' in *England, a Nation: being the Papers of the Patriots' Club* (1904), 47.
3 G. S. Jones, *Outcast London: a Study of the Relationship between Classes in Victorian Society* (1971), 13. See also, for example, R. Lawton, 'An Age of Great Cities,' *Town Planning Review*, XLIII (1972), 220–21; E. E. Lampard, 'The Urbanizing World,' in H. J. Dyos and M. Wolff (eds.), *The Victorian City: Images and Realities*, 1, (1973), 27–8; and M. B. Katz, *The Irony of Early Schools Reform* (1968), 49.
4 Quoted in T. S. and M. B. Simey, *Charles Booth: Social Scientist* (1960), 80.

Worse still, a shocking ignorance of the disparities in conditions of life which existed in different parts of the city persisted throughout the century.[5] The poorer districts, and particularly the East End of London, acquired the public image of distant exotic lands,[6] or even of the nether regions.[7] As Booth himself asserted: 'It is not in country, but in town, that "terra incognita" needs to be written on our social maps.'[8]

However the symptoms of urban malaise were diagnosed, whether they were of runaway population increase, crime, or other social and political unrest, education was a favoured emollient. In fact interaction between urban growth and educational provision was reciprocal. On the one hand, education was mandated to deliver solutions to social problems, while on the other, hyperactive population change created acute difficulties for educational planning. The most glaring stemmed from the escalating numbers of children, generating new demands for school accommodation, intensified by the growing trend towards compulsory attendance. The population of England and Wales had risen from nine million in 1801 to 32 million in 1901. It was increasingly concentrated in the towns: roughly 33 per cent in 1801, 50 per cent in 1851, and over 75 per cent in 1901. To match the increase in demand, a massive infusion of resources was required. To a considerable extent these resources were found. The global achievement, however, masked the presence of unequal distribution of resources and opportunities, both between[9] and within towns and cities.

The main intention of this paper is to provide an overview of the disparities in educational opportunity which arose out of the splintering of towns and cities in the nineteenth century and particularly the late nineteenth century, into distinctive social areas. Residential segregation became a potent influence on attitudes towards education and on the nature of the provision of educational facilities. Together with religious differences, social distinctions added significantly to the complexities which the planners of urban education had to face.[10]

In the 1920s the Chicago school of urban sociology, considerably inspired by Booth's work, used a spatial-ecological approach in their investigations of functional and residential segregation of cities,[11] an approach which can be adapted to the study of home–school relations in a nineteenth-century urban context.[12] The dynamics of temporal and spatial change were interpreted through Darwinian concepts such as competition, invasion, succession, dominance, adaptation, web of life, and the survival of the fittest. As one of the leaders of this school, Robert Park, wrote:

> 'In the course of time every sector and quarter of the city takes on something of the character and qualities of its inhabitants. Each separate part of the city is inevitably stained with the peculiar sentiments of its population.'[13]

---

5 See, for example, J. Garwood, *The Million Peopled City: or One-Half of the People of London Made Known to the Other Half* (1853).
6, 7 See, for example, *The Pall Mall Gazette*, 31st July 1891, which heads its review of an early Booth volume, 'A City very much like Hell'; also J. London, *The People of the Abyss* (London, 1903); C. F. G. Masterman, 'The Social Abyss,' *Contemporary Review*, LXXI (1902), 23–35; and G. Gissing, *The Nether World* (1889).
8 C. Booth (ed.), *Life and Labour of the People in London*, Vol. V, *Population Classified by Trades* (1895), 19–20. See also F. Bédarida, 'Urban Growth and Social Structure in Nineteenth-Century Poplar,' *The London Journal*, I (1975), 163.
9 See W. B. Stephens, *Regional Variations in Education during the Industrial Revolution, 1780–1870* (1973).
10 See D. Rubinstein, *School Attendance in London, 1870–1904: a Social History* (1969), 18.
11 R. E. Park, *Human Communities: the City and Human Ecology* (1952), 166 and 170.
12 W. E. Marsden, 'Social Environment, School Attendance and Educational Achievement in a Merseyside Town 1870–1900' in W. P. McCann, (ed.), *Popular Education and Socialisation in the Nineteenth Century* (1977), 193–230.
13 R. E. Park, op. cit., (1952), 17. See also C. Booth (ed.), op. cit., (1891), Vol. I, 66. Note how Booth's language anticipates that of Park: 'Each district has its character—its peculiar flavour....

In British towns and cities, the evolution of secluded social areas was more characteristic of the second than the first half of the century,[14] when desperate slums could often be found in close proximity to the homes of the affluent. This became less true as improved transport facilities reduced the friction of distance, opening up a wider range of residential choice.[15] As early as the 1850s, Garwood was alert to some of the consequences of this process:

> 'I am disposed to consider very important . . . the gradual separation of classes which takes place in towns by a custom which has gradually grown up, that every person who can afford it lives out of town. . . . Now this was not so formerly; it is a habit which has, practically speaking, grown up within the last half-century. The result of the old habit was, that rich and poor lived in proximity, and the superior classes exercised that species of silent but very efficient control over their neighbours. . . . They are now gone, and the consequence is that large masses of population are gathered together without those wholesome influences which operated upon them when their congregation was more mixed; when they were divided, so to speak, by having persons of a different class of life, better educated, among them. . . .'[16]

A more objective understanding of the process of the social stratification of the city was made possible by Booth's social survey of London. Its final seventeen volumes were garnished by the most evocative set of social maps ever produced.[17] The street by street details were aggregated into school board divisions and blocks. The general map of London poverty was based on 134 blocks and sub-divisions, with darker tints of brown used to depict the areas of most acute poverty. A pattern of distress was revealed, concentrated on riverside areas, the East End and on the northern fringes of the City and the West End.[18]

At the detailed street level a colour coding system was introduced to represent a residential kaleidoscope of varying degrees of poverty, comfort and affluence. Seven colours were employed, ranging from the black and blues of poverty, through the purple of mixed poverty and comfort, to the red and yellow of affluence. This degree of detail, and the revision of the maps at two distinct times, enabled Booth and his team to interpret very closely the centrifugal forces at work, impulses from the centre pushing people into the inner ring, then from the inner to the outer ring, changing the social maps of the city.[19]

> 'The red and yellow classes are leaving, and the streets which they occupied are becoming pink and pink-barred; whilst the streets which were formerly pink turn to purple, and purple to light blue.'[20]

Geographical mobility within the city had obvious consequences for educational provision. Inner areas once under-subscribed might even find themselves over-subscribed with schools. In his report on the City of London in 1871, for example, H. M. I. Morell noted that the current school accommodation was about equal to need. The following year he drew attention to the 'peculiarity' of the City as an area

---

14 See D. Ward, 'Victorian Cities: How Modern?', *Journal of Historical Geography*, I (1975), 135–51. But change was very much in progress by the middle of the century. See, for example, 'The Language of Class in Early Nineteenth Century Britain,' in A. Briggs and J. Saville (eds.), *Essays in Labour History* (1967), 47–8.
15 See, for example, D. J. Olsen, 'Victorian London: Specialization, Segregation and Privacy,' *Victorian Studies*, XVII (1974), 267–8; F. Sheppard, *London 1808–1870: the Infernal Wen* (1971), 84 and 109.
16 J. Garwood, op. cit., (1853), 9–10.
17 See R. Hyde, *Printed Maps of Victorian London, 1851–1900* (1975), 29–31; and B. Webb, *My Apprenticeship* (1926), 239.
18 C. Booth (ed.), op. cit., (1891), Appendix to Vol. 2.
19 See, for example, C. Booth, (ed.), op. cit., (1891), Vol. I, 28–30; Vol. II, 393; and 3rd Series, Final Volume, *Notes on Social Influences* (1902), 182–3 and 205; also C. Booth, *Improved Means of Locomotion as a First Step towards the Cure of the Housing Difficulties of London* (1901), 10–11.
20 C. Booth (ed.), op. cit., (1902), *Religious Influences*, Vol. 5, South-east and South-west London, 194. For a useful summary of this aspect of Booth's thinking see H. W. Pfautz, (ed.), *Charles Booth on the City: Physical Pattern and Social Structure* (1967).

of declining population, yet one enjoying the largest endowments and the greatest provision of efficient schools.[21]

Clark has described the earlier 'close and fortuitous juxtaposition of rich and poor' as 'the geographical basis of the ragged school movement in London.'[22] However, as people migrated to the suburbs, they took their resources with them. The impact on the voluntary sector was serious and cumulative. In his report for 1878–79 on the schools of Lambeth, Fitch pointed out that already more children were attending board schools than voluntary schools in his area, with the ratio increasing in favour of the board schools. The reason was clear:

> '... in the densely peopled districts of Walworth, Kennington and North Camberwell there are few or no rich residents, the inhabitants are chiefly shopkeepers and others who form the class most keenly sensible of the pressure of the rates, and most likely to regard the existence of the education rate as a reason for withholding all subscriptions from Church or other voluntary schools. . . .'[23]

Figure 1 illustrates the crisis which faced the London school board in 1871. Only the City and Westminster came anywhere near to matching supply and demand. Marylebone and Chelsea just about met the needs of junior boys. Provision for girls was in most cases less than adequate, and that for infants critically short. Fifteen years later, the greater efforts of the London School Board on behalf of the more needy

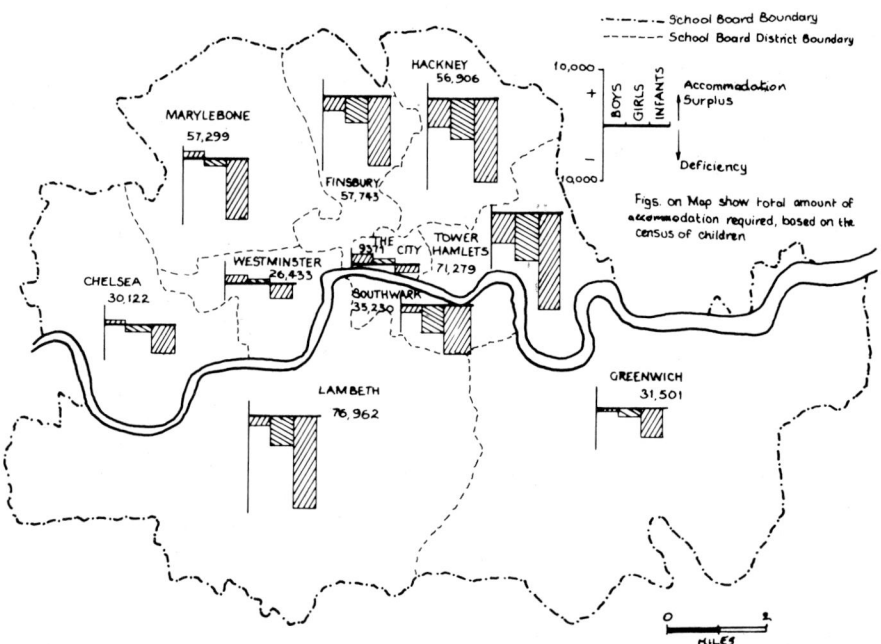

Figure 1. Accommodation problems faced by the London School Board in 1871. (*R. Hunt*).

21 J. D. Morell, 'General Report on the Schools Inspected in the City of London and the Metropolitan District of Greenwich,' *Report of the Committee of Council on Education 1871–2* (1872), 65. Also *RCCE, 1872–3* (London, 1873), 106. For reference to a comparable situation in Liverpool, see E. Midwinter, 'The Administration of Public Education in Late Victorian Lancashire,' *Northern History*, IV (1969), 62.
22 E. A. G. Clark, 'The Ragged School Union and the Education of the London Poor in the Nineteenth Century,' (University of London, unpublished M.A. Dissertation, 1967), 16–18.
23 J. G. Fitch, 'General Report on the Schools Inspected in the Eastern Half of the District of Lambeth, *RCCE, 1878–9* (1879), 548. See also C. Booth, (ed.), op. cit., Vol. 2, *London North of the Thames: the Inner Ring*, 53.

areas, such as parts of Tower Hamlets, Southwark, Hackney, Lambeth and Greenwich, were bearing fruit. They are depicted on Figure 2, a map portraying the ratio of School Board as against voluntary provision by districts. Its responsibility was smaller in the well-endowed cities of London and Westminster, while the voluntary resources of north-west London lessened the demands made on the Board in that area. The 'filling in the gaps' principle can thus be redefined in considerable part in terms of the resolution of spatial inequalities.

A common determinant of social decline was the invasion of an area by industry and its attendant workers, often unskilled, who speedily colonized existing property by multi-occupation, rented hastily thrown up terraces of tenements, or moved into common lodging houses. A classic example can be found in north Merseyside where Bootle, later to become a music-hall joke, was in the first half of the century a thoroughly respectable watering place. Yet by 1900 its estuarine bathing area had been destroyed by the northward migration of the Mersey docks, accompanied by a rapid decline in status of the population.

Table 1. Bootle: Changing socio-economic grouping of child population, 1851–1871[24]

	I/II	III	IV/V
1851	31·6	31·3	37·1
1861	26·4	37·6	36·0
1871	14·9	36·9	48·2

From a balanced socio-economic structure in 1851, when almost one-third of parents of children aged 3–15 were middle class, the situation had declined by 1871 to one in which only 15 per cent belonged to this group, while the semi- and un-skilled working-class population had risen from 37 per cent to 48 per cent in the same period. To meet the population growth and socio-economic change, three new voluntary schools were required in the 1860s.

By the end of the century, the former middle class zone along the shore had virtually disappeared, and only the Merton Road–Breeze Hill enclave survived as a high quality residential zone. Most of the domestic property in the borough was rated at £15 or less.

A more detailed analysis of the socio-economic groupings of the children in 1871 indicates a high proportion of middle-class children (essentially (i) and (ii) on the key of Figure 3(a)) in enumeration district 3, which covered the Merton Road–Breeze Hill area, and a considerable residue of such population in district 8, which at that time was being threatened but had not yet been overtaken by dock expansion.

---

[24] The socio-economic grouping of the child population referred to here reflects that of the head of the family, whether parent or guardian. It is worth mentioning the caution that needs to be exercised in translating the occupational data of the census returns into socio-economic categories, as has been attempted here, more or less following the lines suggested in relevant texts indicated below. For discussion of this and related problems see, for example: H. J. Dyos and A. B. M. Baker, 'The Possibilities of Computerizing Census Data,' in H. J. Dyos, (ed.), *The Study of Urban History* (1968), 87–112; M. Anderson, 'Standard Tabulation Procedures for the Census Enumerators' Books,' 134–45; W. A. Armstrong, 'The Use of Information about Occupation,' 191–310, and other articles in E. A. Wrigley, (ed.), *Nineteenth Century Society: Essays in the Use of Quantitative Methods for the Study of Social Data* (1972); A. Armstrong, *Stability and Change in an English Country Town: a Social Study of York, 1801–51* (1974); R. Lawton and C. G. Pooley, (eds.), *Methodological Problems in the Statistical Analysis of Small Area Data* (1973), Mimeo. For pioneer attempts to apply nineteenth century census enumeration data in the educational context, see T. W. Bamford, *The Evolution of Rural Education, 1850–1964* (1965), 16–18; B. I. Coleman, 'The Incidence of Education in Mid-Century,' in E. A. Wrigley, (ed.), op. cit., (1972), 197–410; and A. Armstrong, op. cit., (1974), 68.

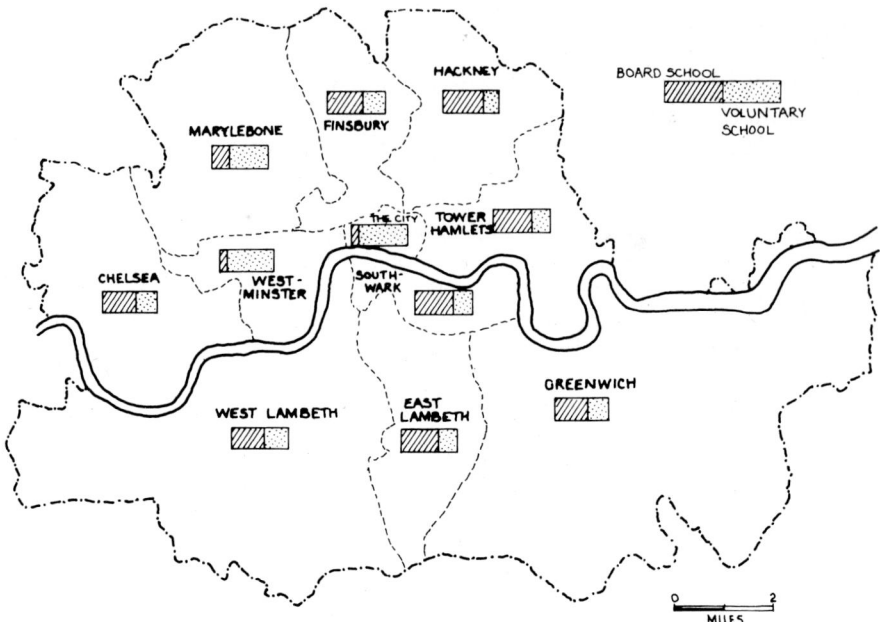

Figure 2. The ratio of Board and Voluntary School provision by districts, 1886. (*R. Hunt*).

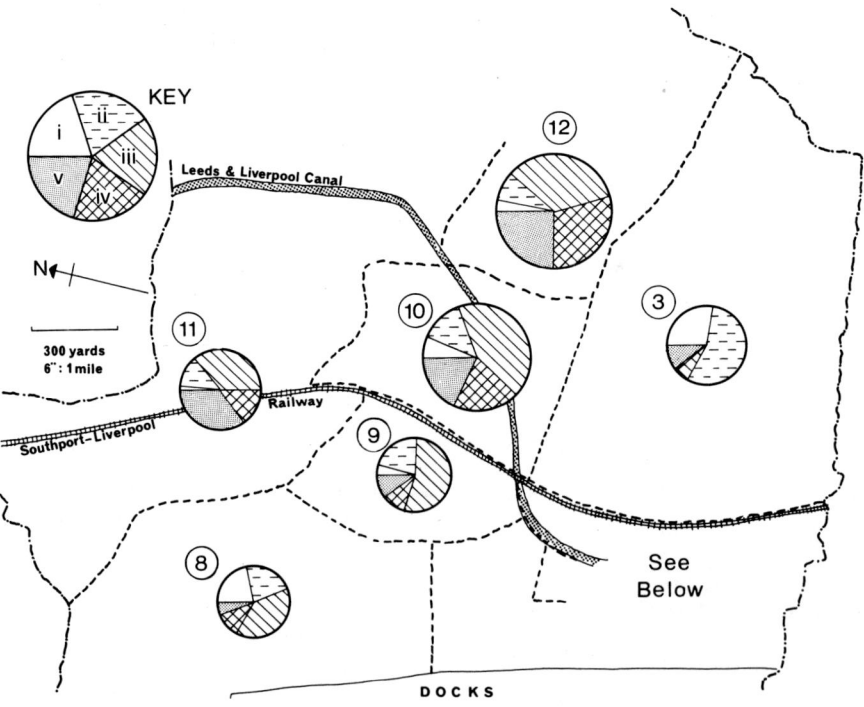

Figure 3a. Spatial variations in the socio-economic grouping of children aged 3–15 in Bootle, 1871. (*R. Hunt*).

Social and environmental disparities are highlighted not only by differences in social groupings, as shown by the divisions of the circles, but also in crowding, as depicted by the sizes of the circles. Thus a separate map (Figure 3(b)) is needed to accommodate the densities of the spatially compact dockland ghetto in districts 5, 6 and 7, the occupational structure of which was dominated by the casual labourer at the docks ((v) on the key). Districts 4 and 13 were more mixed, representing transitions to more favoured zones, though in neither was the highest socio-economic group represented.

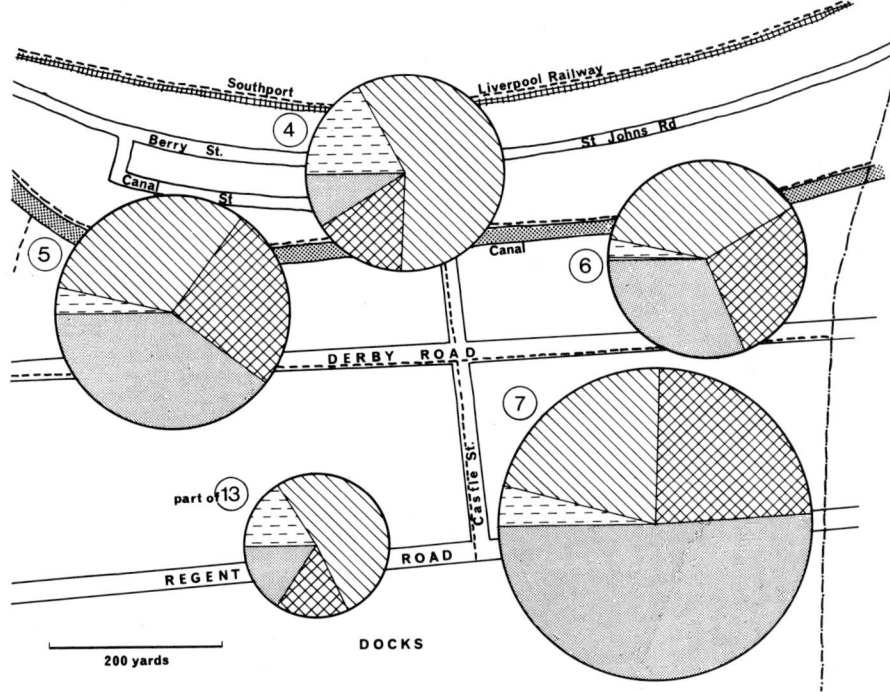

Figure 3b. Socio-economic grouping of children in the South-West corner of Bootle, 1871. (*R. Hunt*).

This south-western corner of Bootle was a quintessential Victorian slum, extending over the municipal boundary into Kirkdale. Dyos has explained the emergence of such slums in the spatial context as a consequence of the nature of urban growth in a *laissez-faire* situation . . . 'without the kind of general control on the spatial development of the city that might have been given, say, by a rectilinear grid, there were bound to be innumerable dead-ends and backwaters in the street plan.'[25] The process was reinforced, as here in Bootle, by the intrusion of canals, railway embankments and cuttings, warehouses and factories.

In Bootle, marked social differences existed within a short geographical compass, and the provision of a physical barrier was needed. Here the double barrier of the canal and the embanked Liverpool–Southport railway was heaven-sent. Similarly in Battersea, Booth described poverty as 'caught and held in successive railway loops.'[26] The closed vista was a ubiquitous feature of the nineteenth-century slum, and in some cases builders of adjacent better class housing deliberately sealed off disreputable areas by either blocking off or off-setting certain streets, as happened in the

---

25 H. J. Dyos, 'The Slums of Victorian London,' *Victorian Studies*, XI (1967), 25.
26 C. Booth (ed.), op. cit., Vol. 5 (1902), 192.

Notting Hill area, to be discussed later.[27] Children had to make detours in their journeys to school to find gaps in the barriers.

The identification of homogeneous social areas as a means of highlighting gross distinctions between middle and working class is a hazardous undertaking, as the detail of Booth's work demonstrates.[28] For within apparently similar built-up areas of terraced housing there normally existed gradations of great subtlety, fully comprehended by the local inhabitants. Roberts, in his study of Salford in the opening years of this century, draws attention to the minutely detailed spatial manifestations of status consciousness:

> '... each street had the usual social rating: one side or one end of that street might be classed higher than another.... End houses often had special status. Every family, too, had a tacit rank, and even individual members within it.'[29]

In the midst of poverty, many working-class families were 'awesomely respectable.'[30] From their analysis of the diary of a Liverpool railway worker, Lawton and Pooley testify to the good name of many a working-class neighbourhood, with patterns and norms of behaviour 'more akin to those of the middle class than to the classes below.'[31] To improve or uphold status, adjustments could be achieved by short range residential moves,[32] lubricated by a flexible rented housing supply. David Brindley's moves in the Everton–Kirkdale–Bootle areas all took place within a one-and-a-half miles radius of his work at Canada Dock goods station. Diary references to friends' removals confirm that such mobility was characteristic of the respectable working class.[33]

There was in addition that 'capricious migration' of socially more slippery groups, which gained them a desired anonymity in the face of the surveillance of the police, debt collectors, medical and school attendance officers. These short-term, short-distance moves made the work of such officers and the teachers more difficult. Alderson, H.M.I. for Marylebone, saw the continually shifting population, however caused, together with irregularity of attendance, as 'the two grand obstacles to the efficiency of London schools.'

> '... Constant removals of the home entail constant removals from school.... The frequency and suddenness with which families appear in a locality, stay some months, and then efface themselves leaving no trace behind, is realized by no-one more fully and sadly than the school teacher on whom the impossible task is laid of teaching their children something *in transitu*.'[34]

27 See L. C. B. Seaman, *Life in Victorian London* (1973), 115–6; P. E. Malcolmson, *The Potteries of Kensington: a Study of Slum Development in Victorian London*, (University of Leicester, unpublished M.Phil., 1970), 41–2. Also P. E. Malcolmson, 'Getting a Living in the Slums of Victorian Kensington,' *The London Journal*, I (1975), 28–55; D. A. Reeder, 'A Theatre of Suburbs: Some Patterns of Development in West London, 1801–1911,' in H. J. Dyos, (ed.), op. cit. (1968), 256 and 264; and F. H. W. Sheppard, (ed.), *Survey of London*, xxxvii, *Northern Kensington* (1973), 340–51.

28 See E. P. Hennock, 'Poverty and Social Theory in England: the Experience of the Eighteen-eighties,' *Social History*, I (1976), 75.

29 R. Roberts, *The Classic Slum: Salford Life in the First Quarter of the Century* (1971), 4. See also Mrs. B. Bosanquet, *Rich and Poor* (1896), 3–4; H. McLeod, *Class and Religion in the Late Victorian City* (1974), 44; D. Rubinstein, op. cit. (1969), 12–13; G. S. Jones, op. cit. (1971), 338.

30 D. Roberts, op. cit., (1971), 10; see also G. Crossick, 'The Labour Aristocracy and its Values: a Study of Mid-Victorian Kentish Labour,' *Victorian Studies*, XIX (1976), 301–28.

31 R. Lawton and C. G. Pooley, 'David Brindley's Liverpool: an Aspect of Urban Society in the 1880's,' *Transactions of the Historical Society of Lancashire and Cheshire*, CXXV (1974), 162.

32 See C. Booth (ed.), op. cit., (1902), Vol. 3, *The City of London and the West End*, 109, for a telling description of the difficulties of keeping up appearances in a declining street.

33 R. Lawton and C. G. Pooley, op. cit. (1974), 153–6. Similar mobility is described in Preston in the 1850s in M. Anderson, *Family Structure in Nineteenth Century Lancashire* (1971), 41; in Leicester in the 1870s in R. M. Pritchard, *Housing and the Spatial Structure of the City* (1976), 49–67; and in Camberwell in H. J. Dyos, *Victorian Suburb* (1961), 59.

34 C. H. Alderson, 'General Report on the Schools Inspected in the Parliamentary Borough of Marylebone,' *RCCE, 1873–4* (1874), 29. See also, C. Booth, (ed.) op. cit. (1891), Vol. 1, 27, where a return of a school board visitor in Bethnal Green is quoted, showing that of 1204 families (with 2720 children) on his books, 530 (with 1450 children) removed in a single year; and D. Rubinstein, op. cit. (1969), 64–5.

The most promising way of applying principles of social area analysis in the educational context would seem to lie in the study of the catchment areas of schools. The catchment area provides a framework within which interaction between the built forms and patterns of the urban environment, the social structure, people's attitudes and behaviour, and the educational system can be investigated in a spatial-ecological approach.

The size of the catchment area is variously related to factors of physical geography, the extent of the built-up area, its population density, the age grouping of the children, administrative control, the prestige of the particular school, and the presence of competing provision. In general terms, the more spatially compact, physically level and densely populated the area, the younger the age group, the lower the prestige of the school, and the more heavily endowed an area is with schools, the smaller the catchment zone.

In *laissez-faire* situations where children have to travel daily to school, a distance decay factor operates: that is, the numbers of children attending the school vary inversely with the distance they have to travel. Figure 4 illustrates travel distance

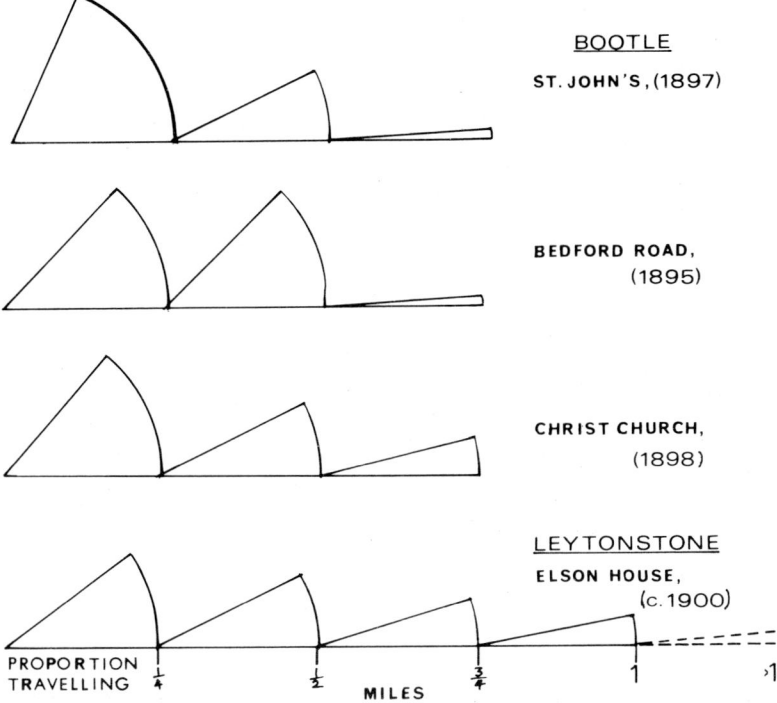

Figure 4. The distance decay factor operating on school catchment areas.

variations between four distinctive schools in different environmental settings in the 1890s, showing the proportion of the total intake at quarter-mile intervals. Three of the schools were Bootle elementary schools. St. John's National school was located in a densely populated working class area, with most of its children living within a quarter-mile of the school. Bedford Road board school drew on a rather more respectable and less densely populated catchment zone, with a considerable portion of the property in its catchment rated between £16 and £19. However, it too had a geographically restricted intake. This was because the School Board in Bootle exercised some control over the placing of pupils, while the middle class sector on the north side and the municipal boundary on the south also squeezed the intake (Figure 8).

By the last decade of the century Christ Church had become a high status elementary school, on the fringe of the middle class sector, to which some parents chose to send their children in preference to schools nearer at hand. Thus Christ Church had a greater proportion of its children travelling over half-a-mile to school. The secondary school in the group, Elson House high school at Leytonstone,[35] demonstrates how the older children of more affluent groups necessarily had to be prepared to travel greater distances to school. The built up area of this London suburb was less compact, and relatively fewer children in this age group required education, particularly where that education was expensive. Thus schools of this type were much thinner on the ground, with consequences which will be analysed later.

Distance from school in spatial terms alone is obviously an over-simple index of access. The inspectorate in the cities was concerned not only by the distances young children and 'timid girls' had to travel, but also by the hazards to be met with on the way. S. N. Stokes, the inspector for Southwark, pointed out that the 'topographical character of the borough' had 'an educational bearing,' and pleaded with the London school board to build moderate sized schools, reminding it that his area was traversed by wide thoroughfares leading to the Thames, and other busy streets, canals and dock entrances.[36] Stokes's advice was not heeded, and huge board schools were built to accommodate the whole child intake of particular districts. Ten years later he was noting, perhaps with some self-satisfaction, that a large proportion of the vacant places were to be found in infants' departments, reiterating that parents of children under five would not suffer them to walk any considerable distance to school.[37]

Catchment zones by definition encompass social areas, some more or less homogeneous, others mixed. It is now regarded almost as anxiomatic that the type of social area its catchment covers has important consequences for a school, and so it had in the nineteenth century. This can briefly be illustrated by reference to two 'celebrity' London slums of the time, the first being the Sultan Street area of Camberwell, made famous in Booth's and Dyos's investigations.[38] In sharp social decline in the second half of the century, this slum acted like a rodent ulcer, eating away at the respectable working class status of nearby streets. Figure 5 shows by horizontal shading areas which Booth had to 'translate down' in the 1890s on his poverty maps, mainly from working class comfort to the mixed comfort and poverty classification.

The school chiefly responsible for the non-catholic children of this district was Leipsic Road board school. The social decay of the area is faithfully reflected in its intake. Of the boys' entry in 1879, roughly 60 per cent came from homes in streets later marked as of working-class comfort,[39] 10 per cent from mixed areas and 30 per

35 M. Sadler, *Report on Secondary and Higher Education in Essex* (1906), 139.
36 S. N. Stokes, 'General Report on the Schools Inspected in the Metropolitan District of Southwark,' *RCCE, 1871–2* (1872), 72. See also T. W. Sharpe, 'Report on the Schools Inspected in the City of London,' *RCCE, 1879–80*, (1880), 375.
37 S. N. Stokes, 'General Report on the Schools Inspected in the Metropolitan District of Southwark,' *RCCE, 1881–2*, (1882), 440–1.
38 C. Booth (ed.), op. cit., (1902), Vol. 6, *Outer South London*, 15–20; H. J. Dyos, op. cit., (1961), 112; H. J. Dyos and D. A. Reeder, 'Slums and Suburbs,' in H. J. Dyos and M. Wolff, (eds.), op. cit., 1 (1973), 373–6.
39 It should be noted that some temporal license has been taken here, in that the earlier set of Booth's maps are not exactly contemporary with the admission register details. It seems likely, however, that if distortion has resulted from this mis-match, it will be in the form of an *under* rather than over-estimation of the changes which took place, as it is unlikely that the streets labelled 'in working class comfort' in the late 1880s would have been in a lower category in the late 1870s (the date of the admissions registers used). But they did decline from working class comfort to a lower category (mixed comfort and poverty) between the 1880s and 1890s.

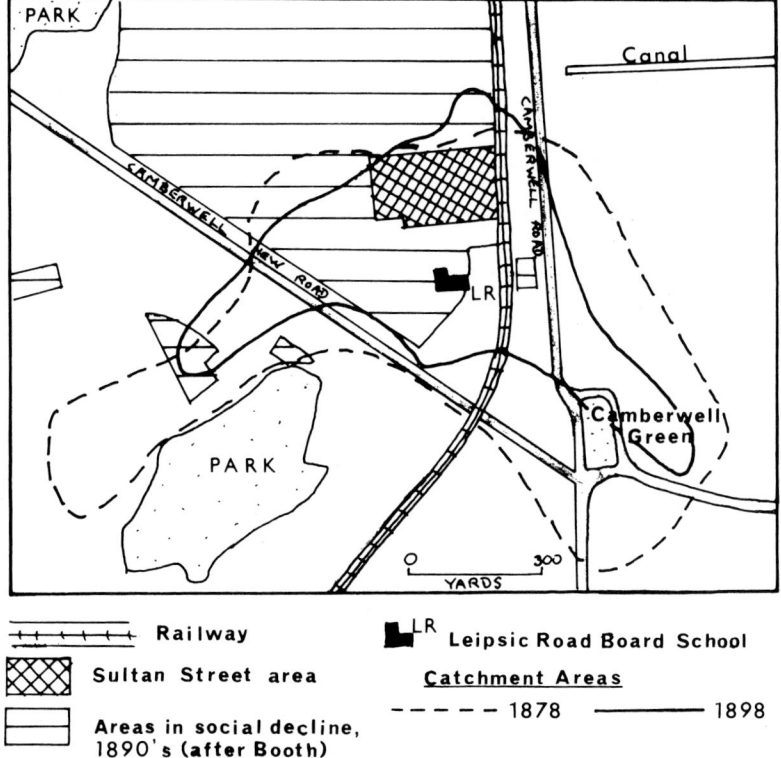

Figure 5. Social change and catchment areas in Camberwell in the late-nineteenth century.

cent from poor. Almost all of the last group lived in the Sultan Street district. By 1898, however, less than 20 per cent came from 'comfortable' areas, 33 per cent from mixed, and almost 50 per cent from poor areas. The map also shows the slight attenuation in the school's catchment area between the two dates, perhaps symptomatic of the fact that the school was losing some of the children from more salubrious neighbourhoods to the south-west and the south-east.

Even starker social disparity was present in the Notting Hill area of Kensington. Here the 'blacks and blues' of Booth's poverty map were in apparently close contact with the 'reds and yellows' of well-to-do districts such as Ladbroke Grove and Holland Park. However, the railway and a series of blind or near blind streets blocked off from more respectable gaze one of the most dissipated slums in London, Notting Dale. The board school serving this area, St. Clement's Road, was one of Booth's 'schools of special difficulty.' The core of disreputable streets, Bangor Street, Crescent Street, William Street, St. Katharine's Road and part of St. Clement's Road, were later singled out by the local authority as a 'special area' (Figure 6), in which infantile mortality, just one index of ill-being, was double that of Kensington as a whole.[40] One of Booth's co-workers, Jesse Argyle, wrote that the 'general poverty of the area may be gauged by the returns of the school. The fee is only one penny and half, the fees are remitted and 500 children receive free meals.'[41]

40 In *Local Government Interviews* (Charles Booth Collection, London School of Economics), Group B, Vol. 260, 43. See also the Annual Report of the Mansion House Council, 1897, *The Dwellings of the Poor* (1898), 21; P. E. Malcolmson, op. cit., (1970); F. H. W. Sheppard, (ed.), op. cit., (1973), 340–9.
41 C. Booth (ed.), op. cit., (1891), Vol. 2, 419. Malcolmson notes that the school was nick-named 'The Penny Board' with children reputedly bribed with sweets to attend, op. cit., (1970), 146.

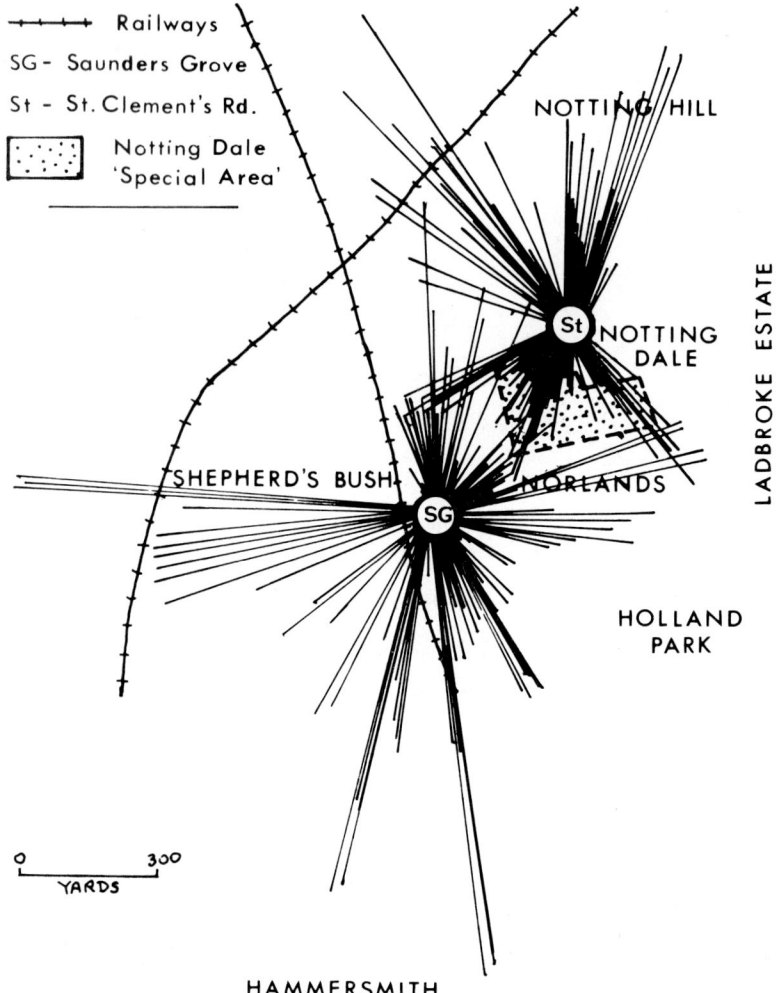

Figure 6. The pupil intake, by area, of two board schools in North Kensington, 1892.

The log books of the girls' department at St. Clement's Road relate the long grapple of the headmistress and her staff with the social conditions of an area notorious for its itinerant and indigent population, its common lodging houses and costers, cadgers, loafers, thieves and prostitutes.[42] Her entries tell of confrontations with drunken and belligerent parents and their periodically insolent children, and of visits to homes to investigate truancy:

> 'I made five calls on Wednesday morning. . . . At the first home, 21 St. Clement's Road, I found the mother with a fearful black eye, and everything looked very dirty and poor, and she told me the girl Margaret was truanting. I obtained the pawn ticket for a pair of boots that I gave Ellen (her sister) on Thursday last and which had been pawned, but I pitied the poor woman more than I could blame her.'[43]

Checking with concurrent admissions registers, one finds that Margaret and Ellen were aged 11 and 9 at the time the visits was made, and that prior to their

---

42 See interviews with Notting Dale grocer in *Local Government Interviews* (Booth Collection), Group B, Vol. 260; and with the police in *Police Notes*, Group A, Vol. 44, 12–13.
43 St. Clement's Road girls' school, Notting Hill, *Log Book* entry, week ending 22nd November 1895. (Greater London Council Record Office.)

present home, the family had recently moved residence twice in the vicinity. Margaret attended the school, apparently irregularly, from the age of 10 to 13. Two further sisters appear in the registers for approximately four years and one year respectively before the family disappears from the school's records.

Children of neighbouring schools were seen as deserving protection from the contamination of this neighbourhood, and not only those in the private sector. Saunders Grove board school (Figure 6), though conveniently located to serve this 'special area,' omitted to take many children from it. Its catchment lay rather in the more respectable working-class districts to the south and west. Children travelled further to this school. The vicar of St. Clement's church pointed out in an interview with Booth that the children attending his own national school were not of the lowest class, and that his parents did not wish their children to mix with those of Bangor Street.[44] Similarly, the nearby Oxford Gardens board school, built in 1884 in a middle class fringe area, was shielded by high fees of sixpence per week, local tradesmen having petitioned that such fees should be charged to keep the school select.[45]

The board schools of London had thus to do more than meet a mere numerical demand. As early as the mid-1870s H. M. I. Morell was affirming that the greater resources of the board would naturally attract 'a large number of children of a grade of population somewhat above those for whom the elementary school was originally intended.'[46] As such people were paying rates, their needs should be accommodated. Town schools could be 'graduated,' with those providing what Morell called a 'middle class' of instruction charging higher fees.

The 'graduated fees' issue was the subject of urgent debate at London school board meetings in the early 1870s.[47] At the other extreme from this 'middle class' of instruction, it was proposed that there should be special schools for 'barbarian' children. One lady member suggested that they needed 'a sort of penal or purgatorial school—something distinctly unpleasant, or at least more unattractive to the unmanageable than the best board schools.'[48] Other members were wholly opposed to such separation of elementary children into grades of social distinction.

The editor of the *School Board Chronicle* made his position clear:

> 'If elementary school children of all sorts can be made to mix without injury to one class or another, and without any demonstration of violent and mischievous repugnance on the part of either children or their parents, then it would obviously be needless and unreasonable to provide separate accommodation of any kind for the barbarian class; but if repugnance, indignation and rebellion are likely to ensue upon the attempt to educate children on the plan of an unqualified admixture of grades, then some other course must be adopted—some special arrangement must be made for the uncivilized. It is useless to attempt to apply agreeable axioms about the breakdown of class distinctions. The School Board must deal with the poor as they find them. They have to instil into the minds of the children Knowledge, not to undertake the Quixotic task of indoctrinating the rising generation of the working and labouring classes with the dogma of equality.'[49]

By 1873, London School Board had provided 28 000 school places, many of them in temporary accommodation, in some cases used by former ragged schools. For nearly 23 000 children the fees were one penny or twopence; for 3670, threepence; for 990, fourpence; and for 870, sixpence.[50] Fees were in part graduated by age, but mainly by social area. The spatial manifestations could be dramatic. Figure 7 shows

---

44 Interview with Rev. C. E. T. Roberts of St. Clement's Church, in *Parish Notes* (Booth Collection), Group A, Vol. 43, 26.
45 L. C. B. Seaman, op. cit., (1973), 117.
46 J. D. Morell, 'Report on Schools Inspected in the City of London and the Metropolitan District of Greenwich,' *RCCE, 1875–6* (1876), 373. See also D. Rubinstein, op. cit., (1969), 94–5.
47 See *School Board Chronicle*, 11th January 1873, 251; 22nd February 1873, 28–9; 8th March 1873, 75–7; 22nd March 1873, 123–5.
48 *SBC*, 9th November 1872, 390.
49 ibid., 399.
50 *SBC*, 11th January 1873, 251.

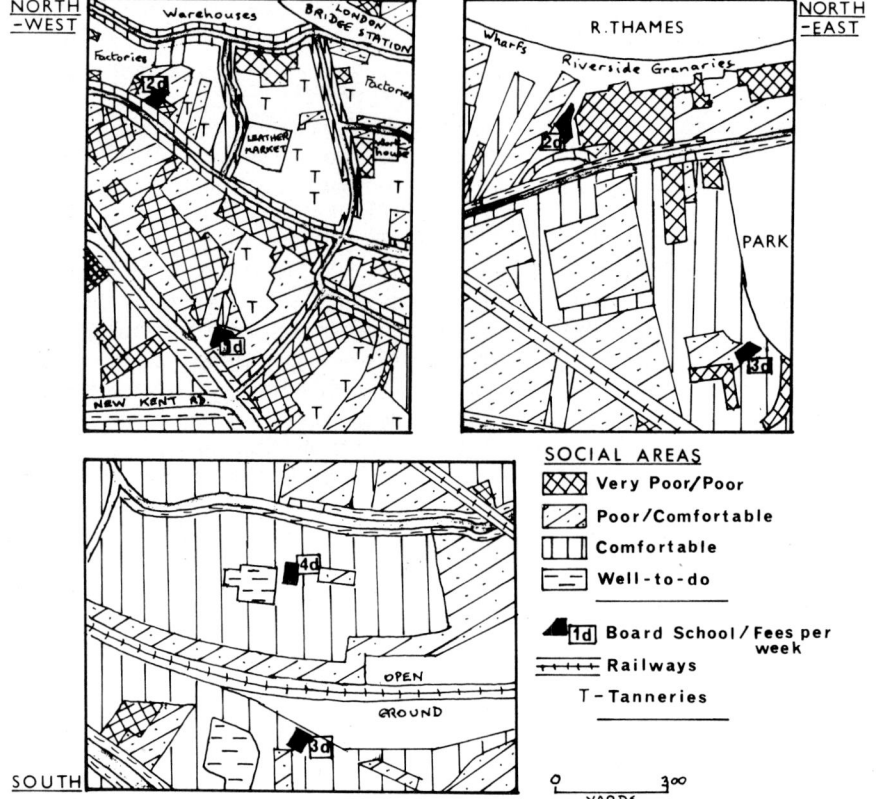

Figure 7. Board School fees and social area differentiation in Bermondsey, 1875.

the sifting process at work in Bermondsey in the mid-1870s. In the poverty-riddled and malodorous tanneries district, an example of a school with fees of only one penny is shown. Schools serving other industrialized and riverside zones were charging twopence, and those in less crowded areas to the east and south threepence. Monmow Road, later to become one of the Board's more prestigious schools, was charging fourpence at this time, benefitting from its location in the middle of an area of working-class comfort.

The concept of elementary schools catering for more or less middle-class needs aroused criticism. There was a case of a London board school headteacher being brought to task for overtly encouraging middle class entry and excluding 'irregular' children, a procedure which outraged a contributor to *The Quarterly Review* in 1879, who also quoted the action of the Bradford School Board, 'the chosen home of caucuses and advanced educational policy,' in establishing two schools to provide a 'superior elementary education.' The fees charged were just within the maximum allowed by the code (ninepence a week). 'By this contrivance,' he wrote, 'well-to-do tradesmen of Bradford are enabled, by the help of other ratepayers there, and of taxpayers all over the country, to get for ninepence such an education for their children as would otherwise cost three or four times that amount.'[51]

The ambitious appearance of some of the board schools, particularly in London, betokened high aspirations. E. R. Robson, architect of one of the more magnificent

---

51 'Our Schools and Schoolmasters,' *The Quarterly Review*, CXLVII (1879), 170–1 and 173.

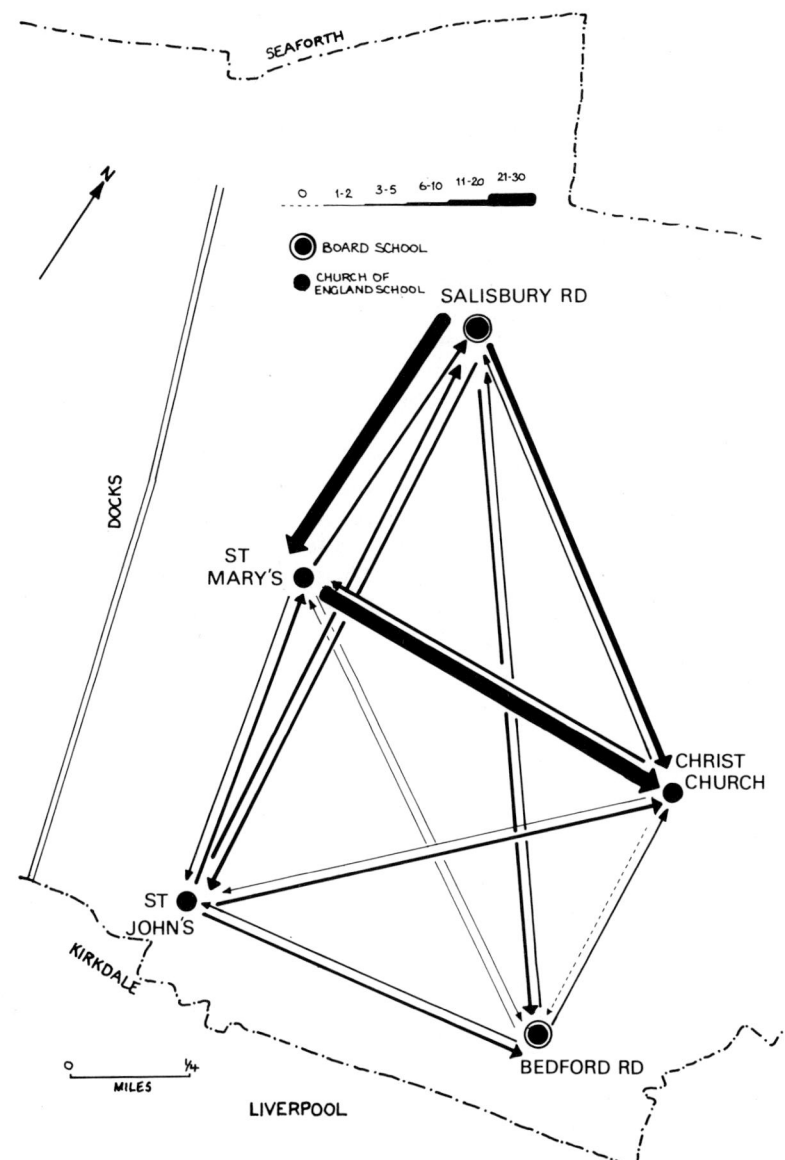

Figure 8. Transfer of children between schools in Bootle—1896–1900. (*R. Hunt*).

examples, Mansfield Place board school in Kentish Town, admitted that its fault lay 'in being somewhat beyond the mark of an Elementary, and suggesting in appearance rather the uses of a Secondary or Grammar school.'[52] By contrast, for the incarcerated Eagle Court slum of Clerkenwell, a lawless district whose inhabitants had violated some of his workmen, Robson asserted that 'the plainest of plain structure could alone be suitable.'[53]

In such ways a hierarchy of elementary schools evolved, highly sensitive to social area needs and changes, with a convenient pricing mechanism to hand. By the time

---

52 E. R. Robson, *School Architecture* (1972, reprint of 1874 publication), 344. See also J. Summerson, 'London, the Artifact,' in H. J. Dyos and M. Wolff, (eds.), op. cit., 1 (1973), 322.

53 E. R. Robson, op. cit., (1874), 315–6. Prints of the schools mentioned are contained in Robson's book.

fees were abolished, the die was cast. In late-nineteenth-century Bootle, for example, some parents were undoubtedly 'working the system,' in consort with headteachers, children being moved between schools for calculative and not capricious reasons. Figure 8 illustrates the transfer of children between the five Bootle schools for which admissions register evidence is available for the 1896–1900 period. The three dominant trends appear to be moves from Salisbury Road to St. Mary's and Christ Church; and from St. Mary's to Christ Church, suggesting Christ Church as a high, St. Mary's as a middle and Salisbury Road as a low status school. The other moves depicted appear inconsequential.

At this time, the Salisbury Road area was in social decline, the docks having reached the northern part of Bootle, which was engulfed by a sea of terraced housing. The headmaster of the school had complained as early as 1887 of the loss from the district of better class parents, and of an increasing entry of 'gutter-snipe' children.[54] The problem was exacerbated in the 1890s by gross over-crowding in the school. A personal comment from an old Bootle resident reinforces the evidence, telling of the relief of her parents when the opening of a new school in nearby Linacre enabled her to be transferred from the unpopular Salisbury Road school. Transfers *to* Salisbury Road were probably of less amenable children, if the situation reflected that of ten years previously, when the head of Salisbury Road was expressing his discontent at the unloading of difficult children from the church schools on to the board school. 'The children admitted at present here consist wholly of outcasts from other schools.'[55]

Figure 9. Population density and elementary school status in London in the 1890s. *Each dot represents 500 persons (from The New Survey of London Life and Labour 1930, pp. 90–91).*
● '*Top 25*' *schools in the L.S.B. scholarship stakes, 1893–1903.*

54 Salisbury Road boys' school, Bootle, *Log Book* entry, 29th April 1887. (Bootle Reference Library.)
55 Salisbury Road boys' school, Bootle, *Log Book* entry, 12th April 1887. (BRL.)

St. Mary's lay in an ambivalent social position, both spatially and temporally. By far the oldest National school in Bootle, it held on to some residual status from its formerly more favoured location, now in the turmoil of dockland expansion. In the late 1890s there were markedly more transfers from St. Mary's to Christ Church than vice versa. Christ Church was by this time firmly elevated at the apex of the elementary school pyramid in the borough, enjoying higher grade status. By 1891 it was charging fees much higher than any other elementary schools in Bootle.[56]

Designation as a higher grade school can well be used as an index of élite status in the elementary school sector. Figure 9 juxtaposes the top 25 schools, many of them higher grade, in the London School Board scholarship stakes over the 1893–1903 period, with population density. It shows them to be located mainly on the less crowded western, northern and eastern fringes of the metropolitan area. Beginning in the mid-1880s, the scholarship scheme was described by Webb as 'one of the most successful developments of the last decade,'[57] establishing a ladder to secondary education. Before attempting the climb, however, children had to have reached Standard V. Figure 10 shows the proportions of candidates eligible to sit the preliminary examination, and brings out spatial variations in opportunity. Leaving aside the City of London, the densely populated central and East End areas stand out as the most disadvantaged.

The most celebrated 'scholarship school' was Fleet Road, in east Hampstead,[58] where the atmosphere on prize days conjured up that of many a middle-class secondary school, with scholarships and other successes proudly acclaimed. At the prize

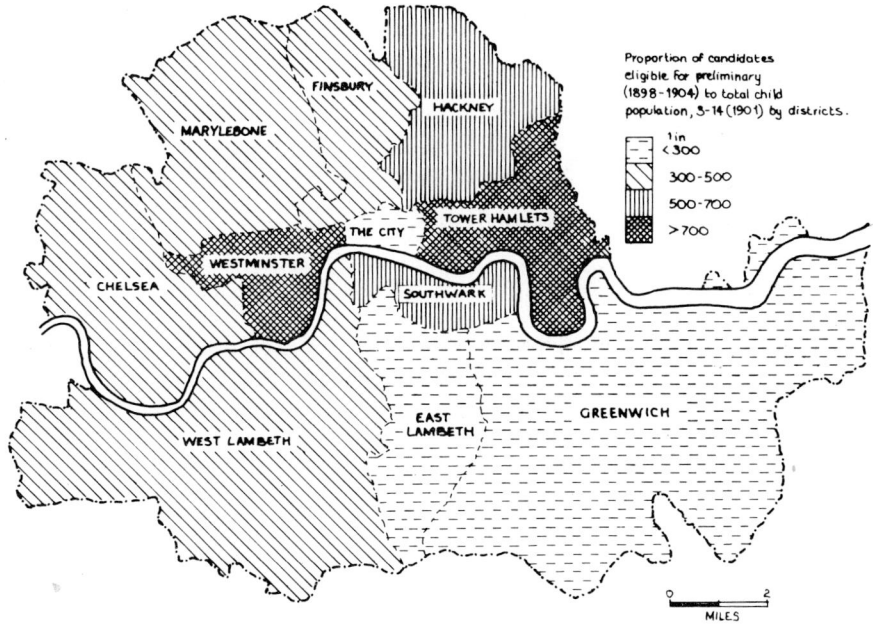

Figure 10. London School Board scholarships. (*R. Hunt*).

---

56 *Bootle Times*, 5th September 1891.
57 S. Webb, 'London Education' (1903), in E. J. T. Brennan, (ed.), *Education for National Efficiency: the Contribution of Sidney and Beatrice Webb* (1975), 116.
58 F. M. L. Thompson, *Hampstead: Building a Borough, 1650–1964* (1974), 416.

giving in 1899, one speaker asserted that no school in the country had done so much to raise the efficiency of elementary schools as Fleet Road.[59] Though Fleet Road was in a middle-class fringe location, with about 16 per cent poverty according to Booth's survey, the immediate vicinity was probably the least salubrious in Hampstead, with many homes in poverty on Fleet Road itself.

The headmaster made it clear to the Cross Commission that his school was by no means in an especially favoured area, though it took only a minority of children from the lowest ranks. Of his catchment area Mr Adams claimed:

> 'The population is a very mixed one; we have the children of bricklayers and labourers: a considerable sprinkling of the parents of the children are employed on the Midland and North-Western Railways. The great industry of the neighbourhood is pianoforte making, Cramer's, Chappell's, and Brinsmead's, and a great number of the parents of the children are employed there. Then we have a new neighbourhood springing up of small villas, which are occupied by people engaged in City warehouses, and so on.'[60]

In his senior board school (later higher grade), Mr Adams had in this mid-1880s period over 250 out of 900 children above Standard V. The successes he achieved over the next fifteen years increasingly attracted a lower-middle-class clientele.[61] Attention here and elsewhere was publicly drawn to criteria of success, particularly the annual government examinations. In Bootle in 1887, for example, the incumbent of St. Mary's caused considerable acrimony not so much by drawing attention to his school's successes, but by making favourable comparisons between his own school and not only the board schools, but also another voluntary school. The latter was going against the code, and the prevailing *rapport* within the voluntary sector was disturbed.[62]

It is well to recognize that while a reasonably favourable social location was of help to a school, it was not a *determinant* of success. The efficiency and high expectations of ambitious heads such as Mr Adams, harmonizing with the values of aspiring parents, were of crucial influence in the process of status acquisition in the elementary school sector.[63]

While the elementary system was spawning its own divisions, a secondary hierarchy was made explicit in official reports, such as that of the Taunton Commission. Educational facilities for the solid centre of the middle class were being provided by reformed grammar schools, proprietary schools and private schools, and the Commission carefully graded schools according to leaving age, fees charged, and the type of curriculum offered.

Liverpool Collegiate typified the large urban proprietary school, established in 1843 in what was then a superior location on the fringe of the city. It served in the first place the merchant quarter which ran up Shaw Street to the heights of Everton. It was created with an upper (classical) school, for the sons of professional people and merchants, paying the highest fees; a middle school, for the better class of shopkeepers and clerks; and a lower school, for small shopkeepers, clerks and educated artisans. As the headmaster informed the Taunton Commission: 'The defining line between the schools is a pecuniary one; people assess themselves at their own status.'[64]

59 *SBC*, 11th March 1899, 257.
60 *Cross Commission*, 2nd Report, 1887, Minutes of Evidence, 14 952–3, 45.
61 S. Maclure, *One Hundred Years of London Education, 1870–1970* (1970), 57.
62 *Bootle Times*, 16th, 23rd, 30th April, 7th May 1887.
63 For other examples see W. E. Marsden, op. cit., (1977), 222; and H. J. Foster, 'The Influence of Socio-economic, Spatial and Demographic Factors on the Development of Schooling in a Nineteenth Century Lancashire Residential Town,' (University of Liverpool, unpublished M.Ed. thesis, 1976) 120, 125 and 131.
64 *Schools Inquiry (Taunton) Commission*, iv (1868), Minutes of Evidence, 2, 572, 165.

Social decline in the Shaw Street area seriously affected the functioning of the school. The merchants were moving to south Liverpool, and some of the boys were having to walk up to eight miles a day to and from school. The headmaster, the Revd. Howson, persuaded the railways, the Mersey ferries and the omnibus proprietors to give concessionary fares for children, and showered south-west Lancashire with maps marked by circles concentric on the Collegiate.[65] The phenomenon of the 'train boy' was even more in evidence in Manchester Grammar School. Its questionable social location, with some of its rooms inhaling the incenses of the polluted rivers Irk and Irwell, had caused its decline as a boarding school.[66] However, it was well placed for the city's railway stations. As Kitchener's map for the Bryce Commission showed, a few of its train boys were travelling daily up to 40 miles each way.[67]

Some schools were favourably located from the start. Thus the old endowed Merchant Taylor's school at Crosby, Lancashire, was ideally placed to serve the

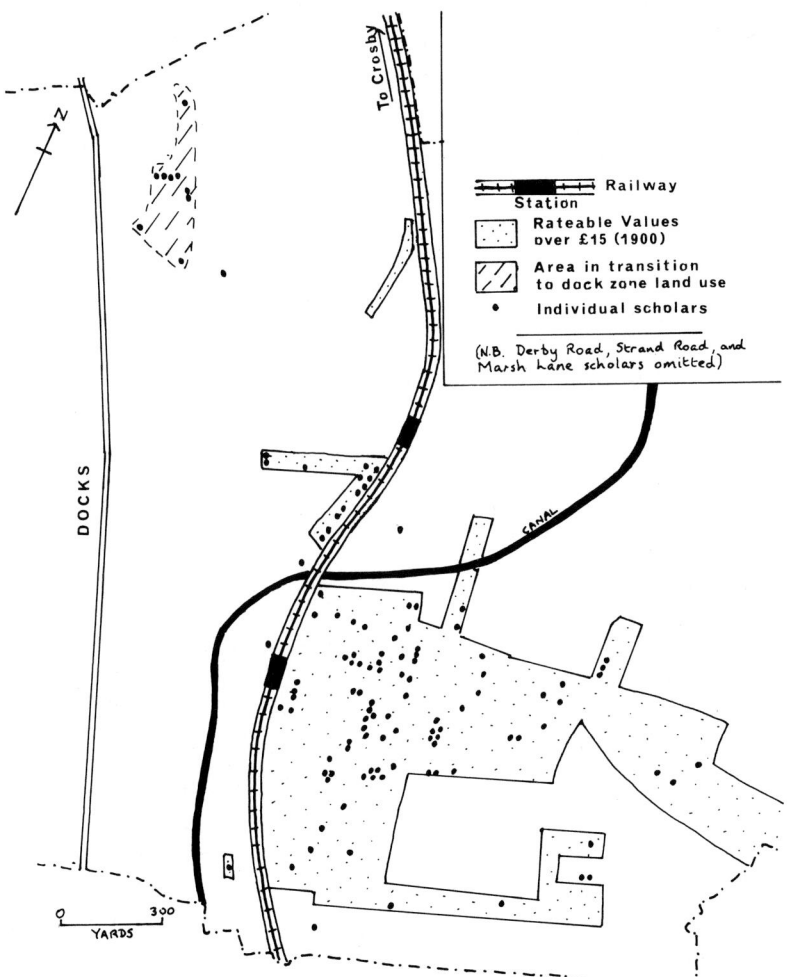

Figure 11. The distribution of scholars attending the Merchant Taylors' (boys) School in Crosby, 1870–1900.

65 D. Wainwright, *Liverpool Gentlemen* (1960), 92–3.
66 J. A. Graham and B. A. Phythian (eds.), *The Manchester Grammar School, 1515–1965* (1965), 28–9, 72.
67 F. E. Kitchener, 'Report on Secondary Education in the Hundreds of Salford and West Derby in the County Palatine of Lancashire,' *Bryce Commission*, vi (1895), 119–20.

needs of the merchant classes of north Merseyside, once its ambitious nineteenth century heads had succeeded in excluding poorer boys and erecting a worthy building.[68] Though much of the school's intake came from the Crosby area itself, it also relied on the Liverpool–Southport railway to bring in pupils. Figure 11 shows the distribution of the homes of Bootle boys using the school in the last 30 years of the century, corresponding well with the more highly rated areas of the borough, conveniently placed for its two railway stations.[69]

The secondary school's answer to social decline in an area was often to follow its clientele. This happened at an early date with Preston Grammar School, for example. Its social intake can be established by examining the distribution of households with servants, based on the 1871 census returns, and the homes of pupils entering the school between 1869 and 1873. Both were concentrated on the Fishergate/Winckley Square area. Crucial to its success was its move in 1844, in this case a short-range one, from the declining Stonygate to the affluent Winckley Square district. The new school building lay in easy reach of much of the intake round about this 1870 period.[70]

Bolton Grammar School (later Bolton School), was located hard by the parish church. The old building was demolished in 1880 and a new one erected on the same site, but used briefly only by the school, from 1883–99. At this stage the school was moved to a large villa in the well-to-do Chorley New Road area in the western suburbs of the town. Here the school remained (becoming the boys' division from 1915) until large new purpose built-schools were erected, also on Chorley New Road, in the 1930s.[71] A number of central London schools were similarly in transit in the late-nineteenth and early-twentieth centuries.

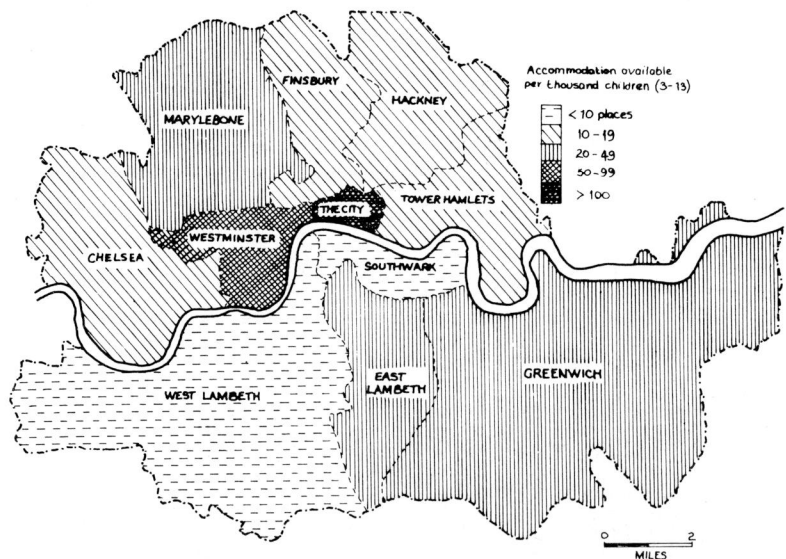

Figure 12. Secondary education provision for boys in London in 1890. (*R. Hunt*).

68 See H. M. Luft, *A History of Merchant Taylor's School, Crosby, 1620–1970* (1970), 160, 191–3; and F. G. Gomez, 'The Endowed Schools Act, 1869—a Middle Class Conspiracy? The South-west Lancashire Evidence,' *Journal of Educational Administration and History*, VI (1974), 11–12.
69 I am indebted to Rev. H. M. Luft for granting me access to the Merchant Taylor's admissions registers, from which source the data on which the map is based were taken.
70 P. J. Dixon, 'Urban Environment, Socio-economic Condition and School Attendance in a Lancashire Borough, 1850–76,' (University of Liverpool, unpublished M.Ed. thesis, 1977).
71 For photographs illustrating the changes, see W. E. Brown and F. R. Poskitt, *The History of Bolton School* (1976), facing 49, 113, 129 and 192–3.

Children in London: Turn of the Century Photographs

Many photographs of children in schools were made for official purposes to record or to demonstrate the achievements of municipal education: some of these are now held in official archives and they can also be found included in commemorative volumes of the city in the period. Some Victorian photographs of children in cities were deliberately posed in order to point up a moral of child neglect and cruelty. These were frequently included in books and pamphlets on slum life in the city. There were other photographs taken, however, simply in order to record the city and its people. These often catch children on the streets in a more natural way revealing interesting or unexpected habits and customs as well as showing the environment in which the children grew up. The following examples are a small selection from the many photographs of London children taken between 1890 and 1912.

Crispin Street and Duval Street, 1912, by C. A. Mathew. The photograph, though rather posed, is an example from a remarkably evocative series taken on the same day of an area straddling Stepney and the City. The area contained a Jewish settlement—some of the children here may have attended the Jews Free School. Further details of this and other photographs are given in the pamphlet published by the Bishopsgate Institute, *The Eastern Fringe of the City* (1974).

Bell Lane looking towards Crispin Street, 1912, by C. A. Mathew. Another example from the Mathew's collection. The children may have just come from the synagogue. Note the posters, including one for the Pavilion Theatre in Whitechapel Road, which was featuring a melodrama entitled *A girl's temptation*, written by Mrs Morton Powell, wife of the manager of the Britannia, Hoxton. (Bishopsgate Institute, p. 19)

Opposite above. Drill for Boys, c. 1912. Drill was a common feature of the activities of voluntary youth organizations and play centres after the turn of the century. Note the lack of footwear, and the use of dummy rifles. This and the next photograph were reproduced in Janet Penrose Trevelyan, *Evening Play Centres for Children* (1920).

Opposite below. A Round Game, c. 1912. The adult organizing the game is one of the voluntary workers in the London Playground movement.

A London square, c. 1902. The children are so busy with their own affairs to be hardly aware of the camera. The photograph is of interest because of the variety of social backgrounds reflected by the clothing and mannerisms of the children. Note also the pram, an ubiquotous feature in this period when older children took responsibility for looking after younger brothers and sisters. (Kodak Museum)

Whitechapel Road, c. 189–. The photograph contains much incidental information about how children and older boys occupied the pavement of this main London thoroughfare. (Greater London Council)

Red Lion Square, Clerkenwell, possibly early 1900s. Note the makeshift toy being pulled by the small children. (Greater London Council)

Above. A Board School Woodwork Class, 1897, Cassell. A set piece, taken of a class at the Kilburn Lane School and probably touched up. It is of interest in being included in Cassell's jubilee volume, *The Queens London*.

Below. Morning Assembly at a Board School, 1897, Cassell. Another example from *The Queens London* with the caption: 'Just as at the large public schools of England the boys meet together for morning prayers, so in like fashion the day begins at the Kilburn Lane Higher Grade School, the carpentry and cookery classes of which have already been illustrated...'.

Jerusalem Court, West End from St. Johns Square by H. W. Fincham, 1899. It is probable that the photographer was mainly interested in the buildings of this dilapidated court in a London slum—the children just happened to be there. Another photograph that is part of the collection held by the Department of Architecture and Civic Design of the Greater London Council.

Predicaments of City Children: late Victorian and Edwardian Perspectives on Education and Urban Society

D. A. REEDER
University of Leicester

The urbanization of the nation has been, and still is, a problematical phenomenon for educational reformers. This is mainly because of the ambiguities which inhere in the idea of the modern city as an agency of civilization and as a suitable environment for bringing up children. Educational changes and innovations have frequently been justified as offering antidotes to the worst features of urban life. This is the theme which is pursued now by discussing how connexions might be made between education and the urban problem in the late-Victorian and Edwardian period. The precedents for studying educational movements and ideas in the context of city developments have been set by American social historians.[1] However, the chief concern in my paper is to discuss similar movements in Britain from the point of view of an historian interested in responses to the urbanism of the later-nineteenth century. One aspect of these responses which began to emerge during research on educational and social movements in late-Victorian and Edwardian cities was the number and variety of apparently separate organizations whose members were, in one way or another, hoping to take a hold on and shape the urban future. It is only possible on this occasion to hint at the common concerns and overlapping membership of some of these groups, which need to be sorted more systematically: what the paper does set out to illustrate is how the connecting threads between them were provided by the city.

In 1900 Michael Sadler was explaining to an audience of teachers how perspectives on education have reflected different social ideals and the differing emphasis given to virtues thought necessary for the development of civilization.[2] These ideals derived from a fundamental Victorian debate about how good behaviour might be achieved and the forms of human settlement and organization most likely to foster it. The experience of urbanization in the nineteenth century provoked conflicting viewpoints and ambivalent feelings about the city as a habitat for man.[3] One tradition of educational thought can be said to have drawn on a critique of the city as an unnatural

---

[1] For example, Sol Cohen, *Progressives and Urban School Reform: The Public Education Association of New York City 1895–1914* (1964); Marvin Lazerson, *The Origins of the Urban School Public Education in Massachusetts, 1870–1915* (1971); A. Platt, *The Child Savers: The Invention of Delinquency* (1969).

[2] M. E. Sadler, 'National Education and Social Ideals,' R. D. Roberts (ed.), *Education in the Nineteenth Century* (1901), 210–39.

[3] B. I. Coleman (ed.), *The Idea of the City in Nineteenth Century Britain* (1973); Stanley Pierson, 'The Way Out,' H. J. Dyos and Michael Wolff (eds.), *The Victorian City Images and Realities*, 1 (1973), 873–89.

and corrupting habitat, made by writers deeply antagonistic to the ethos of commercial and industrial life. Radical criticisms of Victorian education frequently embodied images of the corrupting city, as in the writings of the evangelical supporters of the ragged schools, whose picture of the precocious child drawn into the vortex of urban immorality depended on eighteenth-century notions of the innocence of nature's children.[4] On the other hand, another tradition of educational thought, represented most clearly in the utilitarian argument for popular education, depended on ideals in which the city was regarded as having an authentic nature (as authentic as nature) and as possessing its own physical and moral economy. It was possible for Robert Vaughan, a Unitarian minister, to represent the rise of the city in 1849 as necessary to the evolution of rationality and culture, and the promotion of economic progress and liberty. He was able to ignore the possibility which Adam Smith had raised earlier to justify elementary schooling, that the division of labour in the urban economy might have the effect of making the town worker 'as stupid and ignorant as it is possible to become.'[5]

The anxieties which were experienced by some of the early-Victorian supporters of urban schooling were mainly about the disturbances to the physical and moral economy of towns from too rapid population growth.[6] Social historians have written about the connexion between support for popular education and the social disorganization threatened by the rapidly growing industrial towns of the first half of the nineteenth century. This connexion can be regarded as an aspect of the development of an ideology of community as the rationale for a wide range of philanthropic and educational endeavour. A paradoxical feature of Victorian reformist effort was that as older paternalistic and particularistic forms of social life were undermined, the family and the community became more and more idealized. The argument for popular education in early and mid-Victorian Britain was frequently under-pinned by a desire to restore the relationships of community in the new industrial urban society, especially in those cities where the physical separation of the rich and poor had already started. The idea that, in some sense, the social controls of localism might be restored by means of philanthropic and educational effort was a strongly held conviction in the nineteenth century. It was expressed, for example, in the claim of the Newcastle Commission that 'a set of good schools civilizes a whole neighbourhood'; and it inspired an Arnoldian offensive—a 'civilizing mission'—on the poor by those who promoted experiments in adult education and provided for 'rational recreation' in mid-Victorian towns and cities.[7]

For a generation of mid-Victorian reformers, of the type who gave papers to the Social Science Association for instance, the evolutionary positivism which that Association tended to uphold, encouraged a mainly abstract and optimistic view of the possibilities of social progress. This is why many of the social leaders in Victorian towns and cities could believe that developing qualities of social citizenship would

---

4 M. May, 'The concept of juvenile delinquency in early Victorian England,' *Victorian Studies*, XII, 2 (1973), 220–45.
5 A. Smith, *An Inquiry into the Nature and Causes of the Wealth of Nations* (1976), V, 1; for R. Vaughan, see B. I. Coleman, op. cit., esp. 87; compare the later pessimism of J. A. Hobson, *The Evolution of Modern Capitalism* (1894), 340–2.
6 See, for example, Thomas Chalmers, *The Christian and Civic Economy of Large Towns*, 3 vols., (1821–26).
7 See the meaning given to this reference in D. Glass, 'Education and Social Change in Modern England,' A. H. Halsey, J. Floud and C. A. Anderson (eds.), *Education, Economy and Society* (1961), 395. For a recent study of cultural provision in a Victorian provincial city (Bristol) with many references to the activities of Dr. Percival, headmaster of Clifton College, see H. E. Mellor, *Leisure and the Changing City* (1976).

foster the moral growth of the nation and the process of civilization.[8] However, warning notes had been sounded even then by members of the Social Science Association about the deteriorative tendencies in urban growth. Joseph Kay had warned, for example, that if children were neglected the city would become the 'training ground for crime and disaffection' instead of being the 'school of civilization,' a process that would 'deteriorate the physical and moral condition of the nation.'[9] The suspicion that physical degeneration might be entailed by urban growth was not uncommon amongst early- and mid-Victorian reformers; and the prospect of it was heralded almost prophetically in papers delivered by medical experts to the Social Science Association from the early 1870s on the possibilities of progressive hereditary degeneration in towns. During this decade, medical theories on the effects of town life on the physical constitution—theories about the lack of oxygenization in the blood and the inhalation of foul air (the two breaths)—were being quoted by writers on school hygiene and physical instruction in schools.[10]

In many respects, the arguments and recommendations of reformers in the late-nineteenth and early-twentieth centuries involved a restatement of older social and educational ideals, but in the context of a consciousness of the city in which images of the corrupting, degenerative and irrational forces in urban life had been transmuted into new and more sinister forms. A falling off in the profits of urban industrialization, allied with fears of the competitive strength of newer and more vigorous urbanizing nations, may have undermined confidence in the wealth producing potential of the city; but it was the publicity given to the social consequences of urbanization which most directly challenged optimistic theories. From the 1880s, radical politicians and social commentators became more impressed by the pathological symptoms of urban life. East London became the symbolic reference point for urban ills, and outcast London seemed to become a threat to the very idea of an urban civilization.[11]

The pessimistic reading of the urban condition was deepened by the realization that urban growth had resulted in a shift in the balance between town and country, such that the city had become the characteristic environment of modern man. Thus it became urgently necessary, according to one group of educational reformers, to develop a form of schooling that would facilitate the adaptation of children to the conditions of working and living in cities, making for a more effective urban life by contributing to the physical health and economic well-being of future citizens. Instrumental and functionalist ideas about education gained much support, but especially amongst those who advocated the introduction of physical, domestic and industrial training in the schools.[12] There were other reformers, however, who still pinned their faith on the importance of education to man's ethical development. This was linked with a continuing belief in the possibility of restoring a sense of community, despite the fracturing effects of urban growth. For many social idealists

---

8 T. H. S. Escott, 'Social Citizenship as a Moral Growth of Victorian England,' *Social Transformations of the Victorian Age* (1878). It is difficult to assess, however, what prospects the mid-Victorians held out for the 'residuum' or, in Sir James Kay Shuttleworth's phrase, the 'sensual classes,' 'who stagnate in the lees of society': *Addresses to Workingmen* (1973 originally printed 1873), 82.
9 Joseph Kay, *The Comparative Condition of Children in England and Foreign Countries* (1851), 46.
10 For example, Henry W. Rumsey, M. D., 'On a Progressive Physical Degeneracy of Race in the Town Populations of Great Britain,' *Trans. National Association for the Promotion of Social Science* (1871); Charles Kingsley, *Health and Education* (1874), 1–2; M. D. Roth, *On the neglect of physical education and hygiene in Parliament and the Education Department as the principal causes of the degeneration of the physique of the population* (1879).
11 See, in general, G. S. Jones, *Outcast London: a study of the relationships between classes in Victorian Society* (1971); Anthony S. Wohl (ed.), *The Bitter Cry of Outcast London*, (1970).
12 For example, the contributions to Lord Brabazon (ed.), *Some National and Board School Reforms* (1887).

the important priority was to restore the moral and civic purposes of schooling, even if they differed on how this might be done, whether by developing education as a spirit of living influence, in Michael Sadler's way of putting it, or by means of what F. J. Gould called, 'the logic of moral instruction.'[13] Concepts of moral and civic education were closely related in the endeavour to supply a new ethical purpose for urban schooling, with the idea of citizenship dependent on Roman definitions of rights and duties to the State (and Empire) as well as upon Greek ideals of ethical and social citizenship. Different forms of citizenship might be taught in different ways —by systematic instruction in social duty, or lessons in civics, or as an adjunct of the teaching of history; or citizenship might be caught by fostering *'esprit de corps.'* The duties of the citizen were relayed to school children through texts and primers, and citizenship was taught in evening schools by citizen volunteers before it was put in the curriculum by A. H. D. Acland. Developing citizens became the aim of many boys' clubs and youth movements from the 1890s onwards.[14]

The idea of citizenship, with all its differing emphases and associations, can be regarded as a particularly important aspect of the ideological concerns of different groups within the reforming establishment. Citizenship came to acquire a more functional purpose and attracted Imperialist sentiments. From recent investigations of the aims of the founders of organized youth movements, it does not seem unreasonable to claim that citizenship training was also an attempt to overcome the antagonisms of class by encouraging a better sense of social as well as national cohesion.[15] At the same time, older ideals of citizenship education, defined in terms of humanizing and elevating the industrial worker, were maintained by some of the liberal intellectuals associated with the settlement movement. Essays published by liberal reformers in 1901 under the title, *The Heart of the Empire. Discussions of Problems of Modern City Life in England* illustrate the persistence of humanist (and religious) aspirations and a preoccupation with character development and moral regeneration. What seems to have most affected the feelings and attitudes of liberal reformers and social idealists was the sense that 'aggregation' had altered the texture of social and cultural life. Such responses were influenced no doubt by those brief gestures of power exhibited by the London multitudes in the 1890s; but it was not so much a sense of impending social disorganization as the undermining of older cultural values which worried them, even if these values were associated with older patterns of authority. The tensions which liberal reformers and social idealists saw in the city were not so much between class and class as between the individual and the mass, and between the individual's inner moral and spiritual life and his outer physical environment. One aspect of that was the premonition that the bonds which had formerly held the working classes prisoners of the city were being loosened.[16] C. F. G. Masterman, journalist and liberal reformer, sensed this earlier than most, and his many writings on London contributed a vision of what a mass society, shaped by the interests of a common humanity, might eventually be like. It was an uncertain vision—although

---

13 Sadler, op. cit. F. J. Gould was the Leicester secularist and chairman of the School Board. For the debate about moral and civic education, see R. J. W. Sellick, *The New Education* (1968), 86–110.

14 For references to citizen volunteers, see Helen Mellor, op. cit. For influential statements about citizenship education, see A. H. D. Acland, *The Education of Citizens* (1883) and James Bryce, 'The Teaching of Civic Duty,' *Contemporary Review*, December (1892); and for one of the more popular texts Arnold Foster's *Citizen Reader and Laws of Everyday Life*, which went through many editions, and also the references, going back to George Combe and 'social economy' in William Jolly, *Ruskin on Education Some Needed But Neglectful Elements* (1907). I am currently preparing a series of reprints on this theme for the University of Leicester series of Victorian classics.

15 See, John Springhall, *Youth Empire and Society, British Youth Movements, 1883–1940* (1977), esp. chap. 4, 'Duty and Discipline'. I did not have the benefit of this volume before giving the talk.

16 See, H. J. Dyos and D. A. Reeder, 'Slums and Suburbs,' H. J. Dyos and M. Wolff (eds.), op. cit., esp. 360, 370–1.

Masterman helped represent the educational interests of West Ham and supported Liberal educational measures, he seemed at times to despair both of the choking life of the ghetto and of the banalities of the suburb: 'Into this mass,' he wrote sympathetically but only half believing, 'the School Boards have attempted to introduce as leaven the Evening Schools, flashing lanterns in their faces, encouraging recreation, abolishing fees, making lessons simple and easy, prepared to adopt any expedients if by any means they may have some.'[17]

The uncertainty about the urban future was expressed even more hysterically in the first decade of the twentieth century by those who led a new moral campaign, focussed almost obsessively on sexual morality, and intended to cleanse the city of its more unwholesome characteristics. As there is little evidence of any pronounced change in sexual morals with late-Victorian and Edwardian urbanization, the 'social purity' campaign might be more evidently regarded as a defensive posture by the custodiens of morality.[18] Nevertheless, it was a campaign which had repercussions on educational thought and policy, as we shall see.

A first step in attempting to understand these perceptions is to notice how movements in social and intellectual thought influenced the diagnosis and remedies of contemporary reformers. The most important initial point to make concerns the relations between biology, social theory and analysis. The extent to which biological analogies saturated the language of social analysis, as well as providing a basis for more systematic theories about the evolution of society, cannot be overstressed. When the facts of urbanization, as recorded in the census returns from 1881, were viewed in the light of these evolutionary theories then what happened in and to the city had more wide ranging implications than ever before. The point was made, somewhat dramatically, by Reginald Bray, a settlement worker and member of the London Education Authority, in the preface to his book, *The Town Child* (1907):

> 'Already more than two-thirds of the people are aggregated in cities, and each census return indicates that the end is not yet. The sphinx of the twentieth century propounds to us the riddle as to what England will do with her town populations, or perhaps, more truly, what these town populations will do with England. . . . I have approached the problem from two points of view. First, as a student of evolution anxious to deduce the characteristics of a coming race, as it slowly emerges on the plane of the world, by examining the reciprocal forces of the environment stamping an influence on the race, and of the race struggling in mortal combat with the environment. Secondly, I have looked at the problem with the eye of a social reformer—confident that to control in some degree the course of events is not altogether beyond the range of united effort.'

The sense which Reginald Bray had of the automatic processes of growth, of the town having 'slipped from the control of its creator' (p. 58), was to be given intellectual support by social psychologists, such as MacDougall, for whom 'aggregation' was due mainly to an almost blind instinct of gregariousness.

On the whole, historians of education have tended to emphasize most the impact of idealist philosophy on liberal thought, pointing to the new justifications which it offered for the extension of State power in education. In other words, philosophers such as T. H. Green provided a rationale for the regulating of an urban system which seemed to be going badly wrong, whilst helping to keep the prospect of moral and

---

17 C. F. G. Masterman, 'Where Ignorant Armies Clash By Night,' *The Commonwealth*, August (1901). The best source for his views on the new social and cultural forces in the city is *From the Abyss* (1902), esp. p. 4. For a discussion of Masterman as the 'uncertain prophet', see E. Hyams, *The Edwardian Frame of Mind* (1968), 57–73.
18 James Marchant (ed., for the National Social Purity Campaign), *The Cleansing of the City* (1908), and for discussion, E. Hyams, op. cit.; also Federation of Working Girls Clubs, *The Perils in the City* (1909), and for an earlier view, Ellice Hopkins, 'Social Wreckage,' *Contemporary Review* (1883).

cultural growth alive.[19] Older versions of an ideal city sustained by voluntary service became compatible with new forms of compulsion. Thus Canon Barnett became the founder member of the Educational Reform Association, which pressed, for example, for compulsory continuation education, whilst still upholding the principle that in a mass society it is necessary to deal with people 'one by one.'[20]

Some attention has been given also to the impact of new evolutionary theories such as social Darwinism mainly on the relations between Imperialism, the doctrine of national efficiency and new measures of educational and social reform.[21] However, the way in which social Darwinism came to be applied or taken into social thought was by no means uniform.[22] There were so many different interpretations of Darwin's theories filtered through the writings of social and political theorists, and they were expressed at so many different levels, that the ramifications of these ideas were bound to be extensive. Herbert Spencer stands out, the arch-social Darwinist, as a mediator of evolutionary theories who interpreted them in educational terms. A related approach, dependent on Darwinian notions and concerned with the happiness of the people, was that represented by 'scientific meliorism,' a phrase coined in the 1880s to denote a method of social progress in which the primary aim of a scientific general education was not culture, but the adaptation of individual character and habits to 'the prosecution and enlargement of social life.' Those who embraced 'scientific meliorism' were less optimistic about the future than some reformers, such as the Fabians, nor did they have such a strongly functionalist theory of education as Sydney Webb; but they were less pessimistic about the possibilities of community action than some of the supporters of Eugenics, the science of race improvement invented by Francis Galton, which relied so much on theories about the transmission of hereditary qualities.[23]

An outcome of the influence of social Darwinism for the debate on education and urban society was to highlight the need for adaptation—whether of the child to the urban environment, or of the environment to the child, and not merely in a functional but a biological sense and in the interests of the evolution of the race. This emphasis was manifested in the argument for the more extensive teaching of domestic subjects and hygiene in order to better prepare girls for what was known as 'after school' life, a negative aspect of which was the strengthening in the case against the intellectual tendencies in the curriculum of girls' education.[24] Eugenic spokesmen also set out to overcome the Victorian reticence about the sexuality of the young, and to promote the cause of sex education, a reform urged by Dr Saleeby (a social representative)

---

19 For a general analysis of social evolutionary thought in Victorian Britain, see J. W. Burrow, *Evolution and Society, A Study in Victorian Social Theory* (1970).
20 See W. S. Fowler, 'The Influence of Idealism upon State Provision of Education,' *Victorian Studies*, X (1961), 46–65. For the reference to the Education Reform League and Canon Barnett's views on mass society and the ideal city, see Henrietta Barnett, *Canon Barnett His Life Work and Friends* (1st edn., 1918, this edn., 1921), 294–5, 465; also Canon and Mrs. Barnett, *Towards Social Reform* (1909).
21 Bernard Semmel, *Imperialism and Social Reform; English Social Imperialist Thought 1895–1914* (1960) is still an essential source, but for education, see also G. R. Searle, *The Quest for National Efficiency, A Study of British Politics and Political Thought, 1899–1914* (1971), and E. J. T. Brennan, *Education for National Efficiency: the contribution of Sydney and Beatrice Webb* (1975), esp. his remarks on Webb's functionalist theory of education.
22 Gertrude Himmelfarb, 'Variations in Social Darwinism' in *Victorian Minds* (1968), chap. 7.
23 Jane Hume Clapperton, *Scientific Meliorism and the Evolution of Happiness* (1885), 431 and the chapter headed Education versus Culture. Professor Banks of the University of Leicester provided this source, and the comparison in the text, in a lecture on Victorian Meliorism given to the Victorian Studies centre at Leicester.
24 See Carol Dyehouse, 'Social Darwinist ideas and the Development of women's education in England, 1880–1920,' *History of Education*, V, 1, (1976), 41–55.

in terms of 'education for parenthood' and as 'positive eugenics.'[25] On the other hand, other educational reformers found common ground with the environmental emphasis as represented by the sociologist and town planner, Patrick Geddes. Educationalists and town planners had a mutual interest in civics, an important element in the more general plans which Patrick Geddes worked out to transform the paleotechnic and deteriorative town into the neotechnic and eugenic city.[26] Another link between ideas about civic education and town planning was the appeal to a refurbished concept of community: the aims of the Garden City movement, Sybilla Gurney explained to the Sociological Society, are 'to transform the modern congeries of persons—into a real community—to make citizens as well as cities—and to restore the interaction of town and country.'[27] These ideas were registered in an educational context in M. M. Penstone's pioneering textbook, *Town Study*, a replacement for nature study and an introduction to school civics, published in 1910.

The next point is that the connexions being illustrated did not exist merely in an abstract world but were effected in pressure group activity to bring educational change. In fact, since the 1870s individuals and organizations had emerged to relay ideas at a more popular level and to bring educationalists and teachers into campaigns intended to stir up opinion about the physical and moral deterioration thought implicit in urban conditions. One example is that of Lord Brabazon, the Earl of Meath, who gave an Imperialist orientation to medical theories about the decay of bodily strength in towns and translated them into social and educational reforms intended to combat deteriorating tendencies: during the 1880s and 1890s he campaigned for colonies for the unemployed, open spaces in cities the building and controlled supervision of school playgrounds, the Children's Ministering League, state feeding of children and compulsory physical training. Lord Brabazon not only publicized these matters, enlisting as he put it, 'wealthy and influential people concerned with the happiness of the people,' but he took a leading part in the councils of such organizations as the Northern Union Schools of Cookery, the Housewifery Association, the National League for Physical Education and Improvement and the National Educational Union for harmonizing home and school training.[28] All these organizations throw light on the personnel recruited for educational campaigns publicized by the Earl of Meath as 'social arrows.' Later on, he switched attention to youth, actively supporting such Edwardian movements as the Boy Scouts, the

---

25 Dr C. W. Saleeby, *Parenthood and Race Culture* (1906). The distinction between constructive or 'positive' Eugenics ('promoting the multiplication of the more fit') and destructive or 'negative' Eugenics ('the endeavour [by sterilization and permanent colonies] to diminish the number of the unfit') was also made by Major Leonard Darwin, 'First Steps Towards Eugenic Reform,' *Eugenics Review*, IV, April (1912), 26–38. The first national conference on sex education was held in 1913 with Major Darwin in the chair. See also, Eugenics Education Society, *The Teaching of Eugenics in Schools* (1913).

26 Fitness and beauty were the criteria for Eu-topia achieved by means of eu-technics: Patrick Geddes, *Cities in Evolution, An Introduction to the Town Planning Movement and the Study of Civics* (1915), 258. Helen Mellor points out that Patrick Geddes stole into the precincts of many organizations and movements (including most of those touched on in this paper relating to morality and the development of youth): for this, and Geddes' views on education, see Helen Mellor, 'Patrick Geddes: An Analysis of His Theory of Civics, 1880–1914,' *Victorian Studies*, XV (1970), 291–315.

27 *The Sociological Review*, III (1910), 35–43. For the persistence of an ideology of community in this and other spheres, see Colin Bell and Howard Newby, 'Community, Communion, Class and Community Action: The Social Sources of the New Urban Politics,' D. T. Herbert and R. J. Johnston (eds.), *Social Areas in Cities*, II, *Spatial Perspectives on Problems and Politics* (1976), 189–207.

28 Apart from School Board Reforms, op. cit., see The Earl of Meath (ed.), *Prosperity or Pauperism? Physical, Industrial and Technical Training* (1888), Earl and Countess of Meath, *Social Aims* (1893).

Lads Drill Association, the National Service League, the National League of Workers with Boys, the Anti-Smoking League and so on.[29]

Another example, J. B. Paton, might be cited to illustrate the origins of a campaign for moral fitness.[30] An Evangelical Nonconformist minister, J. B. Paton pioneered the inner mission of his church in the world, with the aim, amongst others, of arresting the moral deterioration affecting the youth of his times. To that end he founded the Recreative Evening Schools Association in Nottingham in the 1880s, which subsequently became significant in changing the evening school codes; he started the Boys' Life Brigade (1899), the Boys' League of Honour, Guilds of Courtesy and the Young Men's Brigade of Service; and he was involved in such national organizations as the Civic League (Social and Educational) for towns and cities. In the 1880s he was associated with Percy Bunting, editor of the *Contemporary Review* in an effort to publicize the immorality of urban working-class youth. Sir Walter Besant's article, '13–17,' was an example, from the founder of the *Peoples Palace*, of a dissertation on the language and behaviour of the foul mouthed 'young Bachantes and raging Maenads' of Hampstead Heath. Paton became especially concerned about the uses of elementary school literacy, setting up the National Home Reading Union in order to combat what he called the 'impure literature industry' especially of 'the perfumed kind.' In later years he associated with the Revd. James Marchant in launching the British Purity Campaign in 1902, subsequently restarted as the Forward Mission of the National Campaign for Social Hygiene in 1907, the progenitor of the National Council of Public Morals. Finally, he helped Michael Sadler along with others, including W. T. Stead and the American purity campaigners, to set up the International Moral Education Congress of 1908–9 at which the two leading moral education organizations in Britain were represented: these were the Moral (subsequently the Civic and Moral) Instruction League, promoted by representatives of the ethical societies, notably the philosopher Bernard Bosanquet; and the Eugenics Education Society, founded in 1907 by a breakaway group from the League in conjunction with scientists, notably J. Arthur Thompson, and medical men, such as Sir James Chrichton-Browne, the first President, and Sir James Barr, the President of the B.M.A., 1911–12.[31]

All of these groups were engaged in the kind of activity to which Augustine Birrell referred when speaking of his time at the Board of Education:

> 'There had been a time when the public elementary school was a place where children were taught reading, writing and arithmetic. But now they lived in another world, and ever since he had been at the Board of Education he had been pursued by deputations of learned and zealous men who looked upon the schools as places where they were to consider the health, future happiness and what he might call the breed of the English speaking race.'[32]

The debate about education and the curriculum ranged beyond narrowly educational circles overlapping with a more general concern about children represented by numerous voluntary societies and the emergence of a scientific (medical and psychological) interest in child development. This concern was the most important factor

---

29 J. O. Springhall, 'Lord Meath, Youth and Empire,' *Journal of Contemporary History*, V, 4 (1970), 97–111.

30 James Marchant claimed that he worked 'for the salvation of the unfit in mind and body': James Marchant, *J. B. Paton, M.A.D.D., Educational and Social Pioneer* (1909), 51, 141–2, 201–9, 216; *John Lewis Paton, John Brown Paton: a biography by his son* (1914).

31 For the Moral Instruction League, see F. W. Hilliard, 'The Moral Instruction League 1897–1919, *Durham Research Review*, 12, September (1961), 53–62. For the formation of the Eugenics Society, *Eugenics Review*, I (1909–1910), 51–54. Dr (later Sir) James Chrichton-Browne came to the fore in the 1880s with the 'over pressure' controversy, and was the foremost medical figure in the child health and child study movements.

32 'The State and the Child,' *Reading Observer*, 9th August 1906, cited in Stephen Yeo, *Religion and Voluntary Organizations in Crisis* (1976), 293, ref., 80.

connecting education and social policy: the predicaments of city children were central themes in educational debates and of national and international conferences on a range of demographic and social subjects, and the internationalism of child concern was one of the factors influencing contemporary British movements.[33] The interrelations between education, child life, and various urban social problems were highlighted particularly by the Fitzroy Committee, set up to investigate allegations of physical deterioration in the aftermath of the Boer War, and also the two great national conferences on destitution held in 1911–12 which brought together voluntary social workers with educationalists and child experts.[34] In his address to the Destitution Conference, Michael Sadler explained that the period since 1900 had been one of the most far reaching, not only because of the building of a system of national education, but also due to the growing conviction that care for the physical condition of children was at least as important as attention to their intellectual development, and because of the belief 'now gaining ground that the responsibilities of the State for the welfare of its younger members must extent beyond the limits of childhood to the frontiers of adolescence.'[35]

Many elements entered into new demands for the State protection of children and the making of the great codifying measure of 1908 (the Children and Young Persons Act); and different interpretations can be made of developments in social policy as they affected children. On the whole, institutional and policy studies have tended to emphasize more the reformist aspects and extensions to childrens' rights, and rather less the connexions which these had with successive revelations of the behavioural patterns of working class 'family' life, and with wider social anxieties, except in a general way.[36] Similarly, less emphasis has been placed on studying the ideological concerns of voluntary workers (especially women) in child 'saving' movements than in corresponding American studies. Yet the very titles of conferences and writings about children in this period, indicate that a range of social dials were being turned, by those who claimed to be registering wider anxieties about how an urban society was handling or failing to handle its children and youth.

One social dial which has been acknowledged by historians of child welfare is that which tuned into anxieties about physical deterioration, a concept that had become an accepted part of the rhetoric of social reformers in the early twentieth century, partly due to the publicity given to the physical condition of the recruits to the Boer War.[37] Even if there were medical experts at the time who refused to accept the evidence on the progressive deterioration of the nation's physique, the popular opinion as represented by the ex-Chairman of the anthropometric committee of the Salford School Board was that the nation had become divided into 'two physical types—that of the well trained and usually well groomed physically fit—and the dwarfed and pollarded masses.'[38] The impact of such ideas on social policy is complicated, however, in being invoked by social reformers of different shades of opinion: S.D.F. and I.L.P. members played on the consequences of deterioration in

---

33 See the bibliography of child life in Margaret Alden, *Child Life and Labour* [Social Service Handbooks, No. 6], (1908). Her husband was a member of the N.C.P.M. and President of the National League of Workers with Boys.
34 *Inter-Departmental Committee on Physical Deterioration*, 1904, xxxii (Cd. 2175) and xxxii (Cd. 2210); Report of the Proceedings, *National Conference on the Prevention of Destitution*, 2 vols., (1911, 1912).
35 ibid., 1911, 217.
36 As, for example, the general account in Ivy Pinchbeck and Margaret Hewitt, *Children in English Society*, II (1976), although some reference is made to physical deterioration and the Boer War on 411.
37 For example, James Cantlee, 'The Health of the People,' The *Practitioner*, March (1902); G. Sale Reaney, 'The Civil and Moral Benefits of Drill,' *Nineteenth Century*, March (1900); George F. Shee, 'The Deterioration in the National Physique,' *Nineteenth Century and After*, May (1903); H. F. Trippel, 'National Physique and National Training,' *New Liberal Review*, April (1903).
38 J. B. Atkins (ed.), *National Physical Training* (1904), 128, 101–116.

support of the principle of the State maintenance of children, whilst conservative social reformers such as Sir John Gorst also supported collectivist measures in the interests of Imperial strength and race regeneration.[39]

The Fitzroy committee helped to focus diffuse anxieties about the upbringing of children in cities, and had a direct importance for educational developments in bringing older demands for physical training and domestic subjects, as well as newer demands for continuation education, to public (and official) notice: the teaching of hygiene and infant care in particular received a boost from this inquiry.[40] However, it is necessary to recognize that no simple historical explanation can be given for the developing concern about the children of the city, and the attempt to do so raises difficult questions about the impact of urbanization on the outlook and perceptions of social reformers. One issue is how far anxieties about children were by-products of adult confusions about an uncertain urban future; and a related, more fundamental question, is the extent to which these confusions and uncertainties were themselves the results of developments that had affected the nature of urban society and the patterns of growing up in cities. What follows now, therefore, are some pointers to how this subject of the concern for child life might be approached in a way that grounds contemporary anxieties more firmly in the urbanizing process.

A helpful notion for studying the urbanization of this period is contained in Professor Lampard's argument, that between the 1880s and the 1920s, industrial society was passing through an urban demographic transition (at different rates in different industrializing countries).[41] Firstly, that the city was moving from a concentrating to a decentralizing unit of population as the balance of urban–rural migration shifted from a situation when the city had grown mainly by recruiting population to one in which urban growth was becoming more self sustaining, as a result of the multiplication of its own inhabitants. Secondly, and related to the former change, movements in urban mortality and fertility rates were taking the nation from a position of high birth and death rates to a position of low birth and death rates, a transition that was, however, only partially completed in Britain before the First World War. This argument is used to illuminate the 'international debate about cities,' especially confusion about the urban future around the turn of the century. Professor Lampard points out that falling urban mortality rates and the move to self sustaining growth in cities averts the dangers of 'race suicide,' but that the demographic changes involved threaten 'a new régime in which the city proletariat outbreeds the higher and more economically productive part of the population.' The argument is complex but relevent since it can be claimed that demographic factors, especially infantile mortality and the birth rate, were key elements in helping to explain why the condition and prospects of city children were a central element in the city debate. One point to make, put in a very summary way, is that whilst the national crude birth rate had been falling since the 1860s this had not much affected the urban working classes. Another point is that the rate of infantile mortality, a discriminating indicator of environmental conditions, had remained high until 1900: actually, the number of deaths per 1000 births went up during the 1890s, falling dramatically thereafter. The two points are related because it was only when infantile

39 See also J. F. Mills, 'The Physical Degeneration of the Masses,' *Clarion*, January 1904: cited, with many other references to labour organizations on this subject, in Derek Riley, 'Physical Deterioration of Young People in Great Britain in the late 19th and early 20th centuries, and suggestions to remedy it, University of Manchester, unpublished M.ED thesis, 1973.' For Sir John Gorst, see *The Children of the Nation* (1906) and *Education and Race Regeneration* (1913), a race and sex pamphlet of the N.C.P.M.
40 Carol Dyhouse, 'Good Wives and Little Mothers: Social Anxieties and the Schoolgirls' Curriculum, 1890–1920, *Oxford Review of Education*, 3, 1 (1977), 21–35, esp. the reference to Alice Ravenhill, lecturer in Hygiene and member of the Eugenics Education Society.
41 Eric E. Lampard, 'The Urbanizing World,' H. J. Dyos and M. Wolff, op. cit., 3–57.

mortality began to decline in urban areas that working-class populations 'were able to exercise a prudential restraint over their own fertility.' In the two decades *after* the turn of the century demographic trends were quite evidently affecting the attitudes of reformers to social issues as anxieties developed about the declining fertility of the middle classes and about Britain's position in the 'world competition for the cradle.'[42] Given the circumstances, it is not difficult to understand why concepts of 'fitness' and 'unfitness' had a special emotive force in Edwardian Britain.

The demographic trends not only influenced how contemporaries regarded the urban condition, they were themselves expressions (the 'behavioural postulates') of ecological developments within large cities: on the one hand, the centripetal and downward tendencies in urban growth registered in the replication of slums; on the other hand, the centrifugal (and mainly upward) tendencies registered by the rise of suburbs. During the two decades *before* the turn of the century the attentions of social reformers were centred not only on infantile mortality and the human waste which this implied, but on the condition of the survivors, as we have seen. Yet even in this period it was not merely the existence of slum populations which caused alarm, but their rate of procreation. H.M.I. Dr Eicholz had made the point to the Fitzroy Committee that it was the proliferation of slums as well as the publicity given to them which had provoked public interest in the physical condition of urban children.[43] As early as the 1880s, the spectre of a proliferating poor had been raised by Samuel Smith M.P. in support of various 'child protection' measures varying from the older remedies of shipping poor children abroad to newer remedies of 'compulsory industrial training for the children of the destitute classes conducted in night schools up to the age of 16.' For Samuel Smith M.P., 'one of the gloomiest elements in the whole case is the extraordinary rapidity with which the degraded population multiplies; the birth rate is far higher in these low slums than in respectable neighbourhoods.' His industrial training plan was an undertaking 'to deodorize, so to speak, this foul humanity.'[44] The image of the poor as a sediment precipitated at the bottom of urban society was reinforced in the 1890s by the discovery that, in the capital, the slums were the settlement tanks for Londoners, the containers of a degenerate class, whose offspring were the products of a cycle of hereditary poverty and associated physical deterioration.[45] The degenerate class contained within it a body of 'loafers,' on some versions, who were both victims and perpetrators of inter-generational decline. The impact of this notion and the hardening of attitudes associated with it caused G. K. Chesterton to remark that ' "This Cry of Save the Children" has in it the hateful implication that it is impossible to save the fathers.'[46]

The Eugenic reformers elaborated further the hereditary coda on the theme of urban deterioration in a lament about racial decay; and in so doing they added variations by extending unfitness to cover mental and moral conditions as well as

---

42 A. Newsholme, *The Declining Birth Rate—Its National and International Significance* [Race and Sex Pamphlet], (1912); S. Low (a critic), 'Is Our Civilization Dying?', *Fortnightly Review*, 99, April (1913); James Marchant (ed.), National Birth Rate Commission [National Council of Public Morals], *The Declining Birth Rate, Its Causes and Effects* (1916).
43 Inter-Departmental Committee, op. cit., evidence, Dr A. Eicholz, M.D., H.M.I., para. 434.
44 'The Industrial Training of Destitute Children,' *Contemporary Review*, January (1885), reprinted in Earl of Meath, op. cit., 64, 66, 76. See also for a social Darwinist view of these problems, Arnold White, *Problems of a Great City* (1886).
45 E. P. Hennock has challenged the view that Booth's characterization of the residuum and its relationship to the rest of the working classes was innovative: see E. P. Hennock, 'Poverty and Social Theory in England: the experience of the eighteen-eighties,' *Social History*, 1, January (1976), 67–91. From the point of view of this discussion it is nevertheless worth stressing the importance of the statistical demonstration that the East London slums were hereditary traps: see H. Llewellyn Smith, 'Influx of population', in C. Booth, *Life and Labour of the People of London*, 1st series, Vol. III, 58–106.
46 *Whats Wrong with the World* (1913 edn.), 198.

physical states. By the time the International Congress on Eugenics was meeting tables of statistics had been drawn up to show that while the most capable and vigorous families barely maintain themselves, feebleminded and degenerate persons were throwing out strains which ramify far and wide throughout the population. Moreover, these strains were thought likely to increase. The problem of feeblemindedness, for example, was its association with other social ailments and 'racial poisons,' the products of urban life.[47]

It is not possible to do more than point to one of the direct educational influences of Eugenic definitions—on the movement to establish special and boarding schools for handicapped and 'feebleminded' children as a first step in the purification of the race.[48] This not to deny that the origins of the movement were diverse and can be traced back to earlier philanthropic endeavour as well as the practical difficulties and humanitarian feelings of medical officers and School Board representatives in large urban centres. Thus Mary Dendy first developed an interest in mentally retarded and mentally defective children from experiences on the Manchester School Board; but her well known plan for the permanent care of feebleminded children was designed to protect some of them from being a danger to themselves and to the community. Mary Dendy was connected with the Social Hygiene movement, and a member of the Liverpool branch of the Eugenic Education Society, her views were approved by Francis Galton, and much quoted by the Eugenic lobby formed to monitor the deliberations of the Royal Commission on the Feeble Minded which had originated from the proceedings of the medical section of the International Congress on this subject chaired by Sir James Chrichton-Browne.[49] The advocacy of permanent care was not unrelated to the demographic anxieties of Eugenic reformers since the 'feeble minded' were thought to be more prolific than other members of the community.[50] It is relevent, therefore, to notice that Professor Sir Cyril Burt, the first psychologist to be appointed to an education authority in order to assist the medical officer in making recommendations about backward children, later admitted that 'like many people at the time I believed that owing to changes in the birth rate, the mentally retarded were multiplying far more rapidly than the normal or supernormal.'[51]

There were, in addition, overlapping connexions between Eugenic reformers and the societies founded in the first decade of this century to study children, especially the Childhood Society which Mary Dendy had assisted in starting in Manchester, with Sir Douglas Galton as President and with a journal edited by M. C. Keylnrick, editor of the *Journal of Inebriety*. F. H. Hayward, the Herbartian critic regarded many current child development theories as linking the 'false psychology' of Froebelian views with the 'paralyzing notions' of heredity developed by the biometricians.

---

47 National Birth Rate Commission, op. cit., Final Report; H. F. Tredgold, medical expert to the Royal Commission on the Feeble Minded, *Eugenics Review*, 1, (1909–10), 99–104. See also L. R. Rentoul, *Race Culture* (1906).
48 R. J. Lloyd, 'The Education of Physically and Mentally Defective Children,' *Westminster Review*, June (1903); Mary Dendy, 'The Feeble Minded,' *Economic Review*, July (1903).
49 For these details on Mary Dendy, see H. McLachlan, *Records of a Family 1800–1933 Pioneers in Education, Social Service and Liberal Religion* (1935), 135–184. Mary Dendy was the grand-daughter of John Relly Beard one of the founders of the Manchester Society for the Promotion of National Education.
50 'The Eugenic Principle and the Treatment of the Feeble Minded,' *Eugenics Review*, II (1910–11), 178–185.
51 C. Burt, *Mental and Scholastic Tests* (1921), preface; 'The Inheritance of Mental Characteristics,' *Eugenics Review*, III (1911–12). Compare the critical treatment of the American connection between social Darwinism, Eugenics and the mental testing movement in Clarence J. Karier, P. Violas and J. Spring (eds.), *Roots of Crisis: American Education in the 20th Century* (1973), 108–17, reprinted in Roger Dale et al., (eds.), *Schooling and Capitalism* (1976), 128–141.

'The notion of heredity,' Hayward wrote, 'tickles the modern imagination in much the same way as the notion of the devil tickled the imagination of medieval men.'[52]

The scientific study of childhood had originated from anthropometric investigations of city children, much extended by medical men and social organizations, as the evidence about the physical defects of children accumulated and social reformers began to realize that the children of the city were no longer the children of peasant fathers but the progeny of an urban race. Helen Dendy (later Helen Bosanquet), sister of Mary Dendy, and a leading supporter of the efforts of the Charity Organization Society in promoting child study, was much impressed by statistics on the contribution of city born children (nearly two thirds) to the annual increase in the population of Greater London in the two decades up to 1891: 'That being so,' she explained, 'restrictions on immigration would affect only a small part of the problem.—A far more serious question presents itself in the infantine army which is advancing upon us and in the physical and mental condition of its members.'[53] The subsequent development of a psychological interest in children's minds, though much stimulated by Herbartians, was also not unrelated to anxieties about the impact of the urban environment on mental development and the influence of the American psychologist, G. Stanley Hall, helped to underline a growing belief that the city had an inferior pedagogic value to the country. Psychological theories developed after the turn of the century contained new charges against the city: on one version that its very attractions—the press of numbers, the shifting kaleidescope of urban scenes—were creating nervous strain and excitability, and, on another version, that the monotony and accidie of the inner suburbs encouraged a restless search for stimulation and excitement. Whatever the version, the complaint was that the urban environment had a disturbing effect on the outlook and mental coherence of children. When J. E. G. de Montmorency made a Special Report for the Board of Education on new initiatives being taken in major cities to take children out of the urban environment—vacation schools, geographical field trips, holiday camps, and country boarding schools for town children—he justified these with older Pestallozian definitions of the educative force of nature and newer arguments about the efficacy of the natural environment on mental development.

The reference to new urban initiatives brings us back into touch with the urban world as perceived by the members of adult voluntary organizations. An aspect of the growth of these organizations very relevent to anxieties about child life in the city, was the increase in the number of women voluntary workers, who came into direct contact with the children of the elementary schools. This had started with the spontaneous development of breakfast and cinderella societies in the 1880s, but had been enlarged after 1902 by the formation (partly as a consequence of legislative enactments) of Care Committees and After Care Committees attached to school districts.[55] Such organizations would repay investigation for the contribution they might have made to generating a groundswell of anxiety. To what extent were voluntary workers relaying changes in child rearing practices and attitudes to children that had been made possible by the declining fertility of the suburban middle class? The example of the Guild of Play might serve to illustrate one of the mechanisms: the

---

52 F. H. Hayward, *Education and the Heredity Spectre* (1908), 1–12, 35.
53 'The Children of Working London,' B. Bosanquet (ed.), *Aspects of the Social Problem* (1895), 58.
54 Board of Education, *Special Inquiries and Reports*, 21 (1907), 'Special Report on School Excursions and Vacations Schools,' iii–iv, 15, 19, 25; also, from many examples, Catherine Dodd, 'School Childrens Ideals,' *The National Review*, February (1900); M. M. Penstone, *Town Study* (1910), 169–170. Compare: 'As our methods of teaching grow natural we realize that the city is unnatural,' G. Stanley Hall, *Aspects of Child Life and Education* (1921 edn.), 10–19, 22–4, cited in Marvin Lazerson, op. cit. (note 1), 43.
55 See the account in Douglas Pepper, *The Care Committee The Child and the Parent* (1914).

Guild of Play was organized in London after 1900 by Mrs Kimmins, wife of the progressive educationalist and Science Inspector for the L.C.C., and it represented an extension of kindergarten practices (which had caught on amongst middle class parents), but in a way that enabled London settlement workers to bring moral pressure to bear on the habits of working-class children. As Sister Grace of the Bermondsey Guild of Play explained, they were trying to combat the 'vulgar street games of the poor,' replacing them with 'character forming games, the heart leaves of the future life.'[56]

The relations between voluntary activity in youth organizations and contemporary perceptions of working-class behaviour have been studied more intensively. Youth provided a common context for many kinds of voluntary organizations seeking to extend their influence by catering for recreational needs in an urban society. One of the earliest of the newer forms (apart from the Y.M.C.A.) designed to ensure a toeing of the line—for church, queen and family—was the Girls Friendly Society.[57] It is a well attested point that the first wave of boys' clubs and brigades afforded opportunities for Public Schoolmen (and boys) to relay their own values of Christian manliness and '*ésprit de corps*,' an endeavour which was associated—significantly—with what the founder of the Boys Brigade described as 'putting the boy back into boyhood' by making his Brigade the 'Eton of the working class boy.'[58] Similarly, the flow of handbooks and guides written to help youth (boys mainly) through the perils of sexual discovery, reflected the experiences and attitudes of Public Schoolmen, such as Canon Lyttleton, headmaster of Haylebury College.[59] The point about youth movements, however, has been elaborated much further in recent studies to the extent that they are regarded as 'offering an antidote to what could be seen, in a self-fulfilling way, as increasing signs of juvenile restlessness.'[60] There is some evidence in a recent study of Oxford, in the decades immediately before and after the turn of the century, that youth movements actively affected the increase in anxiety about delinquency of which one symptom was the more stringent police enforcement of new moral standards. There is also some contemporary testimony from the unexpected source of the Commission on Youth and the Cinema which suggested that the apparent rise in juvenile crime in the first decade of this century may have been related to the fact that 'a greater number of persons is now engaged in keeping the young in the right way, sometimes with too great a zeal.'[61]

One of the difficulties about interpreting youth movements, as both a response to and a reinforcement of a distinctive cycle of anxiety, is that we know very little about whose anxieties they were registering. What evidence there is from local studies suggests that lower-middle-class children (and parents) were particularly well represented, and it might be possible to infer from this representation that youth organ-

---

56 'Childhood' in *The Monthly Record of the Bermondsey Settlement*, II, 5, May (1896), Mrs Kimmins was the wife of Dr C. W. Kimmins, a member of the Settlement, secretary to the London Society for the Extension of University Teaching and then Science Inspector London County Council—he was an Herbartian. Mrs Humphrey Ward (Tavistock Settlement) was also prominent in the play movement and vacation schools. It was the standardizing of children's play which Norman Douglas criticized in the preface to *London Street Games* (1st edn., 1916, new edn., 1931).
57 Described by Brian Harrison in *Past and Present*, 61 (1973), 107–38.
58 William McEager, *Making Men: a history of boys clubs and related movements in Great Britain* (1951). References to the Boys Brigade are cited in unpublished M.A. thesis, University of Leicester, 1976. See now John Springhall, op. cit., chap. 1.
59 However, many of the *Creative Life* booklets of the Moral Instruction League were by women. For Hon Lytllleton's ideas (a member of the E.E. Society), see *Training of the Young in the Laws of Sex* (1900), one of his later works.
60 John Springhall, op. cit., 15.
61 See John Gillis, 'The Evolution of Juvenile Delinquency in England, 1890–1914,' *Past and Present*, 67 (1975), 96–126; James Marchant (ed.), National Council of Public Morals, *The Cinema Its Present Position and Future Possibilities* (1917), xxxviii.

izations were catering substantially for a new suburban class anxious about the behaviour and friends of their own adolescent children. Certainly, the efforts which the leaders of movements such as the Boy Scouts made to present the movement as encouraging respect of parents, orderly behaviour and the self reliant youth would have appealed to lower middle class parents judging from contemporary descriptions (or caricatures) of the suburban lower middle class as the bulwark of old fashioned values and upholders of respectability.[62] This point, though conjectural, has application probably to other aspects of the anxiety about child life.

A more general point about youth movements is that they represented the 'institutionalization of adolescence,' and in doing so defined 'normal' adolescent behaviour in terms of a contrast between organized and to an extent dependent youth, and unorganized and independent youth.[63] This is an interpretation which fits the more general strategy that has been developed to account for the predicaments of city children in contemporary eyes, because it credits to this period another kind of demographic transition, one that was affecting phases of the life cycle. Put very summarily, the old pre-urban phase of youth as a period of semi-dependency or semi-autonomy was being replaced, at least in part, by a more prolonged, regulated, and institutionalized dependency, known as adolescence, a development affecting first the children of the upper middle class but spreading downwards through the layers of society. Thus anxieties about children in cities may have been reflecting, though in a distorted way, variations in the patterns of growing up as children from different social groups adjusted to new demographic and social situations. An example, in the case of the working classes, but of varying significance to different strata, was the importance which the street had to children as playground and working area, and as the centre of operations for the peer group and courtship rituals of older children or youths. One suspects that even our own image of the city as almost over run with children derives as much from their visibility as from their numbers. The need to obtain some sort of living from the streets was especially important for children in port and commercial cities, and in this respect, patterns of growing up were affected not only by institutional developments, such as the enforcement of school attendance, but also by structural changes in the urban economy represented most obviously by the expansion of an habitual but short term market for juvenile labour which served to keep elementary school leavers from attaining full adult status whilst creating tensions between them and adults (their own parents possibly as well as schoolteachers, youth and social workers). Children had always formed, of course, part of the reserve labour force in the urban economy, but in many respects the opportunities for casual or specifically juvenile employment expanded during the later nineteenth century with the growth in the commercial and distributive operations of the city.[65]

These economic factors affected both the life style of the young and lay behind contemporary perceptions of the 'problem' of youth, or, as it was often rendered, the 'problem of boy (and girl) labour.' In London, a range of new jobs were available for school children as well as for school leavers, for which the main qualifications were smartness and a youthful appearance. Large organizations emerged employing

---

62 This impression has since been confirmed by Geoffrey Crossick (ed.), *The Lower Middle Class in Britain* (1977), 28, 34, 39–40.
63 Gillis, op. cit.
64 There is a growing literature in support of this thesis, see in general, Michael Katz, *The People of Hamilton* (New York, 1976), ch. on 'Growing up in the Nineteenth Century,' esp. 307–8; John Gillis, *Youth and History: tradition and change in European age relations, 1770–present* (1974); F. Musgrove, *Youth and the Social Order* (1964); Bernard Davies and Alan Gibson, *The Social Education of the Adolescent* (1967), chap. 2.
65 For comments on the juvenile employment market, see Stedman Jones, op. cit., 69–71; Springhall, op. cit., 76–77; Gillis, *Youth and History*. op. cit.

telegraph and messenger boys; at the outposts of business there were innumerable boy jobs to be had, most of them unskilled and more or less fugitive but yielding better immediate wages often than apprenticeships. According to a departmental return of 1899 of a representative sample of London school-leavers, less than a third would take up apprenticeships leading to jobs classified as 'skilled' whilst 40 per cent became errand or van boys; in Glasgow no less than 53 per cent became lorry or milk boys.[66] The figures refer to first jobs and some transfers occurred at 16. Over the country as a whole the extent of transfer depended mainly on the demand for juvenile work from manufacturing concerns—but in port and commercial cities there was much less transfer than in manufacturing centres such as Leicester where many of the 'boy labourers' were absorbed at 16 into the hosiery industry.[67] The discontinuity between juvenile and adult employment was an endemic feature of the occupational structure of late-Victorian (and Edwardian) London, and the chief source according to the Majority Report of the Poor Law Commission of the casuality of the adult labouring force. Anxieties about employment prospects for children were also connected with fears that apprenticeship was eroding with the decline in traditional crafts and the substitution of 'learnerships' in the new suburban industries affected by technological processes. This anxiety was not limited to manual work, since another feature of discontinuity was the apparent 'over supply' of office jobs creating what might be called a white collar 'residuum.'[68]

The recognition of adolescence in the late-nineteenth and early-twentieth centuries in Britain was directly related to the discovery of the boy and girl labour problem.[69] At the same time, moves to extend control over adolescent youth by means of raising the school leaving age and measures of compulsory continuation education, were an extension of the recognition already made of the educators' responsibilities for the 'after life' of city children. This recognition was increasingly reinforced by new psychological insights into child development and by anxieties about the effects of urban living on ideals of moral and civic conduct. Thus, the youth problem was part of the larger urban problem; and the writings on it brought together ideas about the city and about child development in an evolving and dialectical relationship. This can be illustrated briefly in a last section so as to refer back to the ideas and movements which formed the starting point for the discussion.

The discovery of the boy (and girl) labour problem was a cumulative process initiated as a by product of enquiries made by the Women's Industrial Council into the work undertaken by children whilst they were still at school, and continued by the Committee on Wage Earning Children which had been formed by A. J. Mundella jun, a leading figure in the National Education Association.[70] More information on

66 See Cyril Jackson, Report on Boy Labour, *Appendix*, Vol. XX, *Royal Commission on the Poor Laws*, 1909, xliv (Cd. 4632), 204–5; R. H. Tawney, 'The Economics of Boy Labour,' *Economic Journal*, December (1909); Reginald Bray, *Boy Labour and Apprenticeship* (1911), 114–118.
67 Jackson, ibid.; A. Greenwood and J. E. Kettlewell, 'Some statistics of juvenile employment and unemployment,' *Royal Statistical Society Journal*, LXXV (1911–12), 744–53.
68 Tawney, op. cit., 517; Jackson, ibid., 87; Bray, op. cit., 141–2.
69 It was the character and unsupervized nature of boy work which mattered to contemporaries. Compare the American experience, where, it has been argued, the technological displacement of youth from jobs in offices, shops, etc., was the most important factor: see Selwyn K. Troen, 'The Discovery of the Adolescent by American Educational Reformers, 1900–1920: An Economic Perspective,' in Lawrence Stone (ed.), *Schooling and Society, Studies in the History of Education* (1976), 239–251.
70 Mrs Hogg, 'School Children as Wage Earners,' *Nineteenth Century*, August (1897); Nettie Adler, 'Children as Wage Earners,' *Fortnightly Review*, May (1903). The Women's Industrial Council was concerned with developing technical education for girls and promoting citizenship classes in girls' clubs. For A. J. Mundella and the N.E.A. interest, see A. P. Derrington, 'Anthony John Mundella—Uncle and Nephew,' *History of Education*, IV, 1 (1975), 32–5. For a general contemporary account, see O. J. Dunlop, *English apprenticeship and child labour: a history* (1912), final chapter.

the occupations of school leavers came out of investigations into the working of the Children's Employment Acts and from private investigations of youth and settlement workers many of whom had personal links with those Liberal politicians, the products of the 'new Oxford' movement, who were interested in these social matters.[71] In the first decade of the new century, the investigations of Charles Russell, a well known Manchester youth worker, on the street trades, earnings and life styles of Manchester boys found a place in the Special Reports of the Board of Education.[72]

Before 1900, commentators were chiefly concerned with the physiognomy and morality of child street trading, the private and public investigations contributing an explanation mainly of how the 'loafers,' the core element in the degenerate class, were being recruited: they were being bred to the life, taking on street jobs as school children and graduating into 'loafer' jobs late on—'six months of the undisciplined street life'—Helen Dendy remarked in observations on working London, 'is more than enough to undo all previous training, and it is extraordinary how a course of lounging will change these lads.'[73] It was the interpretation put on the situation, the prism through which it was refracted, that mattered. In the 1870s, John Morley had made a young street trader into the hero of his Board School studies—'citizen carrots,' quick, intelligent, knowing all the answers in the civics class—and one reporter on working London in the 1880s had found much to admire in the enterprise and nimble wits of the little capitalists of the streets.[74] By the next decade, the street trader was generally being portrayed in a very different fashion, a flashy type, with a 'slang' character, restless and unstable, notorious for gambling in billiard saloons, out of parental control, living in cheap lodging houses, roaming the streets in marauding gangs. An aspect of these changing perceptions was the public discussion of Hooliganism, a term said to be a derivative from Hooley's gang, and much used in an alarmist way in newspaper reports around the turn of the century. Whilst Charles Russell pointed out that gangs of Hooligans, Ikeys and Peaky blinders were more taken up with their own territorial conflicts than with deliberately anti-social acts, the problem of the hooligan and the street trader was represented in more popular and some official writings too as a threat for which the best answer was that of discipline. This diagnosis was reflected in the harder line that had been adopted, between 1900 and 1904 particularly, when various recommendations were made for compulsory forms of physical, industrial and military training for youth.[75] Even Cyril Jackson, of the London based Municipal party, concluded his major report on Boy Labour for the Royal Commission on the Poor Laws by suggesting that the

---

71 For example, A. H. D. Acland and H. Llewellyn Smith.
72 Board of Education, *Special Reports*, VIII, 22 (1902) and supp. (1903).
73 Helen Dendy, op. cit.; G. Sims(?), *The Childrens Labour Question* (1899).
74 John Morley, *Board School Studies* (1879); Anon, 'The Children of Working London,' *Strand Magazine*, reprinted in B. Jones (ed.), *Scenes from the Strand* (1975).
75 A. W. Drew, 'Industrial Schools and Juvenile Crime,' *Contemporary Review*, 63 (1893); W. Douglas Morrison, *Juvenile Offenders* (1896); Thomas Burke, 'The Street Trading Children of Liverpool,' *Contemporary Review*, November (1900); Rosa M. Barrett, 'Hooligans at Home and Abroad,' *Good Words*, June (1901); John Trevarthen, 'Hooliganism,' *Nineteenth Century and After*, January (1901); Sir Robert Anderson, 'How To Put Down Hooliganism,' June (1902); Charles E. B. Russell, *Manchester Boys Sketches of Manchester Lads at Work and Play* (1901), esp. 54; and note how J. W. Adamson refers to all this (and cites the example of the Hooligan family in Lambeth as an alternative to Hooley's gang) in *A Short History of Education* (1919), 350. A related topic which I didn't have time to go into is the impact of this agitation on Reformatory and Industrial School policies and the debate about the 'Assylum' theory of reform—one point to note is how efforts were being made to raise the age of supervisory control to 18.

solution lay partly in raising the school leaving age, so taking an age cohort entirely off the market, and partly in compulsory military training for youth.[76]

By the time of the Poor Law Report, the subject of boy employment had been taken up by economists and sociologists, who approached it in two distinct but overlapping ways. First, there was the approach of the economists and Fabians— R. H. Tawney, W. Beveridge, and Sydney Webb—for whom boy labour was not so much a problem of particular faulty industrial arrangements as a problem of the more fundamental dysfunctional relations between education and the economy— leading to the wholesale 'manufacture of inefficiency' between boyhood and manhood, in Arnold Freeman's social Darwinist language.[77] The economists supplied arguments for technical education (and the improved mobility of labour) as the solution to the boy labour problem, although they sometimes wrote 'as though technical education might in itself provide an answer to under employment.'[78] The approach of the technical educationalists overlapped, however, with the wider concerns in boy life of the sociologists, youth and settlement workers, for whom the main problem was the effect of 'dead end' and 'blind alley' jobs on the character of youth. These wider concerns were graphically illustrated in the studies of the Toynbee Trust on boy life in the cities, edited by the sociologist, E. J. Urwick, which, apart from revealing the uncertainties of social reformers about the value of boys' clubs, showed also how they regarded the employment question as simply one factor in the making of a young urban population whose life had little meaning or conviction. Urwick, drew on the social psychology of instincts to bring out the irrationality of urban forces making for the alienation of youth in the city, and he made a plea that educationalists should concentrate on the adaptation of the 'species of man–child' to new urban conditions.[79] For social and moral reformers, technical education was but an element in a scheme of adolescent education, a State apprenticeship for youth, which should give 'systematic care' through the critical years, including instruction in matters of hygiene and conduct.[80] This kind of thinking accounts in part for the popularity of the German educationalist Georges Kerschensteiner, whose theories of the continuation school, combined vocational education with character training in the preparation of citizens. The Munich Continuation Schools were much admired by the Liberals, in line with their more general admiration for German education and municipal enterprize, and the connexions between these two aspects of German achievement were commented on by town planners especially T. C. Horsfall, the leading Manchester town planner and the chief publicist of Kerschensteiner in Britain. After Mary Louch, the founder of the Child Study Association, had moved to Manchester, she began to recommend T. C. Horsfall to child centred educationalists as the pioneer of the wholesome civic life and of 'the wholesome education as part of

---

76 Cyril Jackson, op. cit., 32. For the part of Jackson and Blair of the London Education Authority in the movement for Day Continuation Schools, see D. W. Thoms, 'The Emergence and Failure of the Day Continuation School Experiment,' *History of Education*, IV, 1 (1975), 39, 41–2. Other officials who supported it were Norman Chamberlain of the Birmingham Authority and Spirley Hey, Director of Education for Manchester.
77 Arnold Freeman, *Boy Life and Labour* (1914).
78 Jose Harris, *Unemployment and Politics, A Study in English Social Policy 1886–1914* (1972), 31–2, 259–61.
79 See his introduction to *Studies of Boy Life in our Cities* (1904). Urwick might be described as a 'scientific meliorist,' influenced, however, by Bergson and MacDougal. E. J. Urwick was Tooke Professor of Economic Science at Kings College, and Director of the School of Sociology in London.
80 M. Sadler (ed.), *Continuation Schools in England and Elsewhere* (1908), xii; also Board of Education, *Report of Consultative Committee on the Attendance compulsory or otherwise at Continuation Schools*, 1909, i (Cd. 4757).

that life.'[81] The wholesome life was the particular aim of the Eugenic reformers of course, whose pre-occupation with such 'racial poisons' as venereal disease had resulted in the formation of a lobby for continuation education, in order to press on the country the importance of interesting the State in the life of adolescent girls and in guiding them to virtue. The 'sex lobby' was organized by Mrs Gotto, later permanent secretary to the Ministry of Health, but at this time secretary of the Eugenics Education Society and of the National Council for Combating Venereal Disease. It was most active during the war period during which time the labour issue had dropped out of the debate.[82] By then, Freudian notions about infantile sexuality were beginning to influence the medical supporters of sex education, thus putting the problem of adolescent youth back into the wider context of child rearing practices. Several medical authorities, to the National Commission on Youth and the Race held in 1924, made clear that they regarded the sex problem as caused by the failure of educationalists to keep up with the times. Dr C. J. Bond, for example, a member of the Leicester City Committee for Mental Deficiency and Chairman of the Leicester Society for Combating Venereal Disease, argued that the *cause* of the failure of parents and the State to provide sex education was due to the fact that education generally had failed to keep pace with the altered conditions of life and 'the great changes in modern society, whereby the social and the human side of the environment now largely supplants the surroundings of Nature and the natural world characteristic of a more rural age.'[83]

After sampling some of the various writings on child life in this period—and there were literally hundreds of them—from the point of view of urban attitudes, the dominant impression which they left was of a belief in the creation of a new kind of city monster: a city that was 'devouring' children, dragging them down into its commercial entrails, burning up their idealism and finer instincts, and processing their minds and characters in all sorts of undesirable ways.[84] An aspect of this picture, the image of the city as a biological furnace, was fuelled by ideas about the 'rising of the sap' in children and the associated idea of the 'effervescence of youth.' Such ideas were invoked in defence of various educational and other experiments for youth, in Baden Powell's claims for the Boy Scouts, and even more strikingly, in the claims made by Cyril Reddie—another prophet of racial decay—on behalf of the New Education, pioneered at the experimental school of Abbotsholme founded by Reddie

81 T. C. Horsfall was President of the Manchester Citizens Association. For his views, see 'Improvement of the Dwellings and Surroundings of the People: The Example of Germany,' in T. E. Marr, *Survey of Housing in Manchester and Salford* (1904), 'Health and Education,' *Contemporary Review*, March (1906), and (for Kerschensteiner) his contribution to J. T. Whitehouse (ed.), *Problems of Boy Life* (1912). It should be noticed that J. T. Whitehouse was editor of *St. George*, a Ruskinite publication to which Horsfall, Geddes, Urwick, et al., all contributed. For Mary Louch, see her contributions in the *Demonstration School Record*, esp. Vol. I (1911), published by the University of Manchester Department of Education.
82 Mrs S. K. Gotto (afterwards Neville Rolfe), *The Changing Moral Standard* (1918), a publication of the National Council for Combating Veneral Disease. In his lecture to the History of Education Society in 1976, Professor Armytage drew attention to the 'sex' lobby when accounting for the origins of the continuation education clauses in the Fisher Act, and the opposition of Lancashire and Labour M.P.s to them. This was part of a more wide ranging discussion of factors affecting the curriculum debate in the war period, not only social Darwinism, science and citizenship, but the reaction against these by humanists. An important source for studying the various interest groups is the annual conference of Educational Associations.
83 Sir James Marchant (ed.), National Birth Rate Commission [National Council of Public Morals], *Youth and the Race, The Development and Education of Young Citizens for Worthy Parenthood* (1923), 214–6. Much more needed to be said about the impact of Freud.
84 Compare Jane Addams, *The Spirit of Youth and the City Streets* (1912) which Patrick Geddes described as 'a psychological analysis of the Dionysiac spirit' in *The Sociological Review*, IV, 2 (1911): Geddes also approved of E. Holmes' strictures on education and the machine culture in *What Is and What Might Be*, in a review, ibid., IV, 4 (1911).

in 1898 in rural surroundings, away from the contaminating influence of the city, in order to cater for the adolescent children of the Directing Class. When G. Stanley Hall visited this country in 1910 he saw Abbotsholme as one of the most hopeful of the growing points in English Education.[85] It is well known that Stanley Hall had attempted to apply a theory of race 'recapitulation,' based on Darwinian biological ideas, to the educational psychology of adolescence, and that his ideas on this subject had a considerable impact in Britain as well as in the USA.[86] The 'culture epoch' theory had a particular attraction to the founders of back-to-nature wood-craft groups, such as Ernest Westlake, but in a more general sense, the theory re-affirmed the need to base urban schooling on a psychology of child development which combined genetic study with the principles of racial biology. One advocate of a pedagogy based on the new psychology was Dr J. W. Slaughter, chairman of the Eugenics Education Society, secretary of the Sociological Society, and an ex-pupil of Stanley Hall.[87]

Finally, reference can be made to Professor Findlay, the most influential of the so-called 'scientific educationists' of the pre-war period, whose Demonstration Schools in Manchester were proving grounds for the new experimental pedagogy. Findlay's own career reflected some of the intellectual influences at work in the new education: a teacher at Bath and Rugby, headmaster of several schools, but as an educationist, influenced by Rein at Jena and the American professors, Stanley Hall and John Dewey. Just as Hall's experimental studies had been financed by a leading (female) philanthropist and Froebelian, so the Demonstration Schools attached to the University of Manchester Department of Education were endowed by Sarah Fielden and supported by the Manchester manufacturer, Sir W. Mather, an advocate of manual training, chairman of the Schools and of the Froebel Institute in London. Some of the staff of Findlay's department were members of the Eugenics Education Society (Liverpool branch), including Mary Louch and Findlay himself, where they came into contact with social and medical reformers; and as Findlay came more under the spell of Dewey, editing his work for English readers, he emphasized more the importance of devizing a curriculum, informed by 'culture epoch' theory, which would replace those primary activities and experiences from which children had been cut adrift with the growth of the city.[88] In a sense, J. J. Findlay's writings and activities, represented the culmination of an educational theory of the urban school. Yet, in 1926, in his last work on a social history of childhood, Findlay seemed unsure of whether the breeding of an entire generation cut off from rural roots could ever succeed. 'Can this adaptation be successful?', he asked, 'that is to say, can the town type become established as a permanent variation of the race?'[89]

I am grateful for suggestions from colleagues and students on earlier versions of this paper.

85 B. M. Ward, *Reddie of Abbotsholme* (1934), 100. See also the introduction by J. J. Findlay.
86 Joseph F. Kett, 'Adolescence and Youth in Nineteenth Century America,' *Journal of Interdisciplinary Studies*, II (1971–2), 283–298.
87 Ernest Westlake, *The Forest School or Evolutionary Education* (published in parts, 1917–25); J. W. Slaughter, *The Adolescent* (1911), with an introduction by J. J. Findlay. For the impact of the new psychology on pedagogics, see Margaret MacMillan, *Labour and Childhood* (1907), esp. the references to the 'hygiene of instruction,' and Ellen Key, *The Century of the Child* (1910)—'pedagogy is a psycho-physiological science allowing variations from the type by encouraging the growth of self directing energy.'
88 Based on his contributions to the *Demonstration School Record*. J. J. Findlay was Professor of Education, University of Manchester 1903–1925 after a career that included teaching posts at Bath College and Rugby School, three headships (two Weslyan proprietory schools, and the high school at Cardiff), and lecturer on education at the College of Preceptors London. He was a student of education in Germany, 1891–3, and reported on the U.S.A. for the Royal Commission on Secondary Education, 1894. [*Who was who*, III, 1929–40 (1947)]. Although Professor Selleck mentions him in connexion with the 'scientific educationists' (*The New Education*, op. cit.), there is much more to be said especially about the Manchester connexion and the Liverpool branch of the E.E.S.
89 *The Children of England* (1913), 164.

Social Conflict and Urban Education in the Nineteenth Century: a sociological approach to comparative analysis

D. Smith
University of Leicester

In 1895, a French professor of education wrote the following:

> Comparative sociology is not a particular branch of sociology; it is sociology itself, in so far as it ceases to be purely descriptive and aspires to account for the facts.[1]

Emile Durkheim, author of those remarks, described as follows the subject matter of the discipline he helped to establish:

> Social life (he wrote) . . . is an uninterrupted series of transformations, parallel to other transformations in the conditions of collective existence; and we have at our disposal data concerning not only transformations of recent epochs but many of those through which extinct peoples have passed. . . . Furthermore, a large number of phenomena exist which occur throughout the entire extent of society but take on diverse forms according to geographic location, profession, religious faiths, etc. Such are, for example, crime, suicide, birth-rate, marriage-rates, practice of thrift, etc. From the diversity of these milieux will result, for each of these orders of facts, new series of variations, outside those which historic evolution produces. . . .[2]

Durkheim was committed to the view that social facts, in their several instances over time and space, exhibit morphological variations and sequences of development whose characteristics could be explored in the course of comparative analysis. It was possible to identify 'types' of social fact and 'stages' in their development. Thus one might, for example, search for different types of educational institutions and practices within and amongst societies and also discover successive stages in educational development. It will be assumed in this paper, also, that there is an intrinsic and discoverable order in social development, including its educational aspects, which comparative analysis may help to define.[3]

---

1 *Rules of Sociological Method*, translated by S. A. Soloway and J. H. Mueller (Free Press, New York, 1964), 139. Durkheim was appointed 'chargé d'un cours' in social science and pedagogy in the Faculty of Letters at Bourdeaux in 1887, a post which became a chair in Social Science in 1895. In 1902 he was appointed to a chair in the Science of Education at the Sorbonne, a post renamed Science of Education and Sociology in 1913. In Paris he lectured annually on education to intending secondary school teachers at the Ecole Normale Supérieure from 1904 to 1913. See S. Lukes, *Emile Durkheim, His Life and Works* (Allen Lane, Penguin Press, 1973), 95, 108, 360, 379.
2 Durkheim, op. cit., 134–5.
3 Substantial literature exists on the theoretical and methodological aspects of comparative sociology. See, for example, A. Etzioni and F. L. Dubow (eds.), *Comparative Perspectives: Theories and Methods* (Little, Brown and Company, 1970); M. Armer and A. D. Grimshaw (eds.), *Comparative Social Research: Methodological Problems and Strategies* (Wiley, 1973); N. J. Smelser, *Comparative Methods in the Social Sciences* (Prentice-Hall, 1976); R. L. Merritt and S. Rokkan (eds.), *Comparing Nations: The Use of Quantitative Data in Cross-National Research* (Yale University Press, 1966); F. W. Moore (ed.), *Readings in Cross-Cultural Methodology* (HRAF Press, 1966); I. Vallier, *Comparative Methods in Sociology: Essays on Trends and Applications* (University of California Press, 1971); R. M. Marsh, *Comparative Sociology* (Harcourt, Brace and World, 1967). The last two volumes both contain extensive bibliographies.

The paper is organized into three sections. In the first section it will be argued that urban education may be understood in the context of shifts within a hierarchy of 'structural levels' in societies and alterations in the constellation of dominant and subordinate social interests. Some interpretative issues raised by the use of the recommended framework will be exemplified briefly from the development of English and American urban education in the nineteenth century, with particular reference to Boston, USA, and Birmingham, UK. The remaining two sections will employ the framework more specifically in a discussion of the incorporation of scientific and technical subjects within secondary and higher education during the nineteenth and early-twentieth centuries. In the second section, two articles by Joseph Ben-David relevant to this question of comparisons amongst societies will be subjected to critical analysis. In the third section, the issues which have been raised will be explored in an English context through a comparison between Birmingham and Sheffield.

It may be helpful to begin by identifying the characteristics of social development with which we are concerned. When societies are examined, a number of different structural levels may be distinguished ranging from inter-societal networks, such as the European Economic Community, to local networks such as urban neighbourhoods, and, lower still, particular households. Intermediate levels include the national society and the provincial city. Comparative analysis is possible at any of these levels. Moving from the highest level identified to the lowest, one might compare, for example, Comecon and the E.E.C., French society and British society, Sheffield and Birmingham, Sparkbrook and Edgbaston, and different households within Edgbaston.[4]

The structural levels consist of sets of roles within institutional orders. The institutional order at a particular level co-ordinates the production and application of energy and resources of various kinds. It also sustains a form of life with a distinctive culture. Participation in such institutional orders develops competencies which are themselves exploitable within power relationships. Such competencies include; particular skills and knowledge based on day-to-day household management, capacity to manipulate neighbourhood gossip, ability to mobilize informal contacts in local government, experience in negotiating bureaucratic obstacles in Whitehall, and so on. Although each structural level contains its own distinctive set of roles (kin, neighbours, town councillors, etc.), higher levels include lower level institutions as constituents. Thus neighbourhoods comprise (*inter alia*) households, cities consist of (*inter alia*) neighbourhoods, national societies contain cities, inter-societal structures include national societies.[5]

Coherence and integration amongst different structural levels are increased to the extent that the same individuals participate in structures at a number of levels from the household upwards. The same person may be a householder, a member of a neighbourhood social network (e.g. at the 'local'), participant in local politics, employee of a national company and so on. By furnishing the principal channel through which people pass from the level of the household to the level of nationally-organized structures, the education system promotes integration amongst different levels. This contribution complements the more widely recognized effect of the

---

4 Sparkbrook and Edgbaston are neighbourhoods within Birmingham.
5 It should be noticed that the structural levels mentioned in this paper are not the only conceivable structural levels nor do the collectivities identified exhaust the constituents of the levels cited. They have been chosen because of their relevance to the sociological problem with whose definition this section of the paper is primarily concerned. By contrast, the levels of parish, municipality and national polity are emphasized by Derek Fraser in his very useful work on urban politics: D. Fraser, *Urban Politics in Victorian England* (Leicester University Press, 1976).

education system in tending to maintain distributive inequalities which are expressed at several structural levels.[6]

Each structural level may also be considered as a network of relationships characterized by *conflictual interdependence*. In other words, within these networks there exists on the one hand a tendency towards specialization and exchange, notably but not merely of an economic nature, and on the other hand a disposition to rivalry and competition. Between nation-states, for example, competition may culminate in warfare. Amongst sub-national groupings such as provincial cities a common manifestation is competition for prestige, partly through the creation of high status institutions, such as universities, in rivalry with each other. At a still lower structural level, neighbouring households also sustain relations of conflictual interdependence. On the one hand they tend to compete with each other, for example in terms of material possessions, the educational performance of their children, the saleability of their houses in the local property market, and so on. On the other hand, they tend to co-operate through the exchange of skills and services and possibly through the exclusion or denigration of 'outsiders'.[7]

Three points may be made about the hierarchy of structural levels. First, social processes occurring at each structural level are *interdependent* with processes occurring at all other levels. Thus, for example, spending patterns in particular Edgbaston households may be related through successive levels to processes occurring within the West European economy and beyond that to the world economy.[8] Second, in the course of social development variations occur in the *degree of complexity and density* exhibited by interactions at different structural levels. Increased complexity and density at a particular level produce tendencies towards more intense competition and conflict, on the one hand, and the development of regulative institutions, on the other. For example, in the mid-nineteenth century, the novel political tier of the municipal corporations was created. The town councils, later supplemented by school boards, were a governmental response to the gigantic problem of controlling and organizing vast urban industrial populations of an unprecedented size, scale and rapidity of accretion.[9] Third, in the course of social development shifts occur in the *relative dominance* of particular structural levels *vis-à-vis* other levels. In other words, variations occur in the preponderant direction and relative severity of constraints exercized amongst levels. Processes and structures at one level may lose their relative

---

6 By 'distributive inequalities' is meant inequalities in the pattern of distribution of rewards amongst households, neighbourhoods, cities and indeed societies. These inequalities express the disposition of power relationships amongst major social interests organised at a number of structural levels. The recent work of Byrne and Williamson presents evidence of the manifestation of these inequalities through a comparison between different cities or, more precisely, local education authorities. In terms of the approach presented here this work is an example of comparison at a sub-national structural level: D. Byrne, B. Williamson and B. Fletcher, *The Poverty of Education: A Study in the Politics of Opportunity* (Martin Robertson, 1975). In the political sphere, 'grass roots' campaigning by 'ghetto' organizations and the activities of the 'women's movement' are directed at the structural levels of the neighbourhood and the household. These groups seek to increase awareness of distributive inequalities expressed at these levels and of the power structures which partly produce and partly depend upon such inequalities.

7 For a relevant analysis see N. Elias and J. Scotson, *The Established and the Outsiders* (Frank Cass, 1965). See also N. Elias, 'Towards a Theory of Communities,' in Colin Bell and Howard Newby (eds.), *The Sociology of Community* (Frank Cass, 1974), ix–xii.

8 For a recent discussion of the interplay between regional, national and continental levels emphasizing economic conflict, specialization and interdependence at each level, see Joan Thirsk, 'Economic and Social Development on a European-World Scale,' Review Essay, *American Journal of Sociology*, 82, 5 (1977), 1097–1102. This discussion is set in the context of a favourable review of I. Wallerstein, *The Modern World-System: Capitalist Agriculture and the Origins of the European World-Economy in the Sixteenth Century* (Academic Press, 1974).

9 Another example is the creation of the European Economic Community.

autonomy while the determining capacity of their counterparts at another level may increase. An illustration of this process, taken from the turn of the century, is the strengthening of central direction in English education through the creation of a national Board of Education and the abolition of the locally-elected School Boards, which had controlled extensive municipal systems of elementary and secondary education.

So far social development has been characterized in terms of its manifestations within a shifting hierarchy of interdependent structural levels. There is another way of looking at social development. It may be considered in terms of the processes of conflict and accommodation that occur amongst major social interests in the course of a society's transition from being a commercialized agrarian polity to becoming an urbanized and industrialized nation state. The principal interests may be readily, if crudely, identified: the peasantry, the aristocracy, the manufacturing and mercantile bourgeoisie, the urban workforce, and the managers of the state apparatus. Urbanization, bureaucratization, commercialization, industrialization and other related processes all profoundly disturbed the established hierarchies of agrarian society, throwing up newly powerful commercial, industrial, professional, and bureaucratic élites.[10] Secondary and higher education (including scientific and technical instruction) played a considerable part in the socialization of both established and emerging élites and thus constituted a major sphere within which their confrontation and mutual accommodation occurred. Such processes within and outside the sphere of formal education may be seen in many societies, European, American, and Asian during the period from the sixteenth century onwards.[11]

When such societies are compared it is clear that they have followed varying trajectories *en route* from being commercialized agrarian polities to becoming urbanized and industrialized nation states. Hierarchies of interdependent structural levels have been transformed in different ways. Conflicts and accommodations amongst major social interests have followed dissimilar courses. Assuming that the structure of a national education system is decisively shaped by its participation in such processes of social development, it follows that cross-national variations in the structure of education systems manifest cross-national differences in patterns of social development.

The *sociological problem* which arises out of the preceding analysis may now be defined. It is to seek the structural logic immanent in the array of routes followed by societies as they develop. This logic may be pursued by comparing in particular cases the interplay between shifts within the hierarchy of structural levels and alterations in the constellation of dominant and subordinate social interests. Urban education is a potentially fruitful area for such analysis since its development has not only called forth the energies of established and emerging economic, political and religious élites but also made a direct impact at the related levels of household, neighbourhood,

---

10 Influential works relevant to a study of these processes include B. Moore, *Social Origins of Dictatorship and Democracy* (Penguin, 1969); R. Bendix, *Nation-Building and Citizenship* (Anchor Books, 1969); P. Anderson, *Lineages of the Absolutist State* (New Left Books, 1974). On British society, see J. Vincent, *The Formation of the British Liberal Party 1857–1868* (Penguin, 1966); J. Foster, *Class Struggle and the Industrial Revolution* (Weidenfeld and Nicolson, 1974).

11 For an entrée to some relevant literature see the following and references therein: L. Stone, 'Education and Modernization in Japan and England,' *Comparative Studies in Society and History*, IX, 2 (1966–7), 208–32. See also Earl Hopper, 'A Typology for the Classification of Educational Systems' in Earl Hopper (ed.), *Readings in the Theory of Educational Systems* (Hutchinson, 1971), 91–110. For a critique see D. Smith, 'Selection and Knowledge Management in Education Systems' in Hopper, op. cit., 139–158. See also R. Collins, 'Some Comparative Principles of Educational Stratification,' *Harvard Educational Review*, 47, (February 1977), 1–27.

city, national society and also, in an age of scientific competition, international relations.[12]

Some issues of interpretation raised by cross-national comparisons set within the framework recommended here may be exemplified by a discussion of American and English urban education. It may first be noted that superficially similar organizational patterns may have quite different sociological implications according to the broader context of social development within which they are set. It has been argued elsewhere that urban education in Birmingham, UK, during the late-nineteenth century appeared on the surface to mirror to a surprising extent the pattern in Massachusetts, USA, at a similar period.[13] This common organizational pattern was one of regulation through a public bureaucracy behaving in a paternalistic manner within the formal confines of local democratic control.[14] However, these similarities coexisted with important variations between the two cases, not only in the disposition of power relationships within the educational bureaucracy, but also in the class and political structures within which this bureaucracy emerged and developed. According to Katz, Massachusetts businessmen effectively monopolized local public secondary schools, imposed a common high school pattern, sent their own children to these schools, but lost effective control over their administration to professional educators or 'schoolmen'. In Birmingham, however, professional rather than the most substantial business families had the largest interest in local secondary schooling for their own children, while the latter were tending to patronize the national public schools. The emerging pattern of local provision was a segregated tripartite one and not that of a common high school. Finally, there is evidence to suggest that in Birmingham splits *amongst* the 'schoolmen', between secondary and elementary teachers, were more prominent than major political wrangles between professional educators and the 'laity.'

Conditioning these quite radical differences between the two cases are two major structural dissimilarities between English and American social development. They are the absence of a powerful aristocracy in the United States in the course of industrialization; and the continuing significance of the 'political stock exchanges' of the major provincial cities in the United States in the face of a weak central-state apparatus. In Britain, the aristocratic interest remained a strong one though subject to gradual decline while the power of central government was not only substantial but also tending to increase. Such differences in terms of 'interests' and 'levels' intertwine in complex ways and have complicated effects upon urban education. For example, David Cannadine has recently argued that British and American cities in the nineteenth century differed greatly in the ways in which residential segregation of the urban population into single-class neighbourhoods occurred.[15] Whereas in the United States the development of mass transport in the 1880s and 1890s coincided with the period of most rapid growth in population, in England population growth was steepest from 1800 to 1830 thus antedating the transport revolution by half a century. Furthermore, in England unlike the United States large blocks of urban land were

---

12 In 1896, the authorities of Sheffield Technical School refused an application by the government of Japan that they should permit the attendance of Japanese students: 'the authorities could not see their way to make the facilities open to students other than British subjects': J. H. Stainton, *The Making of Modern Sheffield 1865–1914* (Westons and Sons, 1924), 138.
13 D. Smith, 'The Urban Genesis of School Bureaucracy: a Transatlantic Comparison,' in R. Dale, G. Esland and M. MacDonald (eds.), *Schooling and Capitalism* (Routledge, 1976), 66–77.
14 See especially M. B. Katz, 'From Voluntarism to Bureaucracy in American Education,' *Sociology of Education*, 44 (Summer 1971), 297–332, *The Irony of Early School Reform* (Harvard University Press, 1968), 'The Emergence of Bureaucracy in Urban Education: the Boston case,' *History of Education Quarterly*, 8 (2) (Summer 1968), 155–188, 8 (3) (Fall 1968), 319–57.
15 D. Cannadine, 'Victorian Cities: How Different?', *Social History*, 4, 1 (January 1977), 457–482.

owned by members of the aristocracy and gentry. By mid century, in towns like Birmingham, such land had been developed as exclusive estates for middle class refugees who could afford to move away from increasingly crowded industrial districts inhabited by labouring men and their families.[16] During the last quarter of the century the tram and the railway allowed the lower-middle classes and artisans to move out also creating class tensions and conflicts. At the centre of such conflicts were the established middle-class residents subject to hostility from those 'below' who they sought to exclude and their landlords 'above' whom they annoyed by seeking other less threatened districts to inhabit. By contrast, in the United States a town like Boston was in 1850 still an amorphous 'walking city.' Half a century later the habit of commuting combined with rapid population growth had made Boston a 'tracked city' characterized by extensive residential segregation. However, the conflicts which attended the encirclement and incipient decay of Edgbaston failed to disturb middle-class Roxbury on the outskirts of Boston when it experienced a similar fate.[17]

One implication of Cannadine's article seems to be that class consciousness and class conflict at the structural level of the neighbourhood tended to be greater in English than in American society during the nineteenth century. Such a generalization, crudely expressed here, requires further clarification and elaboration of its implications. Cannadine, himself, notes that in towns such as Birmingham, which had extensive residential segregation by 1850, a 'pre-industrial' economic structure was retained until well into the second half of the nineteenth century.[18] The sociological issues raised here are relevant to processes which Antony Giddens has labelled as the 'mediate structuration' and 'proximate structuration' of class relationships.[19] Both refer to ways in which social categories characterized by distinct market capacities (notably property ownership, technical or educational qualifications, and manual labour power) become identifiable social groupings with cohesion and consciousness. Mediate structuration refers to the degree to which movement amongst different social categories is possible. The more closed is each category to 'outsiders' the more rigid are class boundaries. Proximate structuration refers to 'localized' factors which tend to create homogeneous groupings whose boundaries parallel those fostered by mediate structuration.

Giddens distinguishes three related sources of proximate structuration: the division of labour within the productive enterprise; the authority relationships within the enterprise; and the influence of 'distributive groupings . . . (which) . . . reinforce the typical separations between forms of market capacity.' He argues that 'the most significant distributive groupings in this respect are those formed through the tendency towards community or neighbourhood segregation.' The structural possibility is recognized that these different sources of proximate structuration may contradict rather than reinforce each other. Analyses such as that carried out by John Foster who investigates all three sets of relationships in Oldham, South Shields and Northampton, will contribute towards a more empirically-grounded under-

---

16 Following the failure of the 'tasteful' Alsop Fields development, the Duke of Norfolk's estate in central Sheffield was given over to artisan dwellings in the early nineteenth century. 'But nothing the Duke of Norfolk could have done would have made central Sheffield attractive to the already suburbanized middle classes of the town': D. J. Olsen, 'House Upon House: Estate Development in London and Sheffield,' in H. J. Dyos and M. Wolff, *The Victorian City: Images and Realities*, I (Routledge, 1973), 333–57, 341, 345.
17 Op. cit., 468, 476; Sam B. Warner, Jr., *Streetcar Suburbs: The Process of Growth in Boston 1870–1900* (Harvard University Press, 1962), 106–116.
18 Cannadine, op. cit., 465, n.54.
19 A. Giddens, *The Class Structure of the Advanced Societies* (Hutchinson, 1973), 107–110.

standing of these questions.[20] Meanwhile a working assumption may be made that the pattern of school provision in a city, like the pattern of domestic residence with which it has an intimate association, tends to respond to, reflect and create forms of class solidarity and conflict both within and between neighbourhoods. A general conclusion of these remarks is that case studies in the development of urban education while focusing primarily on the structural level of the city must have cognizance of the complementary levels of the national society on the one hand and the neighbourhood on the other.[21] Political struggles and class conflicts were fought out at each of these levels with complex educational manifestations.

Within the broad terms of the general sociological problem identified in the first section the particular manifestation to be examined in the remaining two sections is the incorporation of scientific and technical subjects within secondary and higher education. How may dissimilarities of kind and extent in this respect be explained in terms of variation in trajectories of social development (when different societies are compared) and modes of participating in such development (when different cities in the same society are compared)? One answer to this question is offered in two articles by Joseph Ben-David which concentrate upon higher education.[22] His analysis will be summarized below and then discussed.

Ben-David focuses upon the ways in which knowledge is organized into disciplines and on the academic systems within which this knowledge is developed and transmitted. He also discusses patterns of social solidarity amongst graduates trained in different disciplines and tendencies towards graduate or professional unemployment. Variations amongst societies in all these respects are discussed in terms of two considerations which may be stated in the form of questions. First, how important, structurally, is the interplay amongst relatively autonomous municipal or regional institutions at a *sub-national* level as opposed to the centralizing tendency manifest in metropolitan agencies which seek or tend to regulate the disposition of energies and resources *nationally*? Second, how important relative to each other are the regulative tendencies of market competition, bureaucratization (notably at the hands of the state), and acquiescence in a dominant status hierarchy? With reference to these two broad considerations he is able to make a systematic comparison of the German, French, Russian, American and English cases as they have developed during and since the nineteenth century.

He argues that the *German* academic system was highly innovative, particularly in the natural sciences, during the first half of the nineteenth century. During this period political decentralization in the 'German cultural area' fostered a fertile competition

---

20 J. Foster, op. cit.
21 Compare the following: 'It is useful to think of the national or society-wide level of social organization as continually subject to two fundamental kinds of disturbing influences, one of which emanates from sub-national levels of organization and one from supra-national levels of organization ... [thus] almost any theory about modernization needs to include variables and even propositions that refer to attributes and processes of both the sub-national units and the supra-national contexts. See Terence K. Hopkins and Immanuel Wallerstein, 'The Comparative Study of National Societies,' *Social Science Information*, 6, 5 (Oct. 1957). An edited version of this article appears under the same title in A. Etzioni and F. L. Dubow (eds.), op. cit., 182–204. See also D. Smith, 'Domination and Containment: An Approach to Modernization with Particular Reference to its Inter-Societal Context,' *Comparative Studies in Society and History* (1978) [forthcoming].
22 J. Ben-David and A. Zloczower, 'Universities and Academic Systems in Modern Societies,' *European Journal of Sociology*, 3 (1962), 45–84 (henceforth referred to as 'Universities and Academic Systems ...') 'Professions in the Class System of Present-Day Societies,' *Current Sociology*, 12 (1963–4), 256–277. For an abridged version see 'The Growth of the Professions and the Class System,' in R. Bendix and S. M. Lipset (eds.), *Class, Status and Power: Social Stratification in Comparative Perspective* (Routledge, 1967), 459–472 (henceforth referred to as 'The Growth of the Professions ...').

amongst universities. However, from about 1850 political power became increasingly centralized and the threat of regulation by the state bureaucracy ever more pressing. In reaction to this threat, German universities developed three institutional characteristics: an emphasis on specialized and systematically ordered disciplines oriented not to practical training but the theoretical aspects of 'basic subjects'; a determination to resist dilution of the charismatic role of the professor; and an insistence upon the doctrine of *wertfreiheit*, classically expounded by Max Weber, which declared that value judgements had no place in scientific enquiry and academic teaching.[23] All three characteristics tended to produce intellectual and organizational inflexibility and isolated the universities from the mainstream of social and political life. However, these institutional and ideological compromises also tended to preserve the relative autonomy of academics in a dangerous political situation for the universities.

The *French* and *Russian* systems are both characterized as having a high degree of political centralization and extensive bureaucratic regulation. In both cases, the state has sought to impose a highly specialized division of labour amongst institutions of higher education in order to exploit their resources more efficiently. Where successfully imposed, this mode of organization has tended both to weaken the social solidarity of the graduate population and diminish the possibility of creating a self-conscious unemployed and alienated intelligentsia through overproduction of graduates in 'traditional' disciplines—such as law—rather than more 'relevant' scientific and technical subjects. However, not only has the French state imposed specialization to a lesser degree than the Soviet state but it has been confronted by powerful academic interests who have resisted a weakening of the dominance of 'traditional' disciplines closely associated with an established status hierarchy.[24]

The *American* system, like the Russian, minimizes graduate unemployment and inhibits the development of a unified and culturally exclusive élite. It does this not through bureaucratic centralization but through the relatively free operation of market competition within a politically decentralized society. Since the mid-nineteenth century the universities have competed with each other to provide instruction and research programmes which would meet the changing demands made upon them in an industrializing society. Law, medicine and other 'traditional' subjects have had to compete on equal terms with scientific and technological subjects. Under these conditions, American universities have developed a complex internal division of academic disciplines and roles, each institution concentrating upon its areas of strength. The principal source of demand has been a middle class, well established before the mid-nineteenth century, which was prepared to patronize the universities as long as they were 'useful' and not dominated by the cultural traditions of a restricted upper class.[25]

According to Ben-David, similar tendencies were not strongly evident in the *English* system during the nineteenth century despite the development of local institutions which were to become the provincial universities. Much more significant than competition amongst localities were the effects of a status hierarchy closely associated with a reinvigorated Oxford and Cambridge. Neither bureaucracy nor market competition but common acquiescence in the dominant status hierarchy with its approved 'ways of doing things' became the central regulating mechanism in the English system. Innovation in subjects and academic roles occurred, albeit to a limited extent and fairly haphazardly, in response to client pressure and subject to

---

23 M. Weber, 'Science as a Vocation' in H. H. Gerth and C. W. Mills (eds.), *From Max Weber: Essays in Sociology* (Routledge, 1967), 129–156.
24 *Universities and Academic Systems* . . . , 80.
25 *The Growth of the Professions* . . . , 472.

the benediction of the ancient universities.[26] Inasmuch as education at Oxford and Cambridge complemented power and privilege already assured, while provincial institutions supplemented existing non-academic systems of apprenticeship to the professions, the basis did not exist for an alienated, unemployed intelligentsia.[27]

Ben-David's argument may be summarized in the following table and the statement immediately below it:

	Dominant Structural Level	Dominant Regulating Mechanism
GERMANY	Initially Local, subsequently National	Initially Market Competition, subsequently Bureaucracy
FRANCE	National	Bureaucracy modified by Status Hierarchy
USSR	National	Bureaucracy
USA	Local	Market Competition
ENGLAND	National	Status Hierarchy

In German universities, internal differentiation of academic roles and disciplines (i.e. within universities) and external differentiation (i.e. between universities) occurred extensively before 1850, to a much lesser degree after that date. In Russia and France, external differentiation was more marked than internal differentiation and both occurred to a greater extent in the former case. In America and England, internal differentiation was more marked than external differentiation and both occurred to a greater extent in the former case. Resistance to the introduction of scientific and technological studies was highest in France and England, particularly the former. However, only in the case of France was this resistance associated with overcrowding and unemployment in the traditional professions, tending to create an alienated intelligentsia.

Ben-David's analysis sustains the general assertion that particular studies of urban education may be understood in terms of specific trajectories of national social development. These trajectories are characterized by the predominance of particular structural levels and social interests. Academic systems are seen to be caught amidst the interplay of class and political 'pressures' whose effects are measured in terms of the constraints of market competition and the norms of status hierarchies on the one hand and the salience of bureaucratic regulation on the other. The influence of bureaucracy is broadly assumed to have a centralizing effect while market competition is associated with decentralization. Status norms may either inhibit extreme centralized bureaucratic control (as in France) or impose central regulation, albeit through informal understandings, on a situation with tendencies towards decentralized market competition (as in England).[28] The major weakness of this presentation, however, is its tendency to treat class and political phenomena in gross terms which obscure the specific outlines of structures of domination, dependence and conflict. In the third section of this paper, an attempt will be made to sketch in some of these outlines at different structural levels in English society. The analysis will differ in

26 *Universities and Academic Systems* . . . , 66–67.
27 *The Growth of the Professions* . . . , 471.
28 For another approach to the form and disposition of power relationships within structures of administrative control; see D. Smith 'Power, Ideology and Transmission of Knowledge' in Hopper, op. cit., 240–261.

significant respects from that presented by Ben-David. Nevertheless, it must also be recognized that a major strength of Ben-David's argument is his assumption that the political apparatus of the state, the structure of class domination and the academic system may articulate with one another in different ways in different societies. This point can be developed with reference to some examples since its implications are as relevant to municipal social structure as they are to that of the national society.

Ben-David suggests, for example, that whereas in Germany academic autonomy was a prize precariously wrested from a jealous state and a hostile dominant class, French academics were much more securely independent, 'outside pressure from the educated middle classes and the government . . . (being) . . . assimilated to the conservative traditions of Paris academic circles.'[29] In Spain, the universities moved from a situation of active co-operation with the state in the seventeenth century, through torpid acquiescence, to a much more conflict-ridden relationship in the nineteenth and twentieth centuries.[30] Frank Parkin has analysed the structural conflict between the intelligentsia and the party hierarchy in East European societies.[31] Through his work on Massachusetts, Michael Katz has demonstrated the capacity of the 'schoolmen' in the educational administration to resist the dictates of the bourgeoisie which brought them into being.[32] Data from Birmingham in the latter half of the nineteenth century indicate that educational institutions, such as the King Edward VI schools, were the object of a competition for control between established and emerging élites, a competition in which teachers themselves took an active part.[33] In his lectures on the evolution of French secondary education, Durkheim traces the success of the Jesuits in establishing their colleges despite opposition from the clergy, the *parlement* and the Faculty of Arts at the University of Paris. They were sustained by a 'public opinion' led by well-to-do families to whose influential 'tastes and needs'

---

29 *Universities and Academic Systems* . . . , 80. This analysis may be compared with Pierre Bourdieu's argument that the relative autonomy of the French education system both creates and depends upon the system's capacity to legitimate and reproduce the prevailing class structure. Bourdieu places a Durkhemian stress on the tendency of education to create 'a general disposition of the mind and will.' Durkheim recognized, for example, that Christianity sought to impose 'a certain attitude of the soul, . . . a certain habitus of our moral being.' Eschewing Christian dogmatism he believed that moral training through education had to act at the level of 'fundamental dispositions . . . those mental states at the root of the moral life,' Moral discipline created personality. A person is not only a being who disciplines himself; he is also a system of ideas, of feelings, of habits and tendencies, a consciousness that has a content.' A major task of education was to develop a spirit in children, which would eventually express itself in appropriate institutions. Bourdieu asserts that the inculcation of habitus takes place within a structure of class domination and in such a way as to both disguise and perpetuate it. This analysis of Bourdieu's work will be developed further in a subsequent paper. See E. Durkheim, *The Evolution of Educational Thought, Lectures on the Formation and Development of Secondary Education in France* (translated by Peter Collins, Routledge, 1977) especially 29–30 and *Moral Education* (translated by E. K. Wilson and H. Schnurer, Free Press 1961), 21, 73, 102–3; P. Bourdieu and J.-C. Passerson, *Reproduction in Education Society and Culture* (Sage, 1977); P. Bourdieu, *Outline of a Theory of Practice* (Cambridge, 1977). For a preliminary attempt to distinguish systematically 'habituation' (defined as as the inculcation of tried and trust ways of doing things) from other educational goals, see D. Smith, *Distribution Processes and Power Relations in Education Systems* (Oxford University Press, 1973), 14–15.

30 See, for example, J. Linz, 'Intellectual Roles in Sixteenth and Seventeenth Century Spain,' *Daedalus* (Summer 1972), 59–108. V. Cacho Viu *La Institucion Libre de Enseñanza* (Ediciones Rialp, 1972).

31 F. Parkin 'System Contradiction and Political Transformation,' *European Journal of Sociology*, XIII (1972), 45–62.

32 M. B. Katz op. cit.

33 D. Smith, 'The Urban Genesis of School Bureaucracy' in R. Dale, G. Esland and M. MacDonald (eds.), op. cit.

their training in strict and orthodox Catholicism appealed.[34] Durkheim was an active participant in contemporary disputes about the educational status of the natural sciences in the wake of both the 1899 reforms, which made 'modern' subjects possible university entrance qualifications, and the 1901 plan of studies which incorporated such studies alongside the classics.[35] His analysis in the lectures leads directly to a set of issues which have immediate relevance to Birmingham and Sheffield in the late-nineteenth century.

Drawing upon a subtle and profound analysis Durkheim argued that the instability of contemporary arrangements reflected three intractable and unresolved problems. The first problem was that of reconciling the tendency for dispersion of students into diverse specialized courses individually chosen and the need to develop 'a certain moral unity, a certain community of ideas and feelings.' The latter 'would be impossible if the different groups lacked all fixity and stability' but were constantly breaking up and recombining in 'a thousand different ways. . . . The truth is that a class is not and should not be a crowd.'[36] Durkheim suggested that subjects should be grouped according to their 'natural affinities' and the 'logical hierarchy amongst the different disciplines.'[37] It may be noted that Durkheim is here raising a problem whose political implications have been interpreted in a different way by Ben-David in his references to the creation of an alienated, self conscious and potentially disruptive intelligentsia. The second problem was the fundamental and persisting opposition between Christian humanism and science whose origins could be traced back to the division between the *trivium* and the *quadrivium*.[38] The political dimensions of this opposition in an English context will be explored in the next section of this paper. The third problem which derived from the first two, was how to 'organize an education especially designed for commerce and industry?' Insofar as recipients of such training required formation of their speculative faculties, they should be taught languages, history, and the natural sciences alongside aspirants for the traditional professions in the same secondary schools. However, merely practical training for industry and commerce beyond the primary level should take place in institutions clearly separate from true secondary schools since such training had different ends, methods and traditions.[39] Durkheim described teachers in contemporary *lycées* as

---

34 These lectures, L'Evolution Pedogogique en France was originally published in 1938 and by Presses Universitaires de Paris in 1969. References will be made to the English translation by Peter Collins, *The Evolution of Educational Thought: Lectures on the Formation and Development of Secondary Education in France* (Routledge, 1977). This reference is to 234–239. Durkheim's view of the development of French education implicitly acknowledged the role of what Bourdieu would describe as 'symbolic violence' and the 'arbitrary' exploitation of cultural capital as carried out by the Jesuits in defence of their own cause and that of their conservative clientele. They bowdlerized the classics and regimented their pupils in the cause of orthodoxy. However he does not regard either educators or their materials as simply being expressions of structures of class domination. His general approach was that of pedagogical doctrines, institutions, and practices should be seen as being partly a manifestation of and partly a response to social currents expressed in the substratum of collective life and the conflictual interplay of institutions and social groups. Both Durkheim and Ben-David give us more guidance than Bourdieu on the question of how the education system is implicated in the continually occurring processes of structural transformation in patterns of class and political domination. Bourdieu and Passeron, op. cit. 6–8; Durkheim, *The Evolution of Educational Thought*, 241–3, 250–1, 254, 258–66 (on the Jesuits) 18–21, 37–41, 64–9, 88–93, 113–24, 166–73, 177–81, 263–64 (for the diverse manifestation of social currents) 19–26, 40–44, 75–87, 121–30, 234–39, 257, 306–10 (on the part played by the French state and the Catholic Church) 166–73 (on the changes in social stratification at the Renaissance) 79–100 (on the strategies of the teaching profession) 101–12, 220 (on the forms of pedagogy types of, organized knowledge and traditions of academic enquiry).
35 ibid., 313.
36 ibid., 302–3.
37 ibid., 303.
38 ibid., 310.
39 ibid., 314–19.

working in a situation where their efforts are dissipated, and (in which they) find themselves paralysed by their isolation from one another. They shut themselves up in their specialism and expound the subject of their choice as if it existed alone, as if it was an end in itself, when it is really only a means to an end which it should constantly have in view and to which it should always be subordinated. Indeed, how should it be otherwise as long as, while they are at university, each group of students are taught their chosen subject separately from the rest and there is nothing to encourage these colleagues of tomorrow to meet and reflect together on the common task that awaits them.

But that is not all. Secondary education has for more than half a century been undergoing a serious crisis which has by no means reached its conclusion. Everybody feels that it cannot remain as it is, without having any clear idea about what it needs to become.... Moreover the question is not peculiar to France; there is no major European state in which it has not risen in almost identical terms. Everywhere educationalists and statesmen are aware that the changes which have occurred in the structure of contemporary societies, in their domestic economies as in their foreign affairs, require special transformations, no less profound, in the special area of the school system.[40]

The complex of interrelated problems with which Durkheim was wrestling bears a striking resemblance to that which exercised his English counter-parts: how should industrialists, men of commerce, counting-house clerks and artisans be schooled? What should be the academic status of science and technology? How could the tendency towards curricular specialization be reconciled with the pursuit of social (or 'moral') integration? Durkheim was both describing and reacting against the emergence of an extreme form of curricular 'collection', to use Bernstein's term.[41] It has been argued elsewhere that the emergence of the English collection curriculum should be understood in terms of shifting power relations, on the one hand between established 'genteel' élites and the social groups indicated above, and, on the other hand between the 'sciences' and the 'arts.'[42] These shifts within the power structure of English society were aspects of a structural crisis to be explored below, a crisis which was fuelled not only by urbanization and industrialization but also by the developments in external relations to which Durkheim makes brief and tantalizing reference in the passage just quoted.

All of the societies discussed in Ben-David's analysis examined in the previous section were in those years entering into steadily intensifying competition with each other, a process which culminated in the First World War. Prussia's growing technological expertise and industrial strength posed an immediate military threat to the Russian and French borders and (at the very least) a pressing economic challenge to England and the United States. In such circumstances, technological education and industrial training could not be elbowed off the political agenda in any of these societies. Weighty vested interests were mobilized on many sides. In England, Birmingham and Sheffield were in the thick of the fight. Some pertinent similarities and differences between the two cities in the second half of the nineteenth century will now be set out.

Birmingham and Sheffield exhibited important similarities in aspects of their demographic growth, élite structure, industrial technology, and educational emphasis. First; both cities were spectacular examples of concentration and growth in population. In 1851 Birmingham contained over 230 000 people, a figure which grow over the next sixty years to 430 000 plus another 95 000 through boundary extension.[43] Sheffield entered the second half of the century with a population of over 135 000 and had expanded by 1911 to 460 000 of which 30 000 was the consequence of boundary extension.[44] Second; in each city considerable social power was wielded

40 ibid., 13–14.
41 B. Bernstein, 'On the Classification and Framing of Educational Knowledge,' in Hopper (ed.), op. cit., 184–211.
42 D. Smith, 'Codes, Paradigms and Folk Norms. An approach to educational change with particular reference to the works of Basil Bernstein,' *Sociology*, 10, 1, (January 1976), 1–19, especially 5–6.
43 Victoria County History, *Warwickshire, vol. VII. The City of Birmingham*, edited by W. B. Stephens (1964) [henceforth *VCH*], 14.
44 S. Pollard, *A History of Labour in Sheffield* (Liverpool University Press, 1959), 89, 184.

by great industrial masters. In Sheffield they were led by the great steel manufacturers, men such as Frederick Mappin, who mass-produced railway springs, Charles Cammell, whose limited company had a share capital of £1 000 000 in 1864, John Brown, like Cammell a major producer of steel rails and armour plating, and Mark Firth, another substantial steel magnate whose firm made a fortune from armaments. Despite its larger population and vigorous productive enterprise Birmingham industry presented a less Himalayan profile than that of Sheffield in the 1860s and 1870s. However, standing clearly above their rivals were manufacturers such as Robert Winfield (brass and engineering), the Elkingtons (electro-plating), Josiah Mason and Joseph Gillott (pen manufacturers), the Nettlefolds and Joseph Chamberlain (screw manufacturers).[45]

Third; the wealth and strength of both Birmingham and Sheffield were based not as in Manchester upon textiles, an industry destined to experience a long-run decline in the decades leading to the First World War, but upon metal manufactures of all kinds and upon engineering, sectors whose importance was to increase steadily. In view, then, of the enormity of the political stakes, considerable interest attaches to the fourth common characteristic, which is that in both cities a number of local businessmen were actively constructing their own systems of municipal education in the late-nineteenth century. One thing they had in mind was the provision of effective training in science and technology. This was to be done through schools and colleges which would offer social promotion (within limits) to those whose merit and usefulness was shown not by birth or even wealth but by performance and achievement. George Dixon, a wealthy Birmingham businessman and chairman of the School Board for twenty years (1876–96) made a large financial contribution to the Bridge Street Seventh Standard School which opened in 1884. Two years later he declared: 'I would invite the manufacturers of the town and neighbourhood to inspect this school and having done so to consider whether it will not be in their best interests to reserve their best places for those who have passed successfully through it.'[46] In 1891, a Municipal Technical School was established, serving as another rung on the educational ladder being constructed during the three decades of the board's existence. At the top of this ladder was Mason College whose founder, the pen manufacturer, had insisted that it should 'promote education adapted to the requirements of the manufactures and industrial pursuits of the Midland district... *to the exclusion of mere literary education and theology.*'[47] In Sheffield the School Board, upon which both Mark Firth and John Brown then served, commissioned an enquiry into local technical education as early as 1871. Three years later the Board instituted science evening classes of its own and by 1880 it had established a Central School which attracted many aspiring artisans and apprentices.[48] In 1886 the structure was capped with a new Technical School providing training in metallurgy and engineering. This school, which owed much to the financial sponsorship of Frederick Mappin, became part of Sheffield University College in 1897.[49]

These four common characteristics indicate the immediacy of the following political questions: how was the co-operation of the workforce to be enlisted in the service of orderly factory production, how were not only the men but also their masters to be reconciled to the maintenance of a social order which protected the

---

45 *VCH*, 126–7, Pollard, op. cit., 162.
46 Address to the School Board, 1886, 9.
47 E. W. Vincent and P. Hinton, *The University of Birmingham. Its History and Significance* (Cornish Brothers Ltd., 1947), 9. My italics.
48 J. H. Bingham, *The Period of the Sheffield School Board 1870–1903* (Sheffield, 1949), 174–182. Pollard, op. cit., 115.
49 A. W. Chapman, *The Story of a Modern University. A History of the University of Sheffield* (Oxford University Press, 1955), 33–44, 68–80.

interests of the aristocratic establishment? In a society whose political controls were focused on the country mansion and the rural vicarage cities such as Birmingham and Sheffield opened up a wild and dangerous frontier. Both represented potential centres of political and cultural challenge to an older genteel order and at the very least imposed a task of containment which could not leave this order unchanged. Before industrialization and the urbanization of the midlands and the north, the 'business' of English society had been largely conducted through multitudinous connexions of kinship and patronage which linked the metropolis to county and parish hierarchies throughout the land. Merchants, bureaucrats and 'professionals' while recognizing other criteria in their occupational ideologies, had accepted and accommodated themselves to the prevailing particularism of the social order.[50] In its operation, the system of kin and client connexions had allowed pragmatic interplay of interests within a rough and ready status hierarchy. However, it could not contain or cope with the dramatic growth of the industrial towns. The very size and concentration of the massed urban population denied the possibility of control through an indefinite extension of particularistic bonds, either those centred upon Anglican land-owning circles or those which cemented the business dealings of Dissenting Industrialists. This problem was not speedily resolved but in the long term the 'master co-ordinates' of social relations and the institutional order within the cities became not kinship nor patronage but universalistic criteria expressed in the cash nexus and bureaucratic regulation. The single class suburb and the elementary school at which attendance was compulsory were two major expressions of these increasingly important modes of integration.[51] Market and bureaucratic networks became increasingly dense and complex, extending outwards from the provincial cities and the metropolis to fill the 'structural space' between. The spread of the railway system, the growth of the popular press, the establishment of national trade unions, political parties and associations of many kinds, the elaboration of an examination system awarding nationally recognized qualifications, the growth of the integrated firm with factories in many towns and shares quoted on the London stock exchange, the eventual arrival of the income tax form, national service, national insurance and even national savings all contributed to these processes. In this way was gradually formed the tissue of the emerging urban industrial nation.

In 1850, a number of questions seemed unresolved which were to appear much nearer settlement in 1914. How were urban configurations such as Sheffield and Birmingham, made potent by dramatic industrial and demographic growth, to 'fit' within the emerging national society? What would be the relationship between the metropolis, seat of the central state apparatus, and the provincial municipalities? How would the county hierarchies and urban regimes articulate with one another? How would the disposition of power relationships develop within national market and bureaucratic networks? Where would the social and political initiative lie? Which groups would wield the major sanctions? France, Germany and the United States demonstrated to contemporaries that a variety of structural outcomes could be envisaged.

The promotion of scientific and technical training in secondary and higher education entailed the assertion of an order of values different from that embodied in the classics and 'mere literary education' and implied a pattern of occupational recruitment and training whose products would have no inbred sympathy with the culture

---

50 See, for example, N. Jewson, 'Medical Knowledge and the Patronage System in 18th Century England,' *Sociology*, 8, 3 (September 1974), 369–385.
51 For a discussion of some possible limitations of the free play of market forces with respect to landownership see G. Rowley, 'Landownership in the spatial growth of towns: a Sheffield example,' *The East Midland Geographer*, VI, 5 (December 1975), 200–213.

of an aristocratic establishment. However, these forms of training developed in very different ways in Sheffield and Birmingham.

When the Sheffield School Board was established in 1870, secondary schooling was provided by three local institutions: the endowed Grammar School, which was a Jacobean foundation, the Collegiate school run on Anglican lines, and Wesley College. The latter two schools were both founded as private ventures in the 1830s. All three moved away from a purely classical curriculum, introducing scientific and commercial subjects. During the 1860s, the Collegiate's headmaster even tried, unsuccessfully, to establish a related technical school which would train engineers. Only Wesley College enjoyed relative prosperity in the subsequent decade, supplying training for about two hundred students. Both the Grammar School and the Collegiate fell on hard times, the latter narrowly escaping closure in 1872.[52]

In 1880 the Sheffield School Board, with great fanfare, opened a Central School for its advanced pupils. At the ceremony, the Lord President of the Council, Earl Spencer said that:

'he understood that the Sheffield scheme was closely identified with the Science and Art departments, a fact which meant that it must have a great and important bearing on the trade and future of Sheffield. It was, he added, worth remembering that a similar association of education and the technicalities of trade had been carried out on the Continent to a very much greater extent than in England, and the example of the Continent was worth studying and copying. It was of the utmost importance that, in England, attention should be turned at once and very fully to the soundest and best possible system of technical education, because of the certainty of increasing rivalry in trade concerns.'[53]

The response of the established secondary schools may be gauged from a pamphlet written in 1883 by S. O. Addy, ex-student and teacher at the Collegiate. He complains that Sheffield could not retain able secondary school teachers: 'one by one they drift away.' Competition between the Grammar School and the Collegiate had weakened both. Now further damage was being inflicted by the Central School, an 'educational palace' built 'illegally' with ratepayers' money. 'What may be the end we may not wholly foresee.'[54] Two years later the Collegiate became part of Wesley College. This consolidation of forces did not stem the progressive decline. In 1898–9 there were more vacancies than candidates at Wesley College and the Grammar School. Finally, in 1905, these two establishments also merged and fell under the control of the School Board's successor, the Sheffield Education Committee.

In sharp contrast, the establishment of Birmingham School Board's Seventh Standard School at Bridge Street and that in Waverley Street seven years later occurred while Revd. E. F. M. MacCarthy, himself a local endowed school headmaster was chairman of the Board's Education Committee. Waverley Road School, a 'show piece,' contained workshops and a science laboratory and among the technical subjects it taught were mechanics, chemistry, machine drawing, geometry, and wood and metal work. The sequel to these events was *not* a decline in support for the endowed schools. Indeed, the nine secondary schools of the King Edward VI Foundation were not only supreme in the local status hierarchy, but also catering for approximately 2500 boys and girls at the time of the Bryce Commission in 1894. Before the Bryce commissioners, MacCarthy felt able to urge not only the building of more 'board secondary schools' with a technical bias but also their freeing from dependence on the Science and Art Department.[55]

---

52 P. J. Wallis, *King Edward VII School* (Sheffield, 1950), E. L. Cotton, *Notes for the history of High Storrs School* (1949) [Sheffield City Library].
53 Stainton, op. cit., 108.
54 S. O. Addy, *Middle Class Education in Sheffield* (1883).
55 A. F. Taylor, 'History of the Birmingham School Board 1870–1903,' (M.A. Thesis, University of Birmingham; 1955), 203, 208, *Secondary Education Commission*, Vol. 2, 178 (evidence of A. R. Vardy).

A similar degree of difference is evident in the sphere of higher education. In Birmingham, Mason Science College and two local medical schools amalgamated in 1892, forming an institution which became a university college six years later and was chartered as the University of Birmingham in 1900. At Sheffield, Firth College was established in 1879 and amalgamated with the local medical school to form a university college in 1897. Eight years later full university status was achieved. Despite these similarities, scientific and technical studies had very different careers in the two cities. Birmingham's University College was dominated by men like R. S. Heath, J. F. Poynting and Bertram Windle who spoke, respectively, for Mathematics, Physics and Anatomy. The Arts Faculty, including E. A. Sonnenschein (Classics), MacNeile Dixon (English) and J. H. Muirhead (Philosophy) was only weakly represented on the Charter subcommittee planning the shape of the future university.[56] Vigorously campaigning to redress the balance, Sonnenschein analysed the college budgetary statistics in 1898. He found that 'comparing Birmingham with other Colleges . . . in no other place was so much as *twice* the amount spent on Science than was spent on Arts.' In Birmingham the ratio was at least five to one in favour of the Science Faculty even though this Faculty 'was numerically inferior in point of students to the Faculty of Arts relatively to the number of Professors employed, and even absolutely, if Evening Classes were taken account of.' Given that laboratories and other equipment made the sciences necessarily more expensive, Sonnenschein and his colleagues claimed not equality but 'some limit to the inequality of expenditure' as existed in other places. They also pointed out that whereas Birmingham had only four arts professors to seven science professors equivalent ratios were 13:9 in Edinburgh, 8:8 in Glasgow, 8:9 in Manchester, 8:6 in Liverpool, 52:34 in Leipzig.[57] Although The Arts Faculty redressed the political balance somewhat through appeals to Joseph Chamberlain.[58] However, the latter insisted that the university would give 'exceptional attention . . . to the teaching of Science in connection with its application to our local industries and manufactures.'[59]

In Sheffield no such pre-eminence was enjoyed by those who taught pure and applied science. When Firth College began its teaching in 1880, the staff consisted of a chemist, a mathematician, two historians, a modern linguist and a lecturer in music.[60] The two aims of the College were avowedly to prepare students for matriculation at Oxford and Cambridge and 'to extend the range of instruction *whenever the needful resources for this shall be available*, so as to include a system of technical education for the due qualification of the artisans of the town, for the several kinds of trade and manufacture in which they are engaged and on which the prosperity of the town so much depends.'[61] Local businessmen were very slow to provide the 'needful resources.' When the Technical School was finally opened in 1886 its funds were kept entirely separate from those of the rest of the college. From 1889 to 1897 the School even ceased to be part of Firth College and fell under the effective control of Sheffield Town Council, establishing in this period close connections with the local board schools. By 1905 it had been reinstated within the university fold but was tucked away on a separate site away from Western Bank.[62]

The predominance of scientific and technical studies at the secondary level in Sheffield during the 1880s and 1890s was matched by the effective relegation of Bir-

---

56 Vincent and Hinton, op. cit., 28.
57 E. J. Somerset, *The Birth of a University. A Passage in the Life of E. A. Sonnenschein* (1934), 9–10.
58 Vincent and Hinton, op. cit., 30.
59 ibid., 34.
60 Chapman, op. cit., 23–4.
61 ibid., 24 [My italics].
62 ibid., 39–40, 131ff.

mingham's thriving 'board secondary schools' at Bridge Street and Waverley Street to the 'third division' below the King Edward VI High School and Grammar Schools.[63] By contrast the supremacy of pure and applied science in the embryonic civic university of Birmingham was complemented by the dismal showing of their equivalent at this higher level in Sheffield. How may these contrary patterns be explained?

Part of an answer which is to be proposed here and explored in further research is that these variations are indications of differences between Birmingham and Sheffield in the internal structure of the newly wealthy and powerful manufacturing bourgeoisie in the two cities and in their relationships with the labouring classes and established genteel and aristocratic social interests. Such relationships manifested themselves on a number of the structural levels indicated in the first section of this paper but here the emphasis will be upon relations between élites at the municipal level and metropolitan élites (in Whitehall, Westminster and the ancient universities) whose sphere of operation was nation-wide. This restriction of emphasis will not be pursued, however, without first noting two major dissimilarities which greatly affected all the others to be mentioned.

Birmingham and Sheffield differed in industrial structure and in their patterns of residential segregation. Without conducting a detailed comparison the broad picture may be drawn. Whereas in Birmingham a high proportion of industrialists were residents of Edgbaston, less than a mile from the business district, in Sheffield the working class neighbourhoods of Attercliffe and Brightside in the north east and the middle class suburbs windward to the west were a good three miles apart each side of the city centre. Furthermore, although both Birmingham and Sheffield were cities of small workshops at mid-century, large units of industrial production were established much earlier in the northern city. In Birmingham a firm like Winfield's was employing 800 people by 1866 while Elkington had over a thousand on the payroll by 1880.[64] However, Brown of Sheffield had a workforce of 5000 in 1872 while another 4000 were employed at Cammell's.[65] The sociological implications of these differences have yet to be fully analysed but they seem to suggest the existence of a closer if not conflict-free relationship between masters and men in Birmingham and greater potential for the development of common understandings manipulable by both. Whereas Birmingham was the home of the quasi-democratic National Liberal Federation encompassing both employers and artisans, Sheffield presented in 1885 'the first clear case of political division following from class housing patterns.' Hallam and Ecclesall were heavily Tory while Brightside and Attercliffe were strongly Radical.[66]

The subtle and divergent interplay of social interests and structural levels in the two cities may be economically suggested by a brief comparison of two enquiries made by Royal Commissions in the sixties, one into affairs at Birmingham and the other concerning Sheffield. Each was an instance of a national agency taking an active interest in a political disturbance rooted in a particular municipal social structure. The Schools Inquiry Commission had before it not only a special report by T. H. Green on the King Edward VI schools at Birmingham but also evidence taken in May 1865 and July 1866 from the major participants in an intensely fought dispute over control and management of the schools.[67] In the following year, 1867, a special Commission of Inquiry sat at the Council Hall, Sheffield between 3rd June and 8th

63 *Secondary Education Commission*, vol. 3, 56–60 (evidence of MacCarthy).
64 *VCH.*, 127.
65 Pollard, op. cit., 162.
66 Vincent, op. cit., 23, n.18.
67 *Schools Inquiry Commission*, vol. 8, 91–145, vol. 4, pt. I, 541–566, 956–1006.

July, hearing evidence on the 'Sheffield outrages' which it made the basis of its subsequent report to the Trades Union Commission.[68]

A preliminary analysis of the dispute over the King Edward VI Foundation has been carried out elsewhere.[69] It was argued that a number of the protagonists could be grouped according to their relative commitment to local as opposed to metropolitan networks of power and prestige and according to whether they belonged to an established, overwhelmingly Anglican élite or were powerful 'outsiders' seeking to build or capture redoubts in the municipal social structure. Businessmen may be found amongst both the established and their challengers. However, their allies and allegiances differed. Joseph Chamberlain, George Dixon, J. S. Wright and others found useful allies locally, downwards within the social order. They adopted styles which were at once populist and paternalistic. By contrast, their opponents on the Foundation's governing body, in the local gas and water companies and elsewhere cultivated exclusivity and the status associations both of Oxford and Cambridge and the neighbouring aristocracy with their metropolitan links. Further investigation will throw light on the manner and extent to which the highly developed ideology and organization of the section of Birmingham's bourgeoisie represented by Chamberlain in the seventies were conditioned by two circumstances: the continuing residual strength of their opponents and the fact that the 'new men' consisted not of a few industrial giants surrounded by pigmies but a network of substantial (rather than gigantic) manufacturers whose impressive *collective* opulence was the product of successful innovation and enterprise.

Sheffield also had its traditional and exclusive social interests resisting the new institutional order associated with industrial growth. In this case they were the artisan trade societies. In 1866, for example, the associations of filesmiths and file grinders were supported by several other Sheffield societies in their resistance to the introduction of file cutting machines. This strike directed country-wide public attention to the violent means by which the societies imposed their rules, extending to a series of gunpowder attacks in the fifties and sixties.[70] One consequence was the Commission of Inquiry in 1867. The contrast between Birmingham and Sheffield is well indicated in the comparison between the powerful provincial initiative displayed in the former's deputation sent to Westminster Hall and the abject passivity of the latter, stigmatized as a disorderly frontier town to be policed by 'federal marshals' dispatched from the civilized home counties.

Note the pessimism in J. P. Gledstone's pamphlet on 'Public Opinion and Public Spirit in Sheffield' published the same year and directed to 'the manufacturers, merchants, and principal tradesmen' of the town.[71] Such men possessed 'the elements of astonishing influence but they are not consolidated . . . (Our) opinions are disfigured by many prejudices and savour of a strong provincialism . . . of public opinion we have none. We are an aggregate of men; we are not a community; we are thousands of Englishmen, but we are not united in our social life.' Of the sixty local trade societies he declared: 'The presence of a crowd of secret societies (numbering thousands of men, and standing in intimate relation to a large proportion of the monied class of the town) and the absence of public opinion! How ominously suggestive!' In his anguish at this mixture of over-regulation on the one hand and lack of moral regulation on the other, Gledstone's tones are almost Durkheimian.[72] Continuing,

68 *Trades Union Commission: Sheffield Outrages Inquiry*, vol. I—Report (1867).
69 D. Smith, 'The Urban Genesis of School Bureaucracy,' in R. Dale, G. Esland and M. MacDonald (eds.), op. cit.
70 Pollard, op. cit., 140–1, 155.
71 J. D. Gledstone, *Public Opinion and Public Spirit in Sheffield* (1867).
72 See E. Durkheim, *The Division of Labour in Society*, translated by G. Simpson (Macmillan, 1920), *Suicide*, translated by J. A. Spalding and G. Simpson (Routledge, 1952).

he notes how helpless local businessmen are 'under pressure of public work; . . . our helplessness under recent trade revelations was simply pitiable.' A recent distribution of prizes for the Cambridge Local Examinations had to be cancelled since a 'suitable gentleman (could) not be found to take the chair . . . were there a lively interest in the great question of education, a town would not be baffled by a miserable difficulty like this.' Where were the noble public buildings to be found in Leeds, Bradford, Manchester, Birmingham, and Liverpool? A recent meeting of the Social Science Congress had been held, for lack of suitable alternatives, in a singing saloon.

The only cure was that 'our men of wealth and education (should) accept this burden of living for others as well as for themselves. A thorough revolution will be effected easily and surely when they play their part.' However, he concluded:

> 'I fail to recognise any young men who are giving promise that they will be active, disinterested friends of Sheffield beyond the trade relationships which they may sustain to it. There may be scores who are developing into quick merchants and enterprising manufacturers; but we have a right to look for more from them. Property and station bring their responsibilities. It is not enough that a man should be responsible in business; his increased wealth, his wider influence, his deep experience are public property in part; and he fails in a serious respect if he simply settles down amongst his riches, and lets the town struggle on.'

The lack of reference to the local Sheffield gentry will have been noted. Were there such they made little apparent impression, providing no staunch 'fifth column' for the aristocratic interest. In Vincent's words, with respect to 'religion, politics, culture, wealth, there (was) almost no community of experience, no possible human solidarity, to unite the 'top ten thousand in Sheffield' with metropolitan 'good society,' that is, with the world of Trollope, Thackeray, and Bagehot, with its extensions in the upper levels of Barsetshire society.'[73] In Birmingham, by contrast, the 'establishment' had citadels worth defending and Charles Evans, headmaster of the King Edward VI Grammar School in the 1860s, thought he had at least a fighting chance of building up a first rate national, public, boarding school.[74]

The outlines of a possible explanation for the differences in scientific and technical education now begin to emerge. In Birmingham, MacCarthy's influence and Sonnenschein's relative isolation both expressed the disposition and influence of the local clientele they sought to serve. There was evidently considerable demand for the classical and literary education purveyed by the King Edward VI schools from families whose off-spring would expect either to enter professional practice locally or perhaps go into the management of old established business houses. Others would use the schools as springboards for Oxford and Cambridge where they could acquire the added *cachet* brought by such degrees and also the chance of a good position in the metropolis. A provincial degree would mean less, and lead to less. In such circumstances, Mason College was dominated by the interests of Birmingham industry and subject to the prevailing influence of bourgeois circles unprepared to accept without criticism metropolitan definitions of 'university education.' The strongest allies of Sonnenschein and his colleagues in the Arts Faculty were not local men but bodies such as the Treasury committee responsible for distributing government grants amongst the university colleges, later to become the University Grants Committee.

---

73 Vincent, op. cit., 18–9. He notes that the phrase 'the top ten thousand' was used by Matthew Arnold in a letter to A. J. Mundella's daughter, 18, n.9.
74 Evans proposed that England and Wales should be organized into nine educational districts each served by central endowed schools supported by fees from paying schools and subscriptions from smaller local endowed schools. For example, Eton and Harrow would serve Oxford, Berkshire, Buckinghamshire and Middlesex. Rugby School and his own would cater for Warwickshire, Leicestershire and Northants. For Evans' scheme, see *Schools Inquiry Commission*, vol. 4, pt. 1, 565–6.

This committee strongly pressed the claims of arts subjects.[75] In contrast, MacCarthy resisted the increased central interference which attended the creation of the Board of Education and chose not to serve on the local education authority which succeeded the school board after its enforced dissolution.

In Sheffield, technical instruction in the higher grade schools held the field almost by default given the weakness of local demand for classical and literary education. However, the pervasive anomie amongst Sheffield businessmen not only yielded little support for education beyond this level but also afforded only weak resistance to metropolitan definitions of its appropriate content. The resulting scope for metropolitan initiative was shown by the success of the University Extension lectures which inspired Firth to establish his college.[76] In the absence of strong local pressure, this college failed to gain admission to the federal Victoria University dominated by Manchester and subsequently experienced the humiliation of the charter provisions of 1905 which required that all ordinances of Sheffield University with respect to the award of degrees should be submitted to the Universities of Manchester, Liverpool and Leeds for approval.[77]

In concluding, it is acknowledged that many relevant questions remain unanswered and still more unasked in the above analysis. However, the usefulness of the framework set out in the first section for exploring the questions posed in the second may have been demonstrated. The argument presented with respect to Birmingham and Sheffield shows that Ben-David has tended to underestimate the significance of the structural level of the provincial city. It also suggests that the interplay amongst bureaucracy, the market and status norms as modes of social regulation have a complexity at which he only hints. The challenge confronting theoretical and empirical investigation remains a powerful one.

---

75 See Chapman, op. cit., chapter six, *passim*. It is worth mentioning that a leading figure in the establishment of the committee was William Hicks, Principal of Firth College and later Principal of the university college of Sheffield.
76 On the role of the University Extension movement in the foundation of Firth College, see Chapman, op. cit., 14–32.
77 ibid., chapters 9 and 14.

The History of Education in the United States: Historians of Education and their Discontents

SOL COHEN

University of California, Los Angeles

'The historiographer ... conserves the scholarship of the past that seems currently relevant. He directs attention to convergent aspects of current scholarship, helping individual historians discover the relation of their own interests to larger currents of thought.

Historiography has also a less routine but more dangerous appeal: it is a critical weapon. Since it blends historical explanation with critical appraisal, it provides a vehicle of emancipation from ideas and interpretations one wishes to supersede. Accordingly it flourishes in response to conflict and revision in historical thought.'[1]

The United States, it has been said, was born in the countryside and has moved to the city. It was during the half century between the Civil War and the First World War that this move was made. In 1860 the whole American population was about 30 000 000. A century later, almost that many people lived in the country's ten largest cities alone. As late as 1860 less than 16 per cent of Americans lived in cities, in 1890, 33 per cent, in 1900, 40 per cent, in 1960 more than 60 per cent did so. In 1890 the U.S. Bureau of the Census announced that the Western Frontier was no more. This transition from a predominantly rural to a predominantly urban pattern of living was one of the most striking and significant of all the social changes which have occurred in the United States. The rise of the city left no basic institution untouched, not the home or family, not the church and certainly not the school. As early as 1889 Dewey was urging that congregation of men into cities was one of the most conspicuous features of the modern world and that no theory of education could possibly disregard the fact of urbanization. Indeed, the problem of education as Dewey saw it in *School and Society* was how to adjust the child to life in the city.

There is available in American urban history a corpus of literature of extraordinary vitality on this great transformation.[2] However, since urban historians in the United States have by and large neglected history of municipal services in general, it is not surprising that with a few recent exceptions they have neglected urban educational

---

1 J. Higham, L. Krieger and F. Gilbert, *History* (1965), 89.
2 See in general, K. T. Jackson and S. K. Schultz (eds.), *Cities In American History* (1972); C. N. Glaab and A. T. Brown, *A History of Urban America* (1967); B. McKelvey, *The Urbanization of America, 1860–1915* (1963); ibid., *The City in American History* (1969); G. E. Mowry, *The Urban Nation, 1920–1960* (1965). There is also what Eric Lampard calls the 'Orbis and Urbis' approach: A. B. Callow (ed.), *American Urban History: An Interpretive Reader With Commentaries* (1969); and A. M. Wakstein (ed.), *The Urbanization of America: An Historical Anthology* (1970), contain nearly all the significant writing on the subject, as well as extensive bibliographies. See also C. N. Glaab, 'The historian and the American city: A bibliographic survey,' in P. M. Hauser and L. F. Schnore (eds.), *The Study of Urbanization* (New York, 1965), 55–80, and R. Mohl, 'The history of the American city,' in W. H. Cartwright and R. L. Watson jun. (eds.), *The Re-interpretation of American History and culture* (1973), 165–205.

history in particular or given it a merely cursory or conventional treatment.[3] Historians of education have been equally deficient. Though the history of education as a specialized field of study coincides with the rise of the city, historians of education in the United States have arrived at the study of urbanization by slow freight. The impact of this great social transformation upon American public education has never been sufficiently explored. The response of American historians of education to the rise of the city has until very recently been largely one of neglect or indifference. In 1973 Stanley K. Schulz started to write a comparative educational history of Boston, Chicago, and St. Louis, but struck 'with the paucity of respectable and useful historical writing on the establishment and growth of one urban school system,' he abandoned the comparative ambition and concentrated on Boston.[4] In fact, the literature on the history of urban education, no matter how broadly defined, is scarcely a decade old, and is represented by little more than a handful of books and perhaps a score of articles.[5] Why historians of American education have devoted such scant attention to the school as an urban institution deserves an essay in itself.

History of education as a special field of study in the United States dates back to about 1890 when it was one of the most widely offered courses in American teachers colleges and schools or departments of education. From the beginning, however, American historians of education have had to face the scepticism of academic colleagues toward the profession of education, the reservations of colleagues in schools or departments of education about the value of history of education in a professional programme, while at the same time they had to cope with the general inadequacies of a field prematurely specialized.[6] These circumstances have severely retarded the development of any significant research interest.

At the outset, few American teachers colleges or schools or departments of education had trained historians on their faculty, and faculty members who taught history of education could not devote themselves to the subject. Most books in the field were largely histories of European educational thought or studies of comparative educational philosophy, emphasizing developments in Europe before the nineteenth century. The only extant works in the history of American education before the First World War were Richard G. Boone's *Education In The United States* (1889) and Edwin Grant Dexter's *A History of Education in the United States* (1904), both essentially chronologies, compilations of facts, largely about educational institutions, laws, and administrative codes. It was little wonder that history of

---

3 The few recent exceptions are M. H. Frisch, *Town Into City: Springfield, Massachussetts and the Meaning of Community, 1840–1880* (1972); E. Feinstein, *Stanford In the Gilded Age; The Political Life of A Connecticut Town 1869–1893* (1973); Z. L. Miller, *Boss Cox's Cincinnati: Urban Politics In the Progressive Era* (1968); and S. B. Warner jun., *The Private City: Philadelphia In Three Periods of Its Growth* (1968).

4 *The Culture Factory: Boston Public Schools 1789–1860* (1973), x–xi. Mohl, in the bibliographical essay cited above, has just one brief paragraph on the history of urban schooling and cites more references in history of urban public health and sanitation. The major reference works in the history of American education cite under 'city' or 'urban' little but the literature of contemporary problems of urban education: J. Herbst, comp., *The History of American Education* (1973); F. Cordasco and W. W. Brickman *et al.* (eds.), *A Bibliography of American Educational History* (1975); and Joe Park (ed.), *The Rise of American Education: An Annotated Bibliography* (1965).

5 The books: Schultz, op. cit.; M. B. Katz, *The Irony of Early School Reform: Educational Innovation In Mid-Nineteenth Century Massachusetts* (1968); M. Lazerson, *Origins of the Urban School: Public Education In Massachusetts 1870–1915* (1971); C. F. Kaestle, *The Evolution of An Urban School System: New York City 1750–1850* (1973); D. B. Tyack, *The One Best System: A History of American Urban Education* (1974); S. K. Troen, *The Public And The Schools: Shaping the St. Louis System 1838–1920* (1975); W. A. Bullough, *Cities And Schools In The Gilded Age: The Evolution of An Urban Institution* (1974).

6 For elaboration see S. Cohen, 'The history of the history of American Education 1900–1976: The uses of the past,' *Harvard Educational Review*, XLVI (1976), 303–308.

education became an increasingly unpopular course, asked to justify itself in the curriculum of American teacher training institutions. Thus Ellwood Cubberley's classic *Public Education in the United States* (1919) must be seen as an attempt to revive history of education in general and to create a viable history of American education in particular. This work endeavoured to overcome the prejudice of educational leaders against history of education by shifting the emphasis from Europe to America, from educational theories to educational institutions, from the past to the more recent present. Cubberley especially sought to secure the place of educational history in the professional programme by making it inspirational—presenting educational history as the story of the inevitable rise and triumph of the public school. Consequently, he provided historians of education with a clear and unambiguous sense of their calling, and his work stood virtually alone among textbooks in the field until the late '40s and early '50s. As late as 1965 Lawrence A. Cremin could write: 'The work is still read, . . . (It) has influenced a vast literature . . . to the most recent scholarly text in American history.'[7] Interest in history of urban education, however, was not part of either Cubberley's outlook or Paul Monroe's; whose students became the second generation of historians of American education.

There was never a large corps of well-trained historians of education in the United States. In 1933 Edgar Wesley claimed that of those who write and teach in the field of the history of education 'only a mere half dozen received their training specifically in history.'[8] According to Cremin, writing thirty years later, though history of education was a widely offered course, yet 'in all but a few instances it is taught by persons who have not been trained as historians, and indeed who do not identify themselves as such.'[9] There was always a shortage of talent for historical research in education in general, let alone in urban education. Then the nature of the subject seemed bewildering, vast in scope, and complex. The energies of most historians of education went into teaching, studying, writing textbooks, or debating the function of history in a school or department of education. The history of education as a field of study also suffered from the geographical and institutional isolation of its practitioners. For years American historians of education had no official organization and no official journal, while neither of the two national historical associations, the Mississippi Valley Historical Association, and the American Historical Association, realized neither their opportunity or their responsibility to provide a forum for history of education. The major organizations in professional education, such as the National Society for the Study of Education and the National Society of College Teachers of Education (NSCTE) provided few outlets for historians of education. To quote Wesley, since historians of education 'did not feel the tingle of competition, nor the stimulation of professional discussion, nor the incentive of writing for publication, they tended to become smug authorities in remote provinces.'[10]

By the late 1950s all the problems and weakness of the field had caught up with it. Historians of education were denounced from within the profession, by a group of educators associated with the enormously influential NSCTE, as irrelevant: and from outside the profession especially by the Ford Foundation's Committee on the Role of Education in American History, speaking for the general historians—as parochial, old-fashioned, anachronistic, and isolated from the mainstream of American historiography. This was the nadir, in the late 1950s.

---

7 *The Wonderful World of Ellwood Patterson Cubberley: An Essay On The Historiography of American Education* (1965), 2, 45.
8 'Lo, the poor historian of education,' *School and Society*, XXXVII (1933), 619.
9 In his review of Bernard Bailyn, *Education In The Forming of American Society* (Chapel Hill, North Carolina: 1960), in *Mississippi Valley Historical Review*, XLVII (1961), 678.
10 'Lo, the poor history of education,' *History of Education Quarterly*, IX (1969), 335.

Ironically, history of education was rescued from oblivion by the same Committee on the Role of Education in American History, and its chief spokesman, Bernard Bailyn.[11] The story is by now well known. Although the committee ran out of funds in 1965, and was terminated in 1966, it had been a most successful project, enormously stimulating the study of the history of education among departmental historians in the United States. What is more, though it was not intended this way, the Committee and Bailyn had enormous influence among historians of education on school of education faculties, giving a boost to their self esteem. When the history of education began to attract the departmental historians, there was an opportunity to reconnect with the rigorous canons of historical scholarship. Historians of education were finally able to renounce the requirement that their work be immediately relevant and provide clear directions for dealing with current problems of contemporary education, and thanks to the publication of Cremin's Bancroft Prize winning, *The Transformation of the School: Progressivism in American Education, 1876–1957* (1961), it became irrelevant to ask whether historians of education were employed in history departments or in schools of education.

In the last ten or fifteen years Bailyn and Cremin's vision of a 'new history of education'—humanistic, broadly conceived, and closely allied with the fields of social and intellectual history—has come true.[12] One result has been a flurry of interest in history or urban education. Sol Cohen's history of school reform in New York City, came out in 1964.[13] As another sign of the growing interest in urban education, in the mid-1960s, three new journals: *Urban Studies, Urban Education*, and *Education and Urban Society* appeared, all aimed at educators and focusing on urban education, and occasionally carrying articles in history of urban education.[14] In 1969 Michael B. Katz organized a symposium on 'Urban Education: Needs and Opportunities for Historical Research' for Division F (History and Historiography of Education) of the prestigious American Educational Research Association.[15] It seemed that history of urban education was ready to take its place as a major research focus for educational historians in America. However, this interest in history of urban education now looks like it may have been short-lived; short-circuited or deflected by the emergence of the conservative revisionists, influenced by Bailyn and Cremin, on the one hand, and the radical or militant revisionists, led by Michael B. Katz, on the other.

The Committee on the role of education in American History, Bailyn, and Cremin, were enormously influential in stimulating interest in the history of American education. However the point is, *not* in the history of urban education. For example,

11 The key works here are: Bailyn's *Education In The Forming of American Society* and the final report of the Committee on the Role of Education in American History, published as *The Role of Education In American History* (1967); and see Cohen, op. cit., 324–25.
12 See, for example, Sloan, *Historiography and the History of Education*, 239–48; Church, *History of Education As A Field of Study*, 415–24; S. Cohen, 'New perspectives in the history of American education, 1960–1970,' *History of Education*, II (1973), 79–96; and D. B. Tyack, 'New perspectives in the history of American Education,' In H. J. Bass (ed.), *The State of American History* (1970), 22–43.
13 *Progressives And Urban School Reform: The Public Education Association of New York City 1895–1954* (1964).
14 E.g., D. F. White, 'Education in the turn-of-the-century city,' *Urban Education*, IV (1969), 169–182; E. B. Gumpert, 'The city as educator,' *Education And Urban Society*, IV (1971), 7–24; R. A. Mohl, 'Urban education in the twentieth century: Alice Barrows and the platoon school plan,' *Urban Education*, IX (1974), 213–237; R. D. Cohen, 'Urban schooling in twentieth century America: A frame of reference,' *Urban Education*, VIII (1974), 423–37.
15 The papers were subsequently published in *History of Education Quarterly*, IX (1969): D. K. Cohen, 'Education And Race'; D. B. Tyack, 'Growing Up Black: Perspectives on the History of Education In Northern Ghettoes'; S. Cohen, 'Urban School Reform'; N. Sutherland, 'The Urban Child'; D. Calhoun, 'The City As Teacher: Historical Problems,' along with a commentary by Katz.

there is no mention of urban education in the Committee's widely read and influential *Education and American History*. The Committee ignored the history of urban education while recommending as a new point of departure, 'the building of communities on the frontier.'[16] Historians like Bailyn and Cremin who in the late 1950s and early 1960s led the revolt against the formalistic, institutional history of education of the Cubberley school, introduced a variety of new subjects and approaches into the discipline, but interest in urban education was not part of their new outlook. Bailyn urged historians to think of education 'not only as formal pedagogy but as the entire process by which a culture transmits itself across the generations.' He urged them to see education 'in its elaborate, intricate involvement with the rest of society.'[17] Cremin defines education only a little less globally, 'as the deliberate, systematic and sustained effort to transmit or evoke knowledge, attitudes, values, skills, and sensibilities. . . .'[18] These definitions are so abstract and encompassing, that they raise the question; what is educational history and what isn't? As Douglas Sloan has put it: 'Where do the educationally significant strands of the total social cultural network begin, interweave, and end? If everything can educate, and if everything affects education, what is educational history about?'[19]

The Committee on the role of education in American History failed to define very clearly a set of intellectual priorities upon which the relatively meagre research resources of history of education in America could be concentrated, whilst the conservative revisionists, by suggesting that historians of American education should be concerned with everything that happens to the young, implied that historians of education were surrounded by historiographical frontiers of equal urgency. This sweeping definition of the field may lead to diffusion and fragmentation of energy, leaving once again a scarcity of resources for research in urban educational history.

In *The Irony of School Reform: Educational Innovation In Mid-Nineteenth Century Massachusetts* (1968), Michael Katz set the tone for the work of the radical revisionists. He examines critically the view that popular education in the United States spread in response to the demands of an enlightened working class and the idealism of a few intellectuals. Katz's point, is that the common-school movement, represented essentially a conservative response to the rapid social changes incident to urbanization and industrialization. School reforms were advocated by an élite of wealth and position largely for their value in the fight to help solve the problems of industrial society. In alliance with this élite were the aspiring middle class who saw the school as an agency of social mobility for their children. Educators joined the fight for school reform to enhance their precarious professional status. The victory of school reformers was complete but, Katz concludes, with decidedly negative benefits. A common school system was established, but it was a system encrusted in a rigid bureaucracy and alienated from the working-class community which comprised its chief clientele.

The computerized findings which occupy a sixty page appendix in Katz's book represent an ingenious attempt at recovering some of the variables which entered into the school debates of the time in Massachusetts. However, it was the tone of the work that was conclusive. Katz deliberately conceived of *Irony of School Reform* as 'a piece of social criticism,' and he offered no apologies for the partisan argument

16 *The Role of Education In American History*, 18.
17 Bailyn, *Education In The Forming of American Society*, 14.
18 *The Wonderful World of Ellwood Patterson Cubberley* 48; 'Notes toward a theory of education,' *Notes On Education*, III (1973), 4.
19 'Historiography and the historian of education,' in F. N. Kerlinger (ed.), *Review of Research In Education*, I (1973), 259; R. L. Church, 'History of education as a field of study,' *The Encyclopedia of Education*, IV (1971), 420; L. R. Veysey, 'Toward a new direction in educational history: Prospect and retrospect,' *History of Education Quarterly*, IX (1969), 343.

except that: 'the crisis in our cities must arouse a passionate response in all those who care about the quality of American life.'[20] He concludes that educational reform and innovation in the past represented the imposition of schooling by a social élite upon an uncomprehending, sceptical, and sometimes hostile citizenry:

> 'The extension and reform of education... were not a potpourri of democracy, rationalism, and humantarianism. They were the attempt of a coalition of the social leaders, status-anxious parents, and status-hungry educators to impose educational innovation, ... upon a reluctant community.'[21]

The *Irony* is pervaded by a powerful action-oriented rhetoric: 'We must face the painful fact that this country has never... known vital urban schools.... We must realize that we have no models; truly to reform we must conceive and build anew.'[22] In the end, he is not interested really in education or in the school: 'The diffusion of a Utopian and essentially unrealistic ideology that stressed education as the key to social salvation created a smoke-screen that actually obscured the depth of the social problems and prevented the realistic formulation of strategies for social reform.'[23] Michael Katz brought a methodological freshness to the field of history of American education through his use of quantitative data and sociological concepts. Unfortunately much of the work that has followed builds on his indictment of urban schools and schoolmen rather than on his conceptualizing or cliometrics.

The radical revisionists appeared on the American scene in the tail-end of the 1960s.[24] The sources of their dissatisfaction were those which produced alienation and rebelliousness throughout American society in the late 1960s and early 1970s: the war in Vietnam, the oppression of the black population, the blighting of cities, the lawlessness of politics, the corruptibility and impersonality of institutions. The radical revisionists have been greatly influenced by the New Left movement in American politics and social thought, as well as by social scientists like James C. Coleman and Christopher Jencks, social and educational critics like Paul Goodman, Edgar Friedenberg, Ivan Illich, and Theodore Roszak, radical economists like Herbert Gintis, Martin Carnoy, and Samuel Bowles, and revisionist general historians like William Appleman Williams, James Weinstein, and Gabriel Kolko. There is among the radical revisionists—militant revisionists might be a better term— an *a priori* commitment to hostility toward American schools, American society, and the liberal/progressive tradition.

The radicals are repelled by American society. Karier proclaims: 'We live... in a fundamentally racist, materialistic society which, through a process of rewards and punishments, cultivates the quest for status, power, and wealth in such a way so as to use people and institutions effectively to protect vested interests.'[25] Hence reform will not do: a fundamental reconstruction of American society and schools is required. According to Katz, 'at this point in history any reform worthy of the name must begin with a redistribution of power and resources. That is the only way in which to change the patterns of control and inaccessible organizational structures that dominate American life. It is the only way in which to make education and other

20 Katz, *The Irony of School Reform:* preface.
21 ibid., 218
22 ibid.
23 ibid., 211.
24 See the following by Katz: *Class, Bureaucracy And Schools: The Illusion of Educational Change In America* (1971); *School Reform: Past and Present* (1971), and *Education In American History: Readings In the Social Issues* (1973). See also C. J. Karier (ed.), *Shaping The American Educational State, 1900 to the Present* (1975); C. J. Karier, P. Violas and J. Spring, *Roots of Crisis: American Education In the 20th Century* (1973); J. Spring, *Education And the Rise of the Corporate State* (1972); E. B. Gumbert and J. Spring, *The Superschool and the Superstate: American Education In the 20th Century 1918–1970* (1974).
25 Karier, *Shaping the American Educational State, 1900 to the Present*, xvii; and Karier, Violas, and Spring, *Roots of Crisis: American Education in the 20th Century*, 5.

social institutions as well, serve new purposes.'[26] Sacrifices may be demanded, but one cannot 'enlist in the cause of justice without sacrifice.'

The radical revisionists view urban schools as pathological, with few redeeming features. Bureaucracy is especially an anathema to them; they use the word as an epithet, heavy with connotations of racism, class domination, and social control. The schools are condemned as 'a fundamental vehicle of social control,' 'a vast social machine for the imposition of values and control.'[27] School reform, especially those reforms usually associated with educational progressivism are another target of the radical revisionists. They see progressive education as the triumph of conservatism, if not of reaction; 'a conservative thrust which in effect contributed to the maintenance of the social system.' School reforms are 'a giant cop-out on the present, an elaborate ritual which focuses on the future as a way of avoiding meaningful action of today's pressing social needs.'[28]

To the radicals, the function of history of education in the present 'crisis' is clear—to serve the cause of social and educational reconstruction. Not only Cubberley, Monroe and their contemporaries and students have to be discredited, but the immediate older generation of American historians in general, and historians of education in particular as well. Thus, not only is liberalism finished, but so is 'liberal history,' that history represented by Bailyn and Cremin, Hofstadter and Handlin, Curti and Commager is, all 'dated and irrelevant.' Karier puts down liberal history as 'short on meaningful criticism and long on apology.' Liberal history 'does not connect with and add meaning to our present world.'[29] For Katz, the major significance of the 'new' history of education is the way it 'links up with, and contributes to, the larger critical, contemporary reappraisal of American life and institutions.' There is, writes Katz, 'no excuse for boredom with a subject that can contribute so significantly to both historical understanding and contemporary reform.'[30] However, sometimes the contribution of history of education to contemporary reform takes priority.

In Katz's *Class, Bureaucracy and Schools* the didactic intent is again frankly admitted, the purpose of the book being 'to proclaim and to account for the illusion of educational change in America.'[31] In the writing of Karier novel canons of historical writing are introduced: 'If one starts with the assumption that this society is in fact racist, fundamentally materialistic, and institutionally structured to protect vested interests, the past takes on vastly different meanings.' The authors of these essays (in *Roots of Crisis*) write from such a conception of the present, which shapes our own view of the past.'[32] Katz ingenuously states: 'Our concerns shape the questions that we ask and, as a consequence determine what we select from the virtually unlimited supply of facts.'[33] In his review of *Roots of Crisis* Katz gives faint praise: given what we know about schooling today there are very good grounds for supposing that the historical vision of the authors is 'generally correct.' Katz concludes, '*In any event*, the burden of proof no longer lies with those who argue that

---

26 Katz, *Education In American History: Readings In the Social Issues* (1973), 348.
27 Karier, Violas, and Spring, *Roots of Crisis: American Education In The Twentieth Century*, 31; Karier, *Shaping The American Educational State, 1900 to the Present* (1975); Katz, *Class, Bureaucracy and Schools: The Illusion of Change In American Education*, xvii–xviii; Spring, *Education And the Rise of the Corporate State*, 149 ff.
28 Karier, *Shaping the American Educational State, 1900 to the Present*; Lazerson, M., 'Social reform and early childhood education,' *Urban Education*, V (1970), 85.
29 Karier, Violas, and Spring, *Roots of Crisis: American Education In The Twentieth Century*, 3, 4, 5.
30 *Education In American history: Readings in the social issues* IX, and his 'Comment,' in *History of Education Quarterly*, IX (1969), 326.
31 p. xi.
32 Karier, Violas, and Spring, *Roots of Crisis: American Education In The Twentieth Century*, 5.
33 Katz, *Class, Bureaucracy, and Schools: The Illusion of Educational Change In America*, xxv.

education is and has been unequal. It lies, rather, with those who would defend the system' (Italics mine).[34] This is history in the service of ideological needs. The 'irony' is that Katz is well aware of what happened once before in America, in the 1950s, when a potentially exciting subject was transformed into an 'insipid methology.' Karier once knew that history speaks only very cautiously and modestly to the present; that in history one seldom finds answers which are completely satisfying.[35]

There are many reasons for revision in history. However, an *a priori* wish to condemn hardly seems legitimate, even if the partisan purpose is masked by the assertion that every generation must write its own history. Of course, our era needs to be interpreted to contemporaries, but there is still a need for detachment, balance, judiciousness, and reasoned historical judgment. The radical revisionists see the world in Manichaean opposites of good and evil, black and white, controllers and controlled. Their focus is peculiarly narrow. Their concern is almost exclusively with the moulding of presumably malleable, passive individuals, and the evils of social control. Moreover, they appear to be unaware of the sociologists' difficulties in establishing meanings for the concept of social control.[36] True, Society in the main often tries to regulate the schools. However it is not to be assumed without proof that society always demands conformity and is inevitably an efficient censor and policeman. In a country where totalitarianism is absent there is room for education to move about.[37] There is clarity, finality and rationality about the work of the radical revisionists that oversimplifies the ambiguities, the incompleteness, the unintentionality and irrationality of historical events. This form of reductionism is most strikingly exemplified in David B. Tyack's *The One Best System: A History of American Urban Education*,[38] which can pass as the *summa* of American revisionist history of urban education.

David Tyack describes his study as an 'interpretive history of the organizational revolution' that took place in American schooling during the last century.[39] In the latter part of the nineteenth century the local, ward system, or community control of schools was prevalent in American cities, a legacy of earlier village or rural patterns. Schoolmen who sought changes in the governance of urban public schools, and their lay allies, an interlocking directorate of university presidents, the new professors of educational administration, leading businessmen and lawyers, the media, and the élite philanthropic and civic groups condemned the ward system as corrupt, inefficient, and uneconomical. The ward system would be replaced by one based on the model of the large-scale industrial bureaucracies rapidly emerging at the turn of the century. The 'administrative progressives,' Tyack's phrase for the men, and they were almost all men, who conceived and led the drive to implement 'the one best system' were convinced that what worked in business and industry was eminently applicable to the schools. Lay, community control of schools was to give way to the 'corporate-bureaucratic model' of control.

---

34 Katz, *Class, Bureaucracy, And Schools: The Illusion of Educational Change In America* expanded ed., (1975), 185.
35 Katz, *Education In American History: Readings In The Social Issues* VII; Karier, *Man, Society, and Education: A History of American Educational Ideas* (1967), x–xi.
36 See, in general, B. Davies, *Social Control And Education* (London, 1976). See also L. W. Banner, 'Religious benevolence as social control: A critique of an interpretation,' *Journal of American History*, LX (1973), 23–42; R. Berthoff, *An Unsettled People: Social Order and Disorder In American History* (1971); and R. H. Wiebe, *The Search for Order, 1877–1920* (1967).
37 Committee on the Role of Education in American History, *Education and American History*, 9.
38 Cambridge, Massachusetts: 1974. I review *The One Best System* at length in the context of American urban historiography in general in 'American History, Urban History, History of Urban Education,' *The Review of Education*, II (1976), 194–206.
39 ibid., 3.

School boards were to be small, non-partisan, elected at large, preferably composed of successful businessmen, and purged of all connexion with political parties and elected officials. Their slogan was 'take the schools out of politics,' that is, increase the power of the 'experts,' the professionals, who would govern the schools for the good of the city as a whole, rather than for the good of special interest groups. This slogan was largely window-dressing. The 'experts' also sought greater power and status for themselves. Urban school reform was part of a broader pattern of élite municipal reform at the turn of the century. The drive to centralize the management of the public schools and to separate public school management from city government was a middle and upper class Protestant reform strategy to keep urban school systems from falling into the hands of the working-class, ethnic-dominated political machine. The new patterns of city school organization spread rapidly as a result of 'informal and formal networks of communication' among leading urban schoolmen and their allies.

In order to make 'the one best system' work, the American schoolmen had to develop a uniform course of study and standardized examinations. Since promotion and grading depended on examinations, and examinations upon curriculum, the entire programme of study had to be carefully structured; 'differentiated' curricula had to be introduced to meet the needs of the various classes of students. The children would be classified, the curriculum 'differentiated.' With differentiated curricula came dozens of new job categories, new programmes of professional preparation, new bureau, new officials. Schoolmen sought to meet the needs of children and the requirements of urban society for stability and order, but they were also seeking 'stable, predictable, reliable structures in which their own role as educational managers would be visible, secure, and prestigious.' The impulse toward centralization and to corporate models of management emerged first in cities in the northeast, then spread south and west, and in time into rural areas as well. Tyack concludes that educational reformers largely succeeded in implementing the 'one best system.' Indeed, 'their success so framed the structure of urban education, that the subsequent history of these schools has been in large part an unfolding of the organizational consequences of centralization.'[40]

This book discusses a wide variety of topics, and there are interesting comparisons of city school systems with police and other municipal organizations. Tyack's insights are frequently penetrating: his description of the nineteenth-century principal and his 'pedagogical harem,' his largely all-female faculty; his analogy between 'Catholic power' in education in the 1830s and 1840s and 'Black power' in education in the 1960s; his depiction of a shift in the theory of urban education from an earlier conception of education as a kind of 'preventive nurture' to a concept of education as a kind of 'preventive detention;' his reminder that in the politics of urban education what is frequently at stake are issues more cultural than economic; his depiction of the architecture of urban high schools—fancy Gothic structures to compete with the most ornate academies in attracting the attention (and the attendance) of the prosperous;'—his analysis of the ties between city school superintendents and university presidents who frequently considered the city school superintent, like themselves, a 'captain of education.'

Tyack's work has many of the strengths then of the so-called 'new' urban history in America—the strong attachment to social science, the effort to interpret well-known data from the perspective of those on the bottom, the bold speculation. *The One Best System* is not only a first attempt to provide a synthesis for American urban educational history in general, it also seeks to provide a showcase for the usefulness of sociology and political science to the historian of education; indeed it is the most

40 ibid., 127.

ambitious attempt yet to marry social science to the history of American education. However to attempt so much, so soon leads inevitably to certain shortcomings. For example, if proof were needed that the complexity and variety of American urban education cannot be subsumed under a single construct, the 'one best system' provides it. In 1969, Katz called attention to the need for case studies, in order to develop the substructure of the history of urban education.[41] That need is still far from being met. Ronald Cohen's studies of the Gary (Indiana) school system reveal that some generalizations about city school systems break down when *individual* schools are examined![42] Tyack's 'the one best system' conceals by its generality, abstraction and vagueness precisely who is doing what to whom and with what results and when. The responsible agents are usually 'they,' or the 'school managers,' or 'the centralizers,' or 'the progressives' or variations thereof. There is also little sense of change or development over time, of the difference say between cities in the nineteenth century and cities in the twentieth century. Further, Tyack's construct leaves too little room for struggle among conflicting tendencies within the same interest groups. For example, a bewildering variety of people, programmes, and philosophies are labelled 'progressives.' What are the 'progressives?' We know that there was conflict among school boards, between school boards and superintendents of schools, between the latter and their associate superintendents, between superintendents and principals, and between 'administration progressives' at city, state, and national levels.[43]

Two recent studies of the politics of urban schooling in America, reveal precisely the inutility of 'the one best system' as an historical construct.[44] Cronin's sketch of the history of the governance of fourteen American city school systems reveals the complex multiplicity of administrative school reform. The organization of city schools varied from decade to decade, from mayoral to mayoral administration in the same decade, and from city to city. Ravitch's history of four 'great school wars' in New York City between 1805 and 1973 also demonstrates how difficult it is to generalize about urban school reform and urban school reformers. The first 'war' took place in the 1840s when Catholics demanded funding for their own schools. The second erupted at the turn of the century when reformers attempted to centralize the local, district or ward school system. The third was waged just before the First World War over the issue of efficiency, economy, and the Gary School Plan. The fourth 'war' was waged in the 1960s over school decentralization and community control of the schools.[45] No single élite dominates the educational system of New York City. The city's schools have through the years been sensitive to community and group demands. These 'school wars' were waged, by a series of interacting and shifting coalitions rather than a monolithic one.[46]

Another criticism that can be made of Professor Tyack's work is that his conception of 'urban education' is sweeping. It reminds one of Roy Lubove's observation that urban history, as understood today, is virtually synonymous with everything that

---

41 'Comment,' *History of Education Quarterly*, IX (1969), 326–27.
42 'Urban Schooling In 20th Century America: A Frame of Reference,' 432.
43 Cf. W. Urban, 'Organized teachers and educational reform during the progressive era: 1890–1920,' *History of Education Quarterly*, XVI (1976), 35–52.
44 J. M. Cronin, *The Control of Urban Schools: Perspective On The Power of Educational Reformers* (1973), and D. Ravitch, *The Great School Wars: New York City, 1805–1973* (1974).
45 I review this volume at length in the context of the politics of urban education in *Teachers College Record*, LXXVI (1975), 505–15.
46 Ravitch's term 'wars' is not really adequate if the word implies an ordered contest between two contending forces. As George S. Counts put it in another but relevant context: 'More commonly the conflict resembles a mêlée or free-for-all fight in which the numerous contestants strive now for this end and now for that, and in the course of the fray freely exchange friend and foe.' *School And Society In Chicago* (1928), 325.

happened in cities. Most of Tyack's findings are more relevant to mainstream historical issues than they are to history of urban education in any generic sense. Tyack treats everything that happens in city schools, from the status of teachers to the emergence of testing to vocational education, as a function of urbanization. Yet urbanization has little to do with some of the educational practices he defines as urban; to take one example, discrimination against female teachers in America in the late nineteenth and early twentieth centuries was no less characteristic of rural areas than urban ones. For Tyack, the enlargement of our understanding of urban education will come only as we approach it anew with the insights, methods, and models of the social sciences. Few would deny the beneficial impact of the methological techniques of the social scientist on historical studies. Tyack's use of social science terminology is often helpful, but too much becomes simply trendy. Thus we have teacher power, black power, Catholic power, women power, sexism, meritocracy, pedagogical harem, the male mystique, etc. In an eagerness to use social science terminology, Tyack's characteristic felicity of style suffers. Moreover, the distinctions between 'governance' and 'politics,' and 'centralization' and 'modernization' are crude and frequently blurred. The key term 'bureaucracy' is vague, and like other historians of the concept, Tyack conceives of it as largely dysfunctional. However, there is another view which strongly qualifies that model in another direction. Michael Crozier argues, for instance, that bureaucracy may not be antithetical to individual goals and may even provide more points of access for relatively powerless groups.[47] In any event, it may be more useful to consider bureaucracy at least in a more neutral way. In the city, bureaucracy becomes an ubiquitous form of organization, and an inevitable and indispensable concomitant of populations of large size and density and high levels of interaction.[48]

Finally, a comment is necessary about the deliberate choice to write present-oriented or usable history. Tyack declares that he does not share the view that urban schools have abysmally declined, 'but in this book I shall stress persistent problems and misconceptions.'[49] Tyack does not deny to public education its value to women, minority groups, and others of the 'dispossessed'; but its redeeming or beneficent features are consistently discounted, its virtues consistently downplayed. Thus, bureaucratization of American urban schools has 'often resulted in displacement of goals' and 'has often perpetuated outworn positions and practices rather than serving the clients, the children to be taught.' Despite 'frequent good intentions,' urban public schools have rarely taught the children of the poor effectively 'and this failure has been systematic, not idiosyncratic.' Finally, American public schools 'have often perpetuated social injustice by blaming the victim, particularly in the case of institutionalized racism.'[50] In his substitution of 'coercive education' with its implications of the use of force, power, violence, for 'compulsory education,' what does Tyack communicate except that he thinks it unfortunate, and that, I suppose, we're all supposed to condemn something. Professor Tyack has earned the debt of all historians of American urban education by this pioneer effort to bring out the 'organizational factor' and to diffuse more widely concepts of sociology and political science. However, in his eagerness to be useful and usable, he sins on occasions in

---

47 *The Bureaucratic Phenomenon* (1964). See also R. R. Alford, *Bureaucracy and Participation* (1969), and F. Musgrave, 'Historical materials for the study of the bureaucratization of education,' in History of Education Society's *History, Sociology and Education* (1971), 33–47.
48 This point is applied brilliantly in D. W. Swift's organizational interpretation of progressive education, *Ideology and Change: Latent Functions of Progressive Education* (1971).
49 *The One Best System*, 11.
50 ibid., 11, 12.

just the ways that he has himself warned against.[51] Another of the 'ironies' of this development, is how much the radical revisionists are trapped by historiographical tradition. Thus Cubberley was convinced that history of education should be directly relevant to present problems. The repudiation of Cubberley was based precisely on the grounds that his version of the past was poor history, anachronistic history. It would be unfortunate if in the desire to clear away old misinterpretations, historians of American education were simply to stand Cubberley on his head: 'to retain his moralistic conflict theory of educational change, merely reversing the labels of children of light and the children of darkness; to substitute for his presentist history, designed to strengthen the public schools, a similarly earnest reform commitment to their demolition. . . . In such an event, the tradition that Cubberley represents would still determine the framework and interests of the historian, and the result would be new myths and anachronistic history.'[52]

'In a sense,' Tyack states in his *One Best System* 'this synthesis is premature, since a new generation of talented scholars is directing its attention to monographic studies of urban schooling. . . .'[53] In the last few years, three of that new generation—Stanley K. Schultz, Carl F. Kaestle, and Selwyn K. Troen—have proved that Tyack was wise to provide so cautious a preamble to his work, since they seriously challenge some of the conclusions of the radical revisionist school.[54] Schultz, Kaestle, and Troen analyse respectively the school systems of Boston, New York City and St. Louis. All three portray the schools as the focal point of idealism as well as self-interest, they abjure the premise that American public schools have been an unequivocal failure, and they use effectively quantitative data as well as concepts from the social sciences. Finally all three demonstrate that there is still much life in institutional history.

The point which is clearly made in these case studies, is that the American public school system emerged as a response to the first shocks of modernization, which were felt earliest and most intensely in America's Eastern coastal cities especially Boston and New York City. The reaction to disorganization, caused by disorderly and rapid urban growth ranged from voluntary organizations to religious revivalism to movements for popular education. The common schools, publicly supported, publicly controlled, and free, were to be a major instrument for re-integration, for a new national cohesion. The schools were to help or substitute for home training, ethical custom, and religion. However, if the schools were to serve as general headquarters for a new moral or social discipline, then all the children had to be got into the school and kept there as long as possible. The rapid expansion in the school population, the swelling economic investment in schools, and the proliferation of schools and school teachers led to a demand for systematization. It was almost inevitable that the model copied would be that of the new and phenomenally successful factory system. The advocates of public schooling set out to shore up their society. They were aided by schoolmen who found in the development of public schools a device by which they could enhance their own professional status and dominance. However, they also

51 'Research arising from contemporary concerns may tempt scholars to read the present into the past, and to concentrate only on those features of our heritage which are pertinent to the problems of today. Disillusionment with institutionalized education and discouragement with the results of schooling in the present, . . . may prompt historians to tell a tale of woe as one-sided as the previous story of the public school triumphant,' in Tyack, 'New Perspectives In the History of American Education,' 29–30.
52 Sloan, '*Historiography and the History of Education,*' 247–48, 261–62.
53 p. 3.
54 Schultz, *The Culture Factory*; C. F. Kaestle, *The Evolution of An Urban School System: New York City, 1750–1850* (1973); S. K. Troen, *The Public and the Schools: Shaping the St. Louis System, 1838–1920* (1975).

believed that education would improve the conditions of the people. Finally, those who established school systems were not following some predetermined paths. Their ramshackle creations illustrate neither the work of the spirit of progress in history nor the conspiracy of one class against another.

Kaestle's *The Evolution of an Urban School System* is an attempt to explain when, why, and how the public schools of New York City became organized into a system. The focus is on institutions of formal instruction. Kaestle reminds us that in colonial America there was a shift in education from a reliance on informal agencies like the family, church, and apprenticeship, to a reliance on deliberate schooling. His study of New York City schools continues the story of that shift as it traces, in an urban setting, a further stage in the transformation: 'the consolidation of schools into a single, articulated, hierarchical system that was amenable to uniform policy decisions.'[55] It was in response to increasing immigration, vagrancy, intemperance, poverty, and crime that New York's leaders organized the Public School Society, and turned to schooling as a deliberate instrument for the acculturation of those individuals whom the colonial arrangements were leaving out, namely the children of the poor. Schools soon became the agents of a 'majoritarian ethic.' Kaestle notes that it is somewhat ironic that the schools became more conformist as the population became more diverse. These developments led to uniform interschool regulation and an explicit hierarchical promotion structure. Examinations, curriculum salaries, and pedagogical routines were standardized, and uniformity became the most essential value of the system. By the time the Public School Society turned over its school to the new, public, New York City Board of Education in 1853, 'schooling services in New York were consolidated, coordinated, and standardized in a process that one is tempted to call a bureaucratic revolution.'[56] However, this revolution happened piecemeal and without a master plan.

Regarding bureaucracy, Kaestle concludes that it was not so much class and cultural bias on the part of school leaders, but 'common sense' which in a large and complex city mandated the consolidation of the schools for economy and efficiency. Of course schoolmen in New York were concerned with efficiency and standardization but there was more involved: 'the desire to be fair to all those who accept the rules of the system, and the desire to raise the quality of teaching.'[57] Standardization was not designed to stifle creativity, rather it was bound up in the process of increasing complexity in society. The roots of educational systematization 'are in the economic system, in economic problems, and in the very demography to which urban school systems must respond.'[58] Standardization may tend to stifle creativity; but it also 'represents an effort to hold in check the personal prejudices and whimsical judgments of individuals by enforcing collective decisions about fair play and opportunity. . . .'[59] Kaestle concludes that New York's public school system is a reflection of the city's persistent institutional approach to urban problems, 'one which has aimed ideally to uplift, hopefully to reconcile, and minimally to control, its turbulent population.'[60]

Schultz's argument is in many ways similar to Kaestle's: 'the public school movement in the United States matured in response to what contemporaries viewed as an urban crisis.' The purpose of public education was 'to secure social order in a disorderly age.' In face of mounting immigration, poverty, and despair about public morality, Boston school reformers turned to the public school as a form of social insurance: 'to assure stability in a time of change.' Rising crime rates, increasing

---

55 p. viii.
56 ibid., 159, 182.
57 ibid., 177–79.
58 ibid., 190.
59 ibid.
60 ibid., 191.

pauperism, and spiralling juvenile delinquency signalled a moral dislocation. Swarms of immigrants challenged the capacities of the city to accommodate and assimilate the newcomers. Those seeking a new urban discipline attempted to create as one of their most useful tools a system of public education. In their attempt to create a 'system,' Boston schoolmen turned to the factories of New England. In 'methods of industrial organization schoolmen saw the perfect model for retooling the schools.'[61] Within this context Schultz examines the growth of school bureaucracy, the continual struggle for funds, and the ethnic and religious tensions which complicated the problem of city school system building.

Both these historians make extensive use of quantitative data to demonstrate that in the Colonial period children from a wide range of socio-economic classes attended urban public schools and that little changed in the nineteenth century. The most significant change was in the organization and purpose of schooling. In organization, increasingly bureaucratized; in purpose, an agency with unlimited potential for solving urban social problems. Both authors are refreshingly aware of European influences on American urban public schools: Schultz stressing the Prussian influence; Kaestle the English. Especially interesting and suggestive are their contributions to a new institutional history—their profiles of nineteenth-century American school buildings, school rooms, pupils, parents, and teachers.

Troen's case study of the St. Louis school system is an extraordinarily valuable mid-west contrast to the studies of New York City and Boston. Troen divides his history into two broad phases: The period between the 1830s and 1880s when 'the major challenge was reconciling contending class, ethnic, sectarian, and racial interests' within the common school, and the turn of the century when the major concern was to enrol the mass of children and teenagers, and adapt the schools to their needs. In the circumstances, bureaucracy was inevitable; there was no alternative. It was imperative to restructure school management if the system was to proceed with the programme of expansion it had embarked on after the turn of the century. Troen distinguishes between curricular reform, and structural reform—reform of the governance of the school system. Though both reforms were often initiated by the same people, these were complementary movements, not 'a co-ordinated programme of reform.'[62]

Troen has a sure feel for change over time. It is easier, he writes, to imagine nineteenth-century-American educators as men of literature, at home with philosophic tracts, while their twentieth-century counterparts emerge as administrators imbued with techniques of scientific management, at home with a slide rule. The change is also manifest in the schools' major documents. Nineteenth century annual city schools reports often had a literary flavour, since they were written for a general audience; in the twentieth century the reports tended to dispense with words in favour of numbers, becoming increasingly unreadable to nonspecialists.[63] Troen rejects what he calls, 'hostile analyses of the interrelationships between schools and corporate society.' Changes in city schools were not foreordained but rather 'flowed from the system's responses to changes in urban life, political pressure, educational theory, and the decisions of students and parents.' Thus he dissents from any 'social control' or 'imposition' model of historiography, rather emphasizing the 'importance of the rationalizing processes that characterized modernizing institutions.'[64] Troen's analysis of the shift in urban school governance from laymen to experts is positive:

---

61 *The Culture Factory*, ix–x.
62 *The Public And The Schools* 208.
63 ibid., 221.
64 ibid., 224.

administrative and curriculum reform were widely supported; they received widespread and enthusiastic endorsement as valid responses to difficult social and educational problems. That administrators were careful to educate the public to the system's work and to seek mass support made the transition relatively quick and free from conflict.[65]

Historians in teachers colleges, or on school or department of education faculties in the United States have always been under particularly acute tension. They carry commitments both to history and to the professional programme and their loyalties are claimed by the demands of both past and present. They are caught, as the late Richard Hofstadter put it in a slightly different context, between 'their desire to count in the world and their desire to understand it.' On the one side their passion for understanding points back to the commitment to detachment, neutrality, and the scientific ideal. However, the urgency of present problems points in another direction, plays upon their desire to get out of history some lessons that will be of use to the world. The problem is one of balance and control. Possessed of a more secure identity, historians of education might learn to live better with this tension between polarities. As it is, there has been an extraordinary proliferation of appraisals of the 'state of history of education' *genre* in the past five or six years, as though historians of education were imposing a moratorium upon themselves, a time to reconsider priorities before they become fatally over-committed to any particular school.

In the United States, history is an important key to ideology. Americans realize that views about the past generally have consequences for the present. It isn't simply that the past 'determines' the present, but that the way one views the past has significant consequences on the way one acts in the present. Since current ideology is based on a particular view of the nature of the past, and present problems are frequently attacked by reference to the way past experience dealt with similar problems, control over the interpretation of the past becomes a burning cultural issue.[66] The question which has really been posed by the radical revisionists is who shall have control over the interpretation of the educational past of the United States. Though enormously influential, the radical or militant revisionists have not been able to dictate the terms of discussion nor establish the norms by which history of American education is to be measured. Many American historians of education are having second thoughts about making their speciality a form of social or political action.[67]

On the other hand, such historians as Katz, Karier and Tyack have made a significant contribution to demythologizing the history of American education. Historians of education are now calling into question stereotyped notions of the words 'reform' and 'progressive' and are thinking in terms of the 'irony' of school reform. Most historians of education are now ready to examine the public schools giving due regard to their possibly restrictive and coercive functions, and they are now disclosing phenomena long hidden by official pieties, e.g., the maltreatment of immigrants and ethnic groups, the discriminatory treatment of women and minority

---

65 ibid., 225–26. See also Troen's 'Strategies for Education In A Technological Society,' *History of Education Quarterly*, XIV (1974), 137–42.
66 'History and the American intellectual: Uses of a usable past,' *American Quarterly*, XVI (1964), 243–63.
67 There has recently appeared a large literature critical of the radical revisionists. Perhaps the most interesting are: R. F. Butts, 'Public education and political community,' *History of Education Quarterly*, XIV (1974), 165–84; M. L. Borrowman, 'Studies in the history of American education,' *Review of Education*, I (1975), 56–66; M. Green, 'Identities and Contours: An Approach to Educational History,' *Educational Researcher*, II (1973), 5–17; See also M. Lazerson, 'Revisionism and American educational history,' *Harvard Educational Review*, 43 (1973), 269–83; W. J. Urban, 'Some historiographical problems in revisionist educational history,' *American Educational Research Journal*, XII (1975), 337–50; and D. Ravitch, 'Ideology and revisionism,' *The Review of Education*, II (1976), 384–91.

groups, the impact of class values, the connexion between schools and politics and education and social stratification, the ways in which educational rhetoric may mask other motives, and the way ideals may be transformed by the very institutions intended to incarnate and perpetuate them. Most important, the radical revisionists have aroused fresh interest in the reading and writing of the history of American education.

Since the late 1950s, the history of education as a field of study in the United States has been 'in a productive state of disarray.' Cremin proceeds from perhaps the broadest conception of education, as we have seen, projecting him far beyond schools and colleges to the multiplicity of individuals, groups, organizations, and institutions that educate, to 'configurations of education' which may be complementary, consonant or dissonant.[68] R. Freeman Butts vigorously urges 'civilization-building and modernization process,' as a framework for the reinterpretation of the history of education.[69] Clifford calls for a new synthesis that places the 'neglected constituents, the school patrons,' at the centre of the story; a 'people—centred institutional history that deals, in significant and sensitive ways, with students, parents, school board members, as well as teachers—warts and all.'[70] Finkelstein calls for a new synthesis that places children at the centre; for it is in the 'primal relationships between parents and children, between teachers and students, between children and their books, and children and the streets that the history of education has proceeded.'[71]

In history of urban education, we know Tyack sees the emergence of bureaucracy and 'the organizational factor' as the key to a new synthesis. Other American historians of education have suggested more modest but still fruitful avenues of inquiry, although the history of American urban education is still one of the classic underdeveloped fields of historical research. For example, of the fourteen largest American cities we have only the beginning of an educational history of four or five of them; we have no comparative studies of American urban school systems. Ronald Cohen calls for more local case studies 'sensitive to the heterogeneity, movement and complexity of urban life.'[72] Neil Sutherland has suggested a novel approach to urban educational history: 'Since debate and conflict about the pathological often lay bare the unstated norms, our first centres of attention should be on children and families in trouble.' The focus here would be on 'special' urban educational institutions like houses of refuge, reform schools, orphanages, juvenile courts, etc.[73] Horlick calls for close analyses of the 'process of educational investments,' e.g., the relationship between municipal budgetary measures, the emergence of teachers' unionism, and the introduction of 'progressive' educational innovations.[74] Dana F. White and William Cutler call for the study of schools, their location, size, and shape as shaping forces in the 'city-building process.'[75] Daniel Calhoun sees great value in studying the city itself as educator: the urban setting may have far greater affects than do urban

---

68 'Further Notes Towards a Theory of Education,' *Notes On Education*, IV (1974), I.
69 'Civilization—Building And The Modernization Process: A Framework for the re-interpretation of the history of education,' *History of Education Quarterly*, VII (1967), 147-74.
70 G. C. Clifford, 'Saints, Sinners, and People: A position paper on the historiography of American education,' *History of Education Quarterly*, XV (1975), 257-268.
71 B. J. Finkelstein, 'Choose your bias carefully: Textbooks in the history of American education,' *Educational Studies*, V (1974), 214.
72 'Urban schooling in 20th century America: A frame of reference,' 437.
73 Sutherland, 'The Urban Child,' 311. In the past few years quite a few historians have been active in this genre: e.g., D. S. Rothman, *The Discovery of the Asylum* (1971); J. M. Hawes, *Children In Urban Society: Juvenile Delinquency In Nineteenth-Century America* (1971); A. Platt, *The Child-Savers: The Invention of Delinquency* (1969).
74 A. S. Horlick, 'Radical school legends,' *History of Education Quarterly*, XIV (1974), 257.
75 The entire issue of *Urban Education*, VIII (1974), is devoted to the topic: 'Schools As City Shapers.'

schools, and the educational historian might ask whether the very variety of urban life may have enhanced the ability of urban Americans to adapt to different settings and people. Might the daily pattern of urban behaviour have influenced general intellectual development? Does investment in schooling do as much to change the mentalities of people than does investment in the more general facilities 'that help to make urban life quick, close, and specialized?'[76]

Stephan Thernstrom's discovery of differences in mobility rates of various ethnic groups in Boston invites speculation regarding urban family life as teacher as well as the role of the city as teacher, especially in the education of minority groups. For example, is religion the critical variable in school success or it is prior urban experience or is it what goes on in urban schools? What was the attitude towards the education of the unskilled and uneducated immigrants who poured into American cities in the early stages of urbanization and industrialization? Timothy Smith portrays a broad social consensus among newcomers and native Americans in his discussion of immigrant social aspirations and American education. The value system of the immigrants centred on their aspirations for success and respectability through education, goals consonant with the 'Protestant Ethic.' Education also served the immigrants' need to create a new structure of family and communal life and their search for a new ethnic identity. These aspirations, according to Smith, 'account for the immense success of the public school system, particularly at the secondary level, in drawing the mass of working-class children into its embrace.'[77] A quite different assessment of the relationship between the American educational system and the children of the immigrants has been advanced by Michael Olneck and Marvin Lazerson. Basing their studies on historical evidence of school performance, they conclude that more important than the differences in educational achievement as between native and immigrant children were the differences among children of various ethnic origins. While Scandinavian, British, German, and Russian Jewish youngsters tended to be as successful in school as those of native parentage, the children of non-Jewish central and southern European immigrants had much higher rates of failure. On every index of educational attainment, children from these nationalities fared much worse than the others. While recognizing the influences of religious and cultural differences on motivation and aptitude, they suggest that the problem may have been the inability of public education to overcome the consequences of poverty or to recognize the legitimacy of working class and immigrant cultures.[78]

A major task for the historian of urban education in America is inquiry into the history of the education of minorities in general. On the regional level we have only one major work: Henry Allen Bullock's masterful *A History of Negro Education in the South: From 1619 to the Present*. We need to know a great deal more about the recruitment and training of the educational establishment with reference to the inclusion or exclusion of minority group members. We should have studies depicting the role of minority group members as teachers, administrators, local school board members and professors of education. We have no profile of the city school administrators, no persuasive analysis of what attitudes toward minorities were conveyed

---

76 'The City As Teacher,' op. cit., 313. See also Calhoun's *The Intelligence of A People* (1973).
77 'Immigrant social aspirations and American education 1880–1930,' *American Quarterly*, XXI (1969), 543. See also Smith's, 'Native blacks and foreign whites: Varying responses to educational opportunity in America 1880–1950,' in D. Fleming and B. Bailyn (eds.), *Perspectives In American History*, VI (1972), 309–32, and 'New approaches to the history of immigration in twentieth-century America,' *American Historical Review*, LXXXI (1966), 1272–74.
78 'The school achievement of immigrant children: 1900–1930,' *History of Education Quarterly*, XVI (Winter 1976), 453–482. See also D. K. Cohen, 'Immigrants and the schools,' *Review of Educational Research*, XL (1970), 13–27.

in the classroom. We do not know how concepts of urban school districting or the 'neighbourhood school,' or of compulsory education, developed. Detailed examinations are needed of the educational history of particular school districts, not only those with statistically significant numbers of minority students, but also those with very few. There is, for example, in San Francisco, a century of experience of a unique kind of educational segregation—the segregation of Chinese—which is almost completely unstudied. There are now more Indians living in Los Angeles and Chicago than in any reservation in the country and the further urbanization of non-reservation Indians is proceeding rapidly, yet this subject too is *terra incognita*.

The whole recent furious conflict over city schools in the United States was largely racial in its inception. Historical inquiry might be given over to efforts to grasp the experience by understanding how it all came to pass. For example, two prospects seem likely to provide opportunities for very useful historical research. One concerns the movement for integration in the schools, and the other has to do with the efforts of schoolmen and educational reformers to eliminate the consequences of differences in social and economic class through programmes of compensatory or remedial education. If any single phenomenon is responsible for the emergence of urban education as a central social and political concern it has been the movement for school integration. But why integration in city schools? How was it that a few men decided that this was the issue on which the back of segregation could be broken? How was that decision—applicable in fact only to the South—translated into an ideology of school reform which continues to have an enormous impact upon schools in the cities outside of the South?[79]

Similarly, we still know little about the Catholic parochial school system. The Catholic school played a crucial role in adjusting many newcomers to the city, and in forming for millions of urban dwellers an alternative loyalty to the public schools. Other denominations also operate schools, but Catholic schools comprise roughly nine-tenths of all private school education in American. The size of the Catholic system alone should make it a matter of pressing historical concern. Yet from a historical point of view, the monographic literature is virtually nonexistent,[80] the same might be said of institutions of higher education, e.g. libraries and city colleges, and other forms of urban adult education.[81] These are some of the areas of research likely to prove fruitful. But this by no means exhausts the subject. Given the current state of research in the history of American urban education, it is probable that only the tip of the iceberg is now visible.

---

79 D. K. Cohen, 'Education and Race,' 281–86, and Tyack, 'Growing Up Black: Perspectives on the History of Education in Northern Ghettoes.' See also the just published history of Brown vs. Board of Education; R. Kluger, *Simple Justice* (1976).

80 V. P. Lannie, 'Church and school triumphant: The sources of American Catholic educational histriography,' *History of Education Quarterly*, XVI (1976), 131–45.

81 But see Troen, *The Public and The Schools*, 132 ff; P. A. Graham, *Community and Class In American Education, 1865–1918* (New York 1974), 175–78, and the entire issue of *Adult Education*, XXVI (1976). See also S. W. Rudy, *The College of the City of New York: A History, 1847–1947* (1949); and T. E. Coulton, *A City College In Action: Struggle and Achievement at Brooklyn College, 1930–1955* (1955).

Select Reading List

This list of titles has been selected to provide further reading and to illustrate some of the writings on the history of urban schooling in the nineteenth century.

URBAN EDUCATION: INTRODUCTORY TEXTS

Claydon, L. F., *The Urban School* (Carlton, Australia, 1975).
Field, Frank, *Education and the Urban Crisis* (Routledge, 1977).
Friedman, John F. and Wulff, Robert, *The Urban Transition: Comparative Studies of Newly Industrializing Societies* (Edward Arnold, 1975).
Herbert, D. T. and Johnston, R. J. (eds.), *Social Areas in Cities* especially D. T. Herbert, 'Urban education: problems and policies,' 2, *Spatial Perspectives on Problems and Policies* (Wiley, 1976).
Hummel, Raymond C. and Nagle, John N., *Urban Education in America, Problems and Perspectives* (Oxford U.P., 1973).
Lauwerys, J. A. and Scanlon, D. G., 'Education in cities,' *The World Yearbook of Education* (Evans Bros., 1970).
Marcus, S. and Rivlin, Harry N., *Conflicts in Urban Education* (Basic Books, 1970).
Mays, J. B., *Education and the Urban Child* (Liverpool U.P., 1962).
Miller, Harry L. and Woock, Roger R., *Social Foundations of Urban Education* 2nd ed. (Dryden Press, 1973).
Raynor, John and Harden, Jane, *Cities Communities and the Young* and *Equality and City Schools*, 2 vols., *Readings in Urban Education* (Routledge, 1973).

URBAN HISTORY AND CITY STUDIES: UNITED STATES

Callow, A. B. (ed.), *American Urban History: An Interpretative Reader with Commentaries* (Oxford U.P., 1969).
Feinstein, E., *Stanford in the Gilded Age: The Political Life of a Connecticut Town, 1840–1880* (Stanford U.P., 1973).
Frisch, M. H., *Town into City: Springfield, Massachusetts and the Meaning of Community, 1840–1880* (Harvard U.P., 1972).
Glaab, C. N., 'The historian and the American city; a bibliographic survey,' in P. M. Hauser and L. F. Schnore (eds.), *The Study of Urbanization* (Wiley, 1965).
Katz, M. B., *The People of Hamilton Canada West: Family and Class in a Mid-nineteenth Century City* (Harvard U.P., 1976).
McKelvey, B., *The City in American History* (Baenes, 1969).
Miller, Z., *Boss Cox's Cincinnati: Urban Politics in the Progressive Era* (Oxford U.P., 1968).
Mohl, R., 'The history of the American city,' in W. H. Cartwright and R. L. Watson jun., (eds.), *The Re-interpretation of American History and Culture* (Washington Social Studies Council, 1973), 165–205.
Ravitch, D., 'The Revisionists Revised: Studies in the Historiography of American Education,' in *Proceedings of the National Academy of Education*, vol. iv, 1977, 1–84.
Thermstrom, S. and Sennet, R. (eds.), *Nineteenth Century Cities: Essays in the New Urban History* (Yale U.P., 1969).
Wade, Richard C., 'Historical Analogies and Public Policy: The Black and Immigrant Experience in Urban America,' in F. Morris and E. West (eds.), *Essays in Urban America* (Texas U.P., 1975).
Warner, S. B., *The Private City: Philadelphia in Three Periods of its Growth* (Pennsylvania U.P., 1968).
Warner, S. B., *The Urban Wilderness: A History of the American City* (Harper Row, 1972).

URBAN HISTORY AND CITY STUDIES: BRITAIN

Anderson, Michael, *Family Structure in Nineteenth Century Lancashire* (Cambridge U.P., 1971).
Church, Roy A., *Economic and Social Change in a Midland Town Victorian Nottingham 1815–1900* (Frank Cass, 1966).
Daunton, M. J., *Coal Metropolis Cardiff 1870–1914* (Leicester U.P., 1977).
Dyos, H. J., Clark, P., Fraser, D., Reeder, D. A., *Urban History Yearbook* (Leicester U.P., 1974).

Dyos, H. J. (ed.), *The Study of Urban History* (Edward Arnold, 1968).
Dyos, H. J. and Wolff, M. (eds.), *The Victorian City Images and Realities*, 2 vols. (Routledge, 1973).
Everitt, Alan (ed.), *Perspectives in English Urban History* (Macmillan, 1973).
Foster, John, *Class Struggle and the Industrial Revolution: Early Industrialism Capitalism in Three English Towns* (Oxford U.P., 1974).
Fraser, D., *Urban Politics in Victorian England* (Leicester U.P., 1977).
Hennock, E. P., *Fit and Proper Persons: Idea and Reality in Nineteenth Century Urban Government* (Edward Arnold, 1973).
Jones, G. S., *Outcast London: a Study of the Relationships between the Classes in Victorian Society* (Oxford U.P., 1971).
McLeod, Hugh, *Class and Religion in the Late Victorian City* (Croom Helm, 1974).
Mellor, H. E., *Leisure and the Changing City* (Routledge, 1976).
Yeo, S., *Religion and Voluntary Organizations in Crisis* (Croom Helm, 1976).

THE HISTORY OF EDUCATION IN TOWNS AND CITIES: UNITED STATES

Bullough, W. A., *Cities and Schools in the Gilded Age: the Evolution of an Urban Institution* (Kennikat, 1974).
Cohen, Sol, *Progressives and Urban School Reform: The Public Education Association of New York City 1895–1954* (Columbia U.P., 1964).
Cronin, J. M., *The Control of Urban Schools: Perspectives on the Power of Educational Reformers* (Harvard U.P., 1973).
Kaestle, C. F., *The Evolution of an Urban School System: New York City, 1750–1850* (Harvard U.P., 1973).
Katz, M. B., *The Irony of Early School Reform: Educational Innovation in mid-19th century Massachusetts* (Harvard U.P., 1968).
Lazerson, M., *Origins of the Urban School: Public Education in Massachusetts, 1870–1915* (Harvard U.P., 1971).
Ravitch, D., *The Great School Wars: New York City 1805–1973* (Basic Books, 1974).
Schulz, K., *The Culture Factory: Boston Public Schools 1789–1860* (Oxford U.P., 1973).
Troen, S. K., *The Public and the Schools: Shaping the St. Louis System 1838–1920* (Missouri U.P., 1975).
Tyack, D. B., *The One Best System: A History of American Urban Education* (Harvard U.P., 1974).

THE HISTORY OF EDUCATION IN TOWNS AND CITIES: BRITAIN THEMATIC AND DOCUMENTARY ACCOUNTS

Bingham, John Hey, *The Period of the Sheffield School Board 1870–1903* (Sheffield, 1949).
Brown, W. E. and Foskitt, F. R., *The History of Bolton School* (The School, 1976).
Carr, J. R., *The Origin, Development and Organization of Certain Lancasterian Schools in London, Middlesex, and Surrey* (M.A., London, 1963).
Cater, P., *Short History of Education in the County of Rotherham, 1871–1974* (Rotherham, 1974).
Chapman, S., 'The Evangelical Revival and Education in Nottingham,' *Thoroton Society Transactions*, 66–7 (1962–3).
Clark, E. A. G., *The Ragged School Union and the Education of the London Poor in the 19th Century* (M.A., London, 1967).
Clark, J. N., *Education in a Market Town: Horncastle 1329–1970* (Phillimore and Co., 1976).
Coleman, B. I., 'The incidence of education in mid century,' in E. A. Wrigley (ed.), *Nineteenth Century Society: Essays in the use of quantitative methods for the study of social data* (Routledge, 1972).
Cowan, I. R., 'School Board Elections and Politics in Salford 1870–1900,' *Durham Research Review*, 23, (1969).
Cruickshank, M., 'The Manchester Mechanics Institute,' in D. S. L. Cardwell (ed.), *Artisan to Graduate* (Manchester U.P., 197).
Duncan, G., 'Adult education in Torquay with particular reference to the contribution of the church,' in Jeffrey Porter (ed.), *Exeter Papers in Economic History* 10 (University of Exeter, 1976).
Foster, H. J., *The Influence of Socio-Economic, Spatial and Demographic Factors on the Development of Schooling in a 19th Century Lancashire Residential Town* (M.A. Liverpool, 1976).
Frith, Simon, *Education and Social Change: Education in Leeds, 1780–1870* (Ph.D., University of California, 1976).
Gammage, M. T., *Newspaper Opinion and Education: A study of the influence of the Birmingham Provincial Press on Developments in Education 1870–1902* (M.Ed., Leicester, 1972).
Gordon, P., 'The school Manager and local history,' *Local History* 10 (1972), 124–5.
Greenwood, Maureen, *Education and Politics in Leicester 1828–1850* (M.Ed., Leicester, 1973).
Hatley, V., 'Literacy at Northampton, 1761–1900,' *Northamptonshire Past and Present* 4 (1966–71) 5 (1974) 397–81 and 129–40.
Hershon, C., *The Evolution of Jewish Elementary Education in England with special reference to Liverpool, 1840–1957* (Ph.D., Liverpool, 1973).

History of Education Society, *Local Studies and the History of Education* (Methuen, 1972) N. Morris especially, 'The Contribution of Local Investigations to Historical Knowledge' and M. Bryant, 'Education from Local Sources.'

Hopkins, Eric, 'Working Class Attitudes to Education in the Black Country in the Mid-Nineteenth Century,' *History of Education Society Bulletin* 14 (1974).

Hunt, J. R., 'The Widnes School Board 1874–1903,' *Historic Society of Lancashire and Cheshire Transactions*, CVI, (1954) 145–7.

Hurt, J. S., 'Education and the Working Class,' *Society for the Study of Labour History Bulletin*, 30, 31.

Inkster, I., 'The development of a scientific community in Sheffield,' *Hunter Archaeological Society Transactions* 10 (1973) 99–131.

Inkster, I., 'Science instruction for youth in the industrial revolution': The informal Network in Sheffield,' *The Vocational Aspect of Education*, 23 (1973) 91–8.

Inkster, I., 'The Social Context of an Educational Movement: A Revisionist Approach to the English Mechanics Institutes 18 –1850,' *Oxford Review of Education*, 2, 3 (1976).

Johnson, R., 'Notes on the schooling of the English Working Class 1780–1850,' in Roger Dale *et al.* (ed.), *Schooling and Capitalism* (Open University P., 1976).

Jones, D. K., *The Lancashire Public Schools Association, later the National Public Schools Association* (M.A., Sheffield, 1965).

Jones, D. K., 'The Educational Legacy of the Anti-Corn Law League,' *History of Education*, 3, 1 (1974) 18–33.

Kitching, J., 'The Catholic Poor Schools 1800–1845,' Parts I and II, *Journal of Educational Administration and History*, 1, 2 (1969) 1–8; 2, 1 (1969) 1–12.

Lawson, J., *A Town Grammar School through Six Centuries* (Oxford U.P., 1963).

MacDonald, P. H. and Tate, J. J. (eds.), *The Liverpool Institute 1825–1875* (The School, 1976).

Maclure, J. S., *One Hundred Years of London Education, 1870–1970* (Allen Lane, 1970).

McCann, Philip (ed.), *Popular Education and Socialization in the Nineteenth Century* (Methuen, 1977)

Midwinter, E. C., 'The administration of public education in late Victorian Lancashire,' *Northern History*, IV (1969), 184–96.

Murphy, James, *The Religious Problem in Education: the Crucial Experiment* (Liverpool U.P., 1959).

Murphy, James, 'The rise of public elementary education in Liverpool.' *Historic Society of Lancashire and Cheshire Transactions*, CXVIII (1966) 105–36.

Parsons, Cheryl, *Elementary Education in the Local Community: A Study of Relationships in the Attercliffe Area of Sheffield 1870–1940* (M.Ed., Leicester, 1975).

Rodgers, C. D., 'Education in Lancashire and Cheshire,' *Historic Society of Lancashire and Cheshire Transactions*, 122 (1971) 39–56.

Roper, N. B., *The Contribution of Nonconformity to the Development of Education in Bradford, 1800–1904* (M.Ed., Leeds, 1967).

Rubinstein, David, *School Attendance in London 1870–1914: a social history* (Hull and New York, 1969).

Salt, J.. 'The Creation of the Sheffield Mechanics' Institute, Educational Advance and Social Pressures in an Industrial Town,' *The Vocational Aspect of Education*, XVIII (1966).

Sanderson, M., 'Social Change and elementary education in Industrial Lancashire, 1700–1840,' *Northern History*, 3 (1968) 131–54.

Sanderson, M., 'Literacy and Social Mobility in the Industrial Revolution in England,' *Past and Present*, 56 (1972) 75–104.

Seaborne, M. and Lowe, R., *The English School Its' Architecture and Organization* 11, *1870–1970* (Routledge, 1977).

Shapin, Steven, 'The Pottery Philosophical Society, 1819–1835: an examination of the cultural uses of provincial science,' *Science Studies*, 2, (1972).

Shapin, Steven, 'Phrenological Knowledge and the Social Structure of Early-Nineteenth-Century Edinburgh,' *Annals of Science*, 32 (1975) 219–43.

Shipley, Stan, *Club Life and Socialism in Mid-Victorian London* (Ruskin College, 1971).

Silver, Pamela and Harold, *The Education of the Poor: the History of a National School 1824–1974* (Routledge, 1974).

Simon, B. (ed.), *Education in Leicestershire: A Regional Study*, (Leicester U.P., 1968).

Skimmider, M., 'Catholic Elementary Education in Glasgow 1818–1918,' *Studies in Scottish Education 1872–1939* (London U.P., 1967).

Smith, D., 'The urban genesis of school bureaucracy: a transatlantic comparison,' in Roger Dale *et al.*, (ed.), *Schooling and Capitalism* (Open U.P., 1976).

Stanford, J. and Patterson, A. T., 'The condition of the children of the poor in mid-Victorian Portsmouth,' *Portsmouth Papers*, 21 (City Council, 1974).

Stephens, W. B., *Regional Variations in Education during the Industrial Revolution 1780–1870* (Leeds Museum, 1973).

Stephens, W. B., 'Early-Victorian Coventry: Education in an Industrial Community, 1830–1851,' in A. Everitt, *Perspectives in English Urban History* (MacMillan, 1973).

Taylor, A. F., *The History of the Birmingham School Board, 1890–1903* (M.A., Birmingham, 1955).
Thackray, A., 'Natural knowledge in a cultural context: the Manchester model,' *American Historical Review*, 79 (1974).
Wadsworth, A. P., 'The First Manchester Sunday Schools,' in M. W. Flinn and T. C. Smout (eds.), *Essays in Social History* (Oxford U.P., 1974).
Wardle, D., *Education and Society in Nineteenth-Century Nottingham* (Cambridge U.P., 1971).
Webster, D. H., *The Ragged School Movement and the Education of the Poor in the Nineteenth Century* (Ph.D., Leicester, 1971).

SCHOOL PROFILES AND CHILDHOOD REMINISCENCES

Barclay, J. B., *The Tounis Schule: the Royal High School of Edinburgh* (Edinburgh, 1974).
Cowan, Evelyn, *Spring Remembered: a Scottish Jewish childhood* (1974).
Cox, M., *A History of Sir John Deane's Grammar School, Northwich 1557–1908* (Manchester U.P., 1975).
Davies, Celia, *Clean Clothes on Sunday* (Terence Dalton, 1974).
Docking, J. W., *Victorian Schools and Scholars* (Coventry H.A., 1967).
Dodd, A. H., 'Keeping school in Victorian Wrexham,' *Denbighshire Historical Society Transactions*, 21 (1972), 11–27.
Foley, Alice, *A Bolton Childhood* (Manchester W.E.A., 1973).
Garlic, S. L., 'The British School, Hollis Lane, Chesterfield,' *Derbyshire Miscellany*, 6 (1971), 47–52.
Gibbard, N., 'Llanelli Schools 1800–1870,' *Carmarthen Historian*, v (1968), 67–83.
Green, E. P., 'A successful schoolmaster in the 1860s,' *Halifax Archaeological Society Transactions* (1962), 29–34.
Heren, Louis, *Growing up Poor in London* (Hamish Hamilton, 1973).
Hickinbotham, E., 'Grantham Methodist Day School,' *Epworth Witness*, (October 1965), 15–16.
Jasper, S. A., *A Hoxton Childhood* (Barrie, 1969).
Jenkins, V. (ed.), *When I was Young; memories of London Childhoods* (Hart Davis, 1976).
Kendal, J. C. U. and Jackson, M. P., *A History of the Free Grammar School, Chesterfield* (The School, 1965).
Liverani, Mary R., *The Winter Sparrows: a Glasgow childhood* (Michael Joseph, 1975).
Markham, John, 'Hendon board school: a study in Victorian elementary education,' *Hendon Local History Society*, 1 (1973).
Niall, Ian, *A London boyhood* (Heinemann, 1974).
Roberts, Robert, *A Ragged Schooling Growing up in the Classic Slum* (Manchester U.P., 1976).
Robertson, David, *The King's School, Gloucestershire* (Phillimore, 1974).
Scannell, Dorothy, *Mother Knew Best: An East End Childhood* (Macmillan 1974).
Smith, Dodie, *Look back with love: a Manchester childhood* (Heinemann, 1974).
Sunderland, N., *The History of the Free Grammar School of Queen Elizabeth* (The School, 1963).
Whitcut, J., *Edgbaston High School 1876–1976* (The School, 1976).

Index

Abbotsholme 93
Acland, A. H. D. 78
Adams, Francis 21
Adams, Mr (Headmaster) 66
Administrative progressives 122, 123
Adolescence 83, 89, 90, 93, 94
Alderson, C. H. 56
Alexander, G. W. 16
American Educational Research Association 118
American Historical Association 117
Andover 36, 37
Anti-Corn Law League 19, 21
Anti-Smoking League 82
Argyle, Jesse 59
Arundel 37
Ashton-under-Lyne 31

Bailyn, Bernard 118, 119, 121
Baines, Edward (Jun.), 15, 19, 20, 22, 23, 25
Bampton 29
Banbury 28
Barnett, Canon S. A. 80
Barr, Sir James 82
Bath 38, 41, 46
Beckett, William 18
Bedfordshire 34
Ben-David, Joseph 96, 101–106, 114
Bermondsey Guild of Play 88
Bermondsey, schooling in 62
Berkshire 36, 44
Besant, Sir Walter 82
Beveridge, W. 92
Bideford 36, 38
Birkdale, social tone of, 70
Birkenhead 4
Birmingham 6, 11, 19, 20, 25, 28, 40, 45, 46, 96, 99 ff
—, Board Schools 111
—, educational politics 21, 24
—, literacy in 45
—, school attendance in 38
—, schooling in 99
—, social structure 111, 112
—, urbanization and insustrialization 106–108
Birmingham Education League 24

Birmingham Municipal Technical School 107
Birmingham School Board 24, 109
Birmingham University College 110
Birmingham Waverley Road School 109, 110
Birrell, Augustus 82
Blackburn 32, 40
Blandford 36
Board of Education 82, 87, 91, 114
Board Schools, Birmingham 111
—, Fleet Road 73
—, Leipsic Road 58
—, London 71
—, Mansfield Place 62
—, Orange Street 72
—, Oxford Gardens 61
—, St Clement's Road 59–61
—, Saunders Grove 61
Boer War 83
Bolton 32, 40
Bolton Grammar School 68
Bond, C. J. 93
Boone, Richard G. 116
Booth, Charles 49, 50, 55, 58, 59, 72
—, —, social survey of London 51, 55, 56, 58, 72
Bootle 64, 65, 66, 67, 72
—, elementary schools in 57, 58
—, St Mary's National School 65
—, schooling in 64
—, social decline in 53–55
Bootle School Board 72
Bosanquet, Bernard 82
Bosanquet, Helen *see also* Dendy, Helen 87
Boston (USA) 96, 100, 116, 126, 131
—, schools in 127, 128
Boy Scouts 81, 89, 93
Bowles, Samuel 120
Boys League of Honour 82
Boys' Life Brigade 82, 88
Brabazon, Reginald (Earl of Meath) 81
Bradford 16, 17, 40, 46, 62, 113
Bradford Charter of I.L.P. 4
Bradford elections 16, 17, 19
Bradford Observer 17
Bradford School Board 4, 62

Bray, Reginald   79
Bridge Street Seventh Standard School   107
Bridgwater   29, 40
Brighton   38
Brindley, David   56
Bristol   31, 33, 34, 38, 39, 41, 46
British Purity Campaign   82
Brixham   28
Brown, John   107
Bryce Commission   4, 67, 70, 109
Buckinghamshire   36
Bullock, Henry Allen   131
Bunting, Percy   82
Bureaucracy   125, 127, 128, 130
Burnley   32
Burt, Sir Cyril   86
Bury   32
Bury St Edmunds   40, 44
Busfield, William   16, 17
Butts, R. Freeman   130
Byles, William   16

Caernarvon   36, 41
Calhoun, Daniel   130
Cambridge   44, 112, 113
Cambridgeshire   44
Cambridge Group for Study of Population and Social Structure   30
Cambridge Local Examinations   113
Cammell, Charles   107
Cannadine, David   99, 100
Cardiff   6
Care Committees   87
Carlisle   40
Carnoy, Martin   120
Catholic school system in USA   132
Chamberlain, Joseph   24, 25, 107, 110, 112
Charity Organization Society   87
Chartism   17
Checkland, S. G.   28
Cheetham, John   16
Cheltenham   38
Cheshire   32, 44
Chester   29, 43
Chesterfield   36
Chesterton, G. K.   85
Chicago   116
Chicago school of urban sociologists   1, 50
Chichester   36
Child development   82, 83, 87
Child labour   32, 45, 89–92
Child life in cities   7–9, 83, 84, 89, 90
Child 'saving' movements   83
Child Study Association   92
Childhood Society   86
Children, State protection of   83
Children and Young Persons Act   83
Children's Ministering League   81

Chipping Norton   38
Chorley   32
Chrichton-Browne, Sir James   82, 86
Cipolla, C. M.   34
Citizenship   78
City of London School   69
Civic League (Social and Educational)   82
Civic and Moral Instruction League   82
Civics   81
Civil War (American)   115
Clifford, G. C.   130
Clitheroe   32
Cobden, Richard   19
Cohen, Ronald   124, 130
Cohen, Sol   118
Colchester   40, 44, 46
Coleman, James C.   120
Commager   121
Commission on Youth and the Cinema   88
Committee on Wage Earning Children   90
Common schools (USA)   126
Contemporary Review   82
Corn Laws   15
Cornwall   29, 36
Coventry   28, 38, 40, 41
—, literacy in   45
Crewe   28
Cross Commission   66, 72
Coulthard, J. R.   31
Cremin, Lawrence A.   117–119, 121
Cronin, J. M.   124
Crossley, Frank   17
Crozier, Michael   125
Cubberley, Ellwood   117, 119, 121, 126
Curti   121
Cutler, William   130

Dale, R. W.   23
Darwinian concepts   50, 80, 81, 94
Deane   32
Deeping   30
Degenerate class   85
Dendy, Helen   87, 91
Dendy, Mary   86, 87
Derby   40, 43, 44, 46
Derbyshire   44
Destitution Committee   83
Dewey, John   94, 115
Devon   29, 31, 36, 44, 45
Devonport   38, 40, 45
Dexter, Edwin Grant   116
Dissenters   15, 17, 22, 23
—, Education Minutes, 1847   14–20
Distance delay factor   57
Dixon, George   21–23, 107, 112
Dixon, MacNeile   110
Dorchester   36, 38
Dorset   36

Dover 40
Durham 45
Durkheim, Emile 95, 104–106
Dyos, H. J. 55, 58

Eardley, Sir Culling 19
East Acklam (Yorks) 31
East Stonehouse 45
Eccleston 32
Eclectic Review 16
Edgbaston 96, 111
—, social decline in 100
Edinburgh 110
Education, history of, USA 116–119, 129, 130
Educational provision, children at school, 36–41
—, children at Sunday School 41
Education, rôle of in American history 117–119
Education and urban politics 11–25
Education Act, 1870 23, 24
Educational reform (USA) 128
Educational Reform Association 80
Edwards, Henry 17
Eggesford 31
Eicholz, Dr 85
Elkington 107
Essex 36, 44
Eugenics Education Society 82, 86, 93, 94
Eugenic reformers 85, 93
European Economic Community 96
Exeter 4, 28, 33, 35, 38, 41, 44, 46
Evans, Charles 113

Factory Acts 46
Factory Bill, 1843 14
Factory system (USA) 126
Falmouth 38
Faversham 36
Fearon, D. R. 69
Feeblemindedness 86
Fielden, Sarah 94
Findlay, Professor J. J. 94
Finkelstein, B. J. 130
First World War 84, 106, 107, 115, 116, 124
Firth, Mark 107
Fitch, J. G. 52
Fitzroy Committee 83–85
Fitzwilliam, Charles 19
Fleet Road School 65, 66
Folkestone 36
Ford Foundation (Committee of) 117–119
Forbes, Henry 17
Forster, W. E. 22
Foster, John 100
Freeman, Arnold 92
Free Trade Hall, Manchester 20

Friedenberg, Edgar 120
Froebel Institute 94

Gainsborough 30
Galton, Sir Douglas 86
Galton, Francis 80, 86
Garwood, J. 51
Gary School Plan 124
Gateshead 29, 40
Geddes, Patrick 81
Geological Society 73
Giddens, Antony 100
Gillott, Joseph 107
Gintis, Herbert 120
Girls Friendly Society 88
Gladstone, J. P. 112
Glasgow 110
Goodman, Paul 120
Gorst, Sir John 84
Gotto, Mrs S. K. 93
Gould, F. J. 78
Grace, Sister 88
Graduated fees' issue 61
Grantham 30
Great Yarmouth 40, 43
Green, T. H. 79, 111
Guild of Play 87
Guildford 36, 38
Guilds of Courtesy 82
Gurney, Sybilla 81

Halifax 31, 33, 41
—, elections 18, 19
—, politics 16
Hall, G. Stanley 87, 94
Hampshire 36
Hampstead 65
Handlin 121
Harrap, Sylvia 31
Haylebury College 88
Hayward, F. H. 86, 87
Hertford 36, 38
Hertfordshire 36
Higher grade schools 65, 66
High Wycombe 36, 38
Hofstadter 121
Hooliganism 91
Hook, W. F. 15, 45
Horlick, A. S. 130
Horsfall, T. C. 92
Housewifery Association 81
Howson, Rev. 67
Huddersfield 4, 16
—, elections 16, 19
Hull 38, 40
Hull Grammar School 4
Hunslet 45
Huntingdon 36, 38

Huntingdonshire 36
Huxley, Thomas 72

Illich, Ivan 120
Industrial Revolution 27–30, 33
Industrial training 85
Industrialization 27, 28, 33, 77, 106, 108, 119
Inglis, K. S. 46, 47
International Congress on Eugenics 86
International Moral Education Congress 82
Ipswich 44

Jackson, Cyril 91
Jencks, Christopher 120
Jewish children 8
Jones, D. K. 7
Jones, Stedman 49
Journal of Inebriety 86

Kaestle, Carl F. 126, 127
Karier, C. J. 120, 121, 129
Katz, Michael B. 99, 104, 118–122, 129
Kay, Joseph 77
Kay-Shuttleworth, Sir James Phillips 21, 22
Kendal 36, 38, 41
Kent 36
Kentisbeare 31
Kerschensteiner, Georges 92
Keylnrick, M. C. 86
Kimmins, Mrs 88
King Edward VI Foundation 109, 111, 112
King Edward VI Schools 104, 111, 113
Kings Lynn 31, 33, 40, 44
Kirkham 32
Kolko, Gabriel 120

Lads' Drill Association 82
Lampard, E. E. 84
Lancashire 27, 28, 34, 36, 38, 40, 42, 44, 45, 46, 67
Lancashire Public Schools Association 20
Lancaster 40
Laqueur, T. W. 41
Lawton, R. 56
Lazerson, Marvin 131
Leeds 11, 14, 19, 20, 34, 40, 46, 113
—, East Parade Chapel 15
—, literacy in 34, 35
—, politics and elections 15, 18–20
Leeds Mercury 15, 16, 18
Leeds School Board 24
Leicester 28, 40, 46, 93
—, literacy in 45
Leicester City Committee for Mental Deficiency 93
Leicestershire 45

Leicester Society for Combating Venereal Disease 93
Liberalism, urban 19
Leigh 32
Leipzig 110
Leytonstone
—, Elson House High School 58
—, schools in, 57
Lincoln 30, 36, 38
Lincolnshire 34
Literacy and illiteracy levels, 1840–1870 34, 35
Literacy and industrialization 32–34
Literacy in towns 28–34, 42–46
Liverpool 4, 7, 8, 11, 12, 14, 38, 40, 46, 110, 113
—, railway worker's diary 56
Liverpool Collegiate 66, 67
Liverpool Corporation 12
Liverpool Corporation Schools 13, 14
Liverpool Girls' College 69
Liverpool Toryism 14
Liverpool Town Council 13, 14
Llandovery 36
Local history 4, 5
London 34, 44, 46, 51, 53, 58 ff, 68, 69, 72, 77, 78, 87, 88 ff
—, City of 65
—, East End of 50, 65
—, poverty in 51, 77
—, school attendance in 52
—, school leavers 90
—, slums: schools in 58–62
—, suburban development 69
—, suburbs; schools in 69, 70
London School Board 52, 53, 61, 65, 72
Los Angeles 132
Louch, Mary 92, 94
Louth 30
Lubove, Roy 124
Lucas, Samuel 20
Ludlow 30, 33
Lymington 36, 38
Lyttleton, Canon 88

Macclesfield 40
MacDougall 79
M'Neille, Rev. J. 13, 14
Maldon 38
Manchester Grammar School 67
Manchester 7, 11, 14, 19–23, 25, 32, 40, 46, 92, 107, 110
—, boys 91
—, Demonstration Schools 94
—, educational politics 19–22
—, school attendance in 38
Manchester Mechanics' Institute and Technical College 4

Manchester School Board   24, 86
Mappin, Frederick   107
Marcham, Rev. James   82
Marlborough   36
Marriage marks   43
Marshall, James G.   18
Mason, Josiah   107
Mason Science College   107, 110, 113
Massachusetts   99
—, schooling in   99
Masterman, C. F. G.   49, 78, 79
Mather, Sir W.   94
Maynooth   14, 16, 17, 20
Medical theories about town life   77
Merchant Taylor's School (Crosby, Lancs.)   67
Merthyr Tydfil   38
Miall, Edward   17
Middlesbrough   28
Migration   56
Military training for youth   92
Ministry of Health   93
Minorities, education of, in USA   131, 132
Minutes, 1846   14, 17
Mississippi Valley Historical Association   117
Modernization   3, 126
Monroe, Paul   117, 121
Montmorency, J. E. G. de   87
Morell, J. D.   51, 61
Morley, John   91
Morpeth   36
Mottram   31
Muirhead, J. H.   110
Mundella, A. J.   90
Municipal history   3
Murphy, James   7

National Commission on Youth and the Race   93
National Council for Combating Venereal Disease   93
National Council of Public Morals   82
National Education Association   90
National Education League   21, 24
National Education Union   21, 24, 81
National Home Reading Union   82
National League for Physical Education and Improvement   81
National League of Workers with Boys   82
National Liberal Federation   111
National Public Schools Association   7, 20
National Service League   82
National Society of College Teachers of Education (USA)   117
National Society for the Study of Education (USA)   117
Nettlefold   107

Newark   41
Newcastle Commission   72, 76
Newcastle-upon-Tyne   4, 29, 38, 40, 43, 44
New Left Movement (USA)   120
Newport   40
New York City   126, 127
—, Board of Education   127
—, schools in   124, 127
Nonconformist   17
Norfolk   44
Norris, Rev. J. P.   45
Northern Union Schools of Cookery   81
Northampton   31, 33, 41, 100
North London Collegiate   69
Norwich   38, 44
Nottingham   28, 31, 32, 33, 40, 45, 46, 82
—, literacy in   45
Nottinghamshire   45
Notting Hill area, schooling in   59
Notting Hill School   69

Oldham   32, 38, 40, 100
Olneck, Michael   131
Oral history   9
Ottery St Mary   34
Oxford   31, 33, 112, 113
Oxfordshire   36

Park, Robert E.   1, 50
Parkin, Frank   104
Paton, J. B.   82
Pembroke   40
Penstone, M. M.   81
Penryn   38
Penzance   30
Peoples Palace   82
Plymouth   40, 45
Plymstock   30, 38
Poole   36
Pooley, C. G.   56
Poor Law   11
Poor Law Commission   90
Portsmouth   38, 41
Poverty, structural levels in   97, 98, 100, 101
Preston   9, 32, 40
Preston Grammar School   68
Protestation returns   29, 30
Protheroe, Edward   17, 18
Public School Society (USA)   127
Punch   73

The Quarterly Review   62

Radford   45
Radical revisionists (USA)   129
Ragged School Union   52
Ravitch, D.   124
Reading   44

Recreative Evening Schools Association   82
Reddie, Cyril   93
Reductionism   122
Retford East   36
Revisionists (USA)
—, conservative   118, 119
—, radical   119–121
Registrar General of Births, Deaths and Marriages   30, 34, 42
Richmond (Yorks)   36
Ripon   36, 37
Roberts, R.   56
Robson, E. R.   62, 63
Rochdale   32, 46
Romsey   37
Roszak, Theodore   120
Roxbury   100
Royal Commission on the Feeble Minded   86
Royal Commission on the Poor Laws   91
Royal Commission on the State of Large Towns   32
Russell, Charles   91
Russell, Lord John   17

Sadler, M. E.   69
Sadler, Michael   4, 75, 78, 82, 83
St Helens   28, 32
St Ives   36
St Louis (USA)   116, 126
—, schools in   128
Saleeby, C. W.   80
Salford   24, 40
—, social distinctions in   56
Salford School Board   83
Salisbury Road School   64
San Francisco   132
Sargent, W. L.   31, 32, 42
Searr, Archie   24
School attendance and urban churchgoing   46, 47
—, catchment areas   57–67
—, and community links   9
—, design   63
—, reformers in USA   119, 121
School Board Chronicle   61
School Board elections   23–25
School boards   79
Schools Inquiry Commission   111
Schultz, Stanley K.   116, 126–128
Science and technology   106
'Scientific meliorism'   80
Scientific and technical education in cities   107–110
Scotland   44
Secondary education in France   105, 106
Sedbergh   34
Shaftesbury   36

Sheffield   6, 8, 40, 46, 96, 105, 107, 108, 111, 112
—, schooling in   109
—, social structure   111, 112
—, urbanization and industrialization   106–108
Sheffield Central School   109
Sheffield Firth College   110, 114
Sheffield School Board   109
Sheffield Technical School   107
Sheffield Town Council   110
Sheffield University College   107
Shrewsbury   44
Shropshire   44
Slaughter, J. W.   94
Sleaford   30
Sloan, Douglas   119
Smith, Adam   76
Smith, Samuel   85
Smith, Timothy   131
Social citizenship   76, 78
Social Darwinism   80
Social decline   58
—, in Liverpool   67
Social development   95–101
Social disorganization   76, 78, 126
Social 'networks'   6
Social hygiene   82, 86
Social history   6
Social Science Association   76, 77
Social Science Congress   113
Social theory   79
Sociological problems   98
Sociological Society   81, 94
Sonnenschein, E. A.   110, 113
Southampton   38
Southend   69
Southampton City Council   5
Southport   70, 71
—, social tone of   70
—, University School   70, 71
South Shields   38, 100
Southwold   38
Sparkbrook   96
Spencer, Herbert   80
The Spectator   72
Stafford   40
Staffordshire   44, 45
Stalybridge   31
Stamford   36, 37
Stansfield, W. R. C.   16
Statistical Society of London   30
Stead, W. T.   82
Stockport   32, 38, 40
Stockton   36, 38
Stokes, S. N.   58
Stone, L.   29
Sturge, Joseph   18

Sudbury   36, 38
Suffolk   44
Sumner, J. B.   44
Sunday schools   7, 29, 41
Sunderland   38, 41
Surrey   36
Sussex   36
Sutherland, Neil   130
Swansea   38, 40
Swindon   28

Taunton Commission   66, 68
Technical education   92, 98
Thernstrom, Stephan   131
Third World   2
Thompson, J. Arthur   82
Thompson, Perronet   15, 16, 17
Torrington   35
Totnes   29, 37
Towns
—, with day-school pupils more than 1-6 of population 1851   35
—, marriage marks and percentage of children at school   43, 47
—, percentage of children at school on census day 1851   39, 40, 41
—, proportion of day-school pupils 1851   37
Tawney, R. H.   92
Towns, English, variety of   28
Toynbee Trust   92
Trades Union Commission   112
Troen, Selwyn K.   126, 128
Truro   41
Tyack, D. B.   2, 122–126, 129

University Extension Lectures   114
University of Cambridge   102, 103, 110
University of Leeds   114
University of Liverpool   114
University of Manchester   114
—, Dept. of Education   94
University of Oxford   102, 103, 110
University of Paris   104
University of Sheffield   114
University Grants Committee   113, 114
Urban bureaucracy   97, 99, 121
Urban community   77
Urban conditions
— —, anxiety about   77, 79, 81, 83, 85
— —, psychological theory of   87, 92
Urban economy   89
Urban education
—, achievements of   71
—, American and English compared   99
—, case studies   101, 126, 130
—, complexity of (USA)   123–125
—, concepts of   1, 12, 15, 124, 125
—, history of

— —, in Britain   1–10
— —, in USA   115–132
—, sociological approach to   95–114
Urban educational planning   50
Urban educational provision
—, elementary schools   71–73
—, higher education   110
—, secondary schools   69–71, 109–111
Urban elementary schools, hierarchy of   63, 64
Urban history   47
—, 'new'   123
—, USA   115, 116
Urban migration   56
Urban mobility   131
Urban politics, nature of   12
Urban problem and youth   90
Urban problems and education   75–95
Urban residential segregation   50, 85, 99, 100
Urban schooling
—, anxieties about   76–79, 94
—, and child literacy   42–46
Urban schools, concept of (USA)   132
Urban slum   55
Urban social decline   53–55
Urban themes
—, in Britain   7–10
—, in USA   130, 132
Urbanism   75
Urbanization   1, 2, 8, 27, 49, 75, 79, 84, 85, 98, 106, 108, 116, 119, 125
—, in the USA   115, 116, 119, 125
Urwick, E. J.   92
U.S. Bureau of Census   115

Vaughan, Robert   49, 76
Victoria County History   5
Victoria University   114
Vincent, E. W.   113
Voluntaryism   14–21

Wakefield   41, 46
—, elections   15
Wales   34, 36, 38, 40, 41, 50
Walmsley, Joshua   12, 13
Walsh, Miss   70
Warrington   28, 32
Warwickshire   45
Webb, Sydney   4, 65, 72, 80, 92
Weber, Max   102
Weinstein, James   120
Wesley College   109
Wesley, Edgar   117
West Bromwich   45
Westlake, Ernest   94
Wetherby (Yorks.)   30, 33
Weymouth   36

Whalley 32
White, Dana F. 130
Wigan 32, 46
Wilderspin, Samuel 13
Williams, William Appleman 120
Wiltshire 36
Windsor 36
Winfield, Robert 107
Winwick 32

Wolverhampton 40, 46
Women's Industrial Council 90
Wood, Sir Charles 17
Wright, J. S. 112

Yasumoto, M. 32
Y.M.C.A. 88
Young Men's Brigade of Service 82
Youth movements 88, 89